H A N D B O O K S

W9-AAV-831

NASHVILLE

MARGARET LITTMAN

Contents

Maps

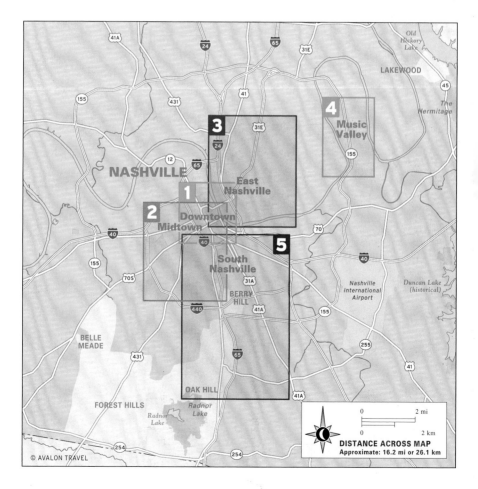

Buena Vista

⊕ **SIGHTS**

11	◖ BICENTENNIAL CAPITOL MALL STATE PARK	43	◖ CIVIL RIGHTS ROOM AT THE NASHVILLE PUBLIC LIBRARY	75	TENNESSEE SPORTS HALL OF FAME
16	TENNESSEE STATE CAPITOL	46	DOWNTOWN PRESBYTERIAN CHURCH	83	THE JOHNNY CASH MUSEUM
18	MILITARY BRANCH MUSEUM	53	HUME FOGG	90	FORT NASHBOROUGH
19	WAR MEMORIAL PLAZA	55	THE RYMAN AUDITORIUM	91	SHELBY STREET PEDESTRIAN BRIDGE
21	TENNESSEE STATE MUSEUM	71	FRIST CENTER FOR THE VISUAL ARTS	95	◖ COUNTRY MUSIC HALL OF FAME
31	THE ARCADE	74	CUSTOMS HOUSE		

🍴 **RESTAURANTS**

4	ROLF & DAUGHTERS	33	KATIE'S MEAT & THREE	81	MERCHANT'S
5	MAD PLATTER	36	MANNY'S HOUSE OF PIZZA	89	THE SOUTHERN STEAK AND OYSTER
6	MONELL'S	37	THE GREEK TOUCH	97	ETCH
7	CITY HOUSE	38	SANTORINI	100	COPPER KETTLE
8	GERMANTOWN CAFÉ	45	PROVENCE	102	HUSK NASHVILLE
9	SILO	61	JACK'S BAR-B-QUE	107	WATERMARK
10	MARY'S OLD FASHIONED PIT BAR-B-QUE	64	◖ DIANA'S SWEET SHOP	112	ARNOLD'S COUNTRY KITCHEN
27	CAPITOL GRILLE	68	WHISKEY KITCHEN	114	FLYTE
30	PUCKETT'S GROCERY & RESTAURANT	72	FRIST CENTER CAFÉ		
		73	THE STANDARD		

🍸 **NIGHTLIFE**

2	NASHVILLE JAZZ WORKSHOP	59	TOOTSIE'S ORCHID LOUNGE	96	COUNTRY MUSIC HALL OF FAME
28	OAK BAR	60	LAYLA'S BLUEGRASS INN	98	THE LISTENING ROOM CAFÉ
40	BOURBON STREET BLUES AND BOOGIE BAR	62	ROBERT'S WESTERN WORLD	99	THE RUTLEDGE
41	FIDDLE AND STEEL	63	THE STAGE ON BROADWAY	103	3RD AND LINDSLEY
42	◖ LONNIE'S WESTERN ROOM	67	WILDHORSE SALOON	104	THE STATION INN
48	JAZZ 'N' JOKES	69	FLYING SAUCER	109	YAZOO TAP ROOM
49	THE BEER SELLAR	77	THE WHEEL	110	CANNERY BALLROOM
50	B. B. KING BLUES CLUB	79	PARADISE PARK TRAILER RESORT	113	JACKALOPE BREWING CO.
51	12TH AND PORTER	86	ROCK BOTTOM RESTAURANT & BREWERY		
56	THE RYMAN AUDITORIUM				
58	LEGENDS CORNER				

🎭 **ARTS AND LEISURE**

1	ACTORS BRIDGE ENSEMBLE	24	TENNESSEE REPERTORY THEATRE	92	TENNESSEE TITANS
12	◖ NASH TRASH TOURS	32	THE ARCADE	93	◖ CUMBERLAND PARK
14	THE ARTS COMPANY	34	TWIST ART GALLERY	94	JAZZ ON THE CUMBERLAND
15	THE RYMER GALLERY	44	WISHING CHAIR PRODUCTIONS	101	◖ NASHVILLE CHILDREN'S THEATRE
17	LIVE ON THE GREEN	57	BLUEGRASS NIGHTS AT THE RYMAN	111	MISS JEANNE'S MYSTERY DINNER THEATRE
20	WAR MEMORIAL AUDITORIUM	76	NASHVILLE PREDATORS		
22	NASHVILLE BALLET	84	SEGWAY TOURS		
23	NASHVILLE OPERA ASSOCIATION	87	NASHVILLE SYMPHONY ORCHESTRA		

🛍 **SHOPS**

3	◖ PETER NAPPI	66	BOOT COUNTRY	85	TRAIL WEST
13	NASHVILLE FARMER'S MARKET FLEA MARKET	78	ERNEST TUBB RECORD SHOP	105	TWO OLD HIPPIES
35	PEANUT SHOP	80	LAWRENCE RECORD SHOP	106	LUCCHESE
65	◖ HATCH SHOW PRINT			108	BULLETS AND MULLETS
				115	◖ THIRD MAN RECORDS

🏨 **HOTELS**

25	DOUBLETREE HOTEL NASHVILLE	39	HOTEL INDIGO DOWNTOWN	54	RENAISSANCE HOTEL
26	SHERATON DOWNTOWN NASHVILLE	47	COURTYARD BY MARRIOT	70	UNION STATION
29	◖ HERMITAGE HOTEL	52	HOLIDAY INN EXPRESS NASHVILLE-DOWNTOWN	82	HILTON NASHVILLE DOWNTOWN
				88	OMNI NASHVILLE HOTEL

SEE MAP 2

Music Row

SEE MAP 2

© AVALON TRAVEL

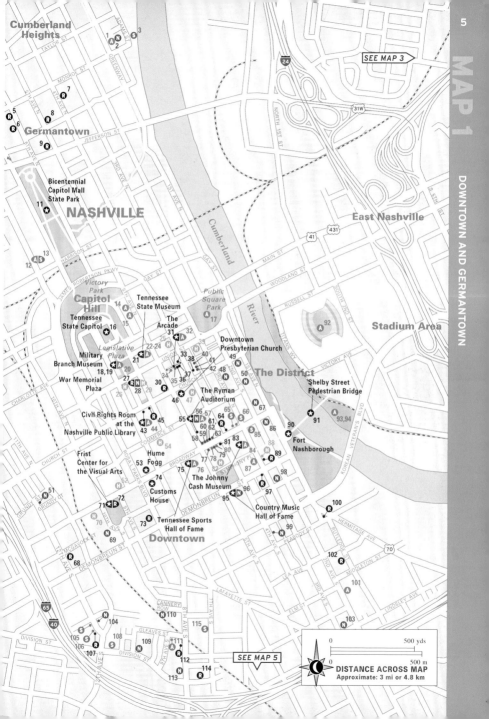

Cumberland
Heights

Germantown

NASHVILLE

Bicentennial
Capitol Mall
State Park

East Nashville

Cumberland River

Public
Square
Park

Victory
Park

Capitol
Hill

Tennessee
State Museum

Stadium Area

Tennessee
State Capitol

The
Arcade

Downtown
Presbyterian Church

Legislative
Plaza

Military
Branch Museum

The District

War Memorial
Plaza

Shelby Street
Pedestrian Bridge

The Ryman
Auditorium

Civil Rights Room
at the
Nashville Public Library

Fort
Nashborough

Frist
Center for
the Visual Arts

Hume
Fogg

The Johnny
Cash Museum

Customs
House

Tennessee Sports
Hall of Fame

Country Music
Hall of Fame

Downtown

SEE MAP 3

SEE MAP 5

0   500 yds

0   500 m

DISTANCE ACROSS MAP
Approximate: 3 mi or 4.8 km

⊙ SIGHTS

1	FISK UNIVERSITY	21	THE UPPER ROOM
2	MEHARRY MEDICAL COLLEGE	39	VANDERBILT UNIVERSITY
6	MARATHON VILLAGE	44	THE PARTHENON
20	RCA STUDIO B	71	BELMONT UNIVERSITY
		72	BELMONT MANSION

⊙ RESTAURANTS

11	SWETT'S	64	SUNSET GRILL
13	SUZY WONG'S HOUSE OF YUM	65	HOT AND COLD
18	THE CATBIRD SEAT	66	FIDO
22	SAN ANTONIO TACO CO.	68	BONGO JAVA
25	TAVERN MIDTOWN	69	PM
27	NOSHVILLE	70	INTERNATIONAL MARKET AND RESTAURANT
33	ELLISTON PLACE SODA SHOP	84	A MATTER OF TASTE
37	JIMMY KELLY'S	85	ATHENS FAMILY
42	ROTIER'S	87	MAFIAOZA'S PIZZERIA AND NEIGHBORHOOD PUB
47	HOG HEAVEN	92	BURGER UP
53	TIN ANGEL	93	LAS PALETAS
58	PANCAKE PANTRY	94	SLOCO

⊙ NIGHTLIFE

5	MARATHON MUSIC WORKS	35	THE GOLD RUSH
7	CORSAIR ARTISAN DISTILLERY	36	CAFÉ COCO
14	TRIBE	46	SPRINGWATER
19	PLAY	61	BOSCOS
19	PATTERSON HOUSE	62	CABANA
31	BLACKSTONE RESTAURANT AND BREWERY	76	THE BASEMENT
		80	ZANIES
		81	DOUGLAS CORNER CAFÉ
34	EXIT/IN	83	THAT'S COOL
		86	12 SOUTH TAPROOM AND GRILL

⊙ ARTS AND LEISURE

3	CARL VAN VECHTEN GALLERY	43	CENTENNIAL SPORTSPLEX
4	AARON DOUGLAS GALLERY	45	CENTENNIAL PARK
16	NASHVILLE PEDAL TAVERN	50	CUMBERLAND TRANSIT
38	HOT YOGA PLUS	55	BLAIR SCHOOL OF MUSIC
40	SARRATT GALLERY	60	BELCOURT THEATRE
41	VANDERBILT UNIVERSITY FINE ARTS GALLERY	73	STEADFAST AND TRUE
		95	12 SOUTH YOGA

⊙ SHOPS

8	ANTIQUE ARCHAEOLOGY	67	FIRE FINCH BOUTIQUE
9	OTIS JAMES	74	HATWRKS
10	BANG CANY COMPANY	75	FLIP
26	MANUEL EXCLUSIVE CLOTHIER	77	GRIMEY'S NEW AND PRELOVED MUSIC
49	SCARLETT BEGONIA	78	HOWLIN' BOOKS
51	BOUTIQUE BELLA	79	EIGHTH AVENUE ANTIQUES MALL
52	UAL	82	GRUHN GUITARS
56	BOOKMAN BOOKWOMAN USED BOOKS	89	KATY K DESIGNS RANCH DRESSING
57	DAVIS COOKWARE	90	MODA
59	PANGAEA	91	IMOGENE + WILLIE
63	HILLSBORO VILLAGE		

⊙ HOTELS

12	MUSIC CITY HOSTEL	32	LOEWS VANDERBILT PLAZA
17	BEST WESTERN MUSIC ROW	48	MARRIOTT NASHVILLE VANDERBILT
23	HILTON GARDEN INN	54	DAISY HILL B&B
24	ALOFT WEST END	88	1501 LINDEN HOUSE BED AND BREAKFAST
28	HUTTON HOTEL	96	12 SOUTH INN
29	GUESTHOUSE INN AND SUITES		
30	HAMPTON INN VANDERBILT		

DISTANCE ACROSS MAP
Approximate: 4.9 mi or 7.9 km

0   500 yds
0   500 m

North Nashville

Meharry
Medical
College

Fisk University

Fisk
University

Capitol Hill

The District

Marathon
Village

SEE MAP 1

Downtown

Music Row

RCA
Studio B

The Upper
Room

Vanderbilt
University

Centennial
Park

Vanderbilt
University

Fort
Negly
Park

Edgehill

Cherokee Park

Hillsboro
Village

Belmont
Mansion

Belmont
University

Belmont University

Bellmont
Hillsboro

Melrose

12 South

SEE MAP 5

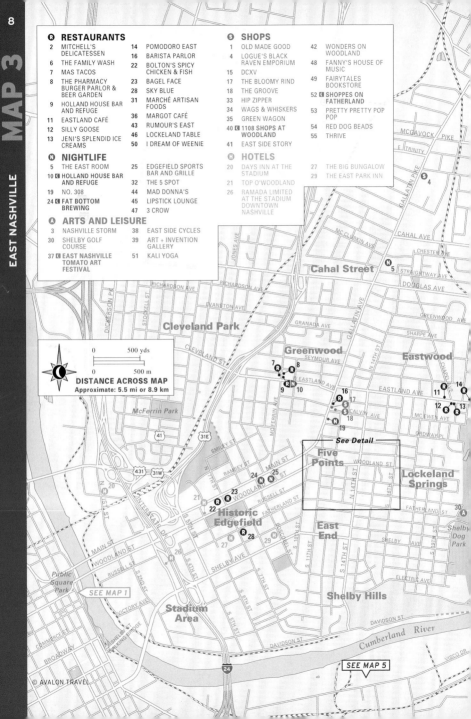

Ⓡ RESTAURANTS

- 2 MITCHELL'S DELICATESSEN
- 6 THE FAMILY WASH
- 7 MAS TACOS
- 8 THE PHARMACY BURGER PARLOR & BEER GARDEN
- 9 HOLLAND HOUSE BAR AND REFUGE
- 11 EASTLAND CAFÉ
- 12 SILLY GOOSE
- 13 JENI'S SPLENDID ICE CREAMS
- 14 POMODORO EAST
- 16 BARISTA PARLOR
- 22 BOLTON'S SPICY CHICKEN & FISH
- 23 BAGEL FACE
- 28 SKY BLUE
- 31 MARCHÉ ARTISAN FOODS
- 36 MARGOT CAFÉ
- 43 RUMOUR'S EAST
- 46 LOCKELAND TABLE
- 50 I DREAM OF WEENIE

Ⓝ NIGHTLIFE

- 5 THE EAST ROOM
- 10 Ⓒ HOLLAND HOUSE BAR AND REFUGE
- 19 NO. 308
- 24 Ⓒ FAT BOTTOM BREWING
- 25 EDGEFIELD SPORTS BAR AND GRILLE
- 32 THE 5 SPOT
- 44 MAD DONNA'S
- 45 LIPSTICK LOUNGE
- 47 3 CROW

Ⓐ ARTS AND LEISURE

- 3 NASHVILLE STORM
- 30 SHELBY GOLF COURSE
- 37 Ⓒ EAST NASHVILLE TOMATO ART FESTIVAL
- 38 EAST SIDE CYCLES
- 39 ART + INVENTION GALLERY
- 51 KALI YOGA

Ⓢ SHOPS

- 1 OLD MADE GOOD
- 4 LOGUE'S BLACK RAVEN EMPORIUM
- 15 DCXV
- 17 THE BLOOMY RIND
- 18 THE GROOVE
- 33 HIP ZIPPER
- 34 WAGS & WHISKERS
- 35 GREEN WAGON
- 40 Ⓒ 1108 SHOPS AT WOODLAND
- 41 EAST SIDE STORY
- 42 WONDERS ON WOODLAND
- 48 FANNY'S HOUSE OF MUSIC
- 49 FAIRYTALES BOOKSTORE
- 52 Ⓒ SHOPPES ON FATHERLAND
- 53 PRETTY PRETTY POP POP
- 54 RED DOG BEADS
- 55 THRIVE

Ⓗ HOTELS

- 20 DAYS INN AT THE STADIUM
- 21 TOP O'WOODLAND
- 26 RAMADA LIMITED AT THE STADIUM DOWNTOWN NASHVILLE
- 27 THE BIG BUNGALOW
- 29 THE EAST PARK INN

0   500 yds
0   500 m

DISTANCE ACROSS MAP
Approximate: 5.5 mi or 8.9 km

Cahal Street

Cleveland Park

Greenwood

Eastwood

McFerrin Park

Five Points

Lockeland Springs

Historic Edgefield

East End

Public Square Park

SEE MAP 1

Stadium Area

Shelby Hills

Shelby Dog Park

Cumberland River

SEE MAP 5

© AVALON TRAVEL

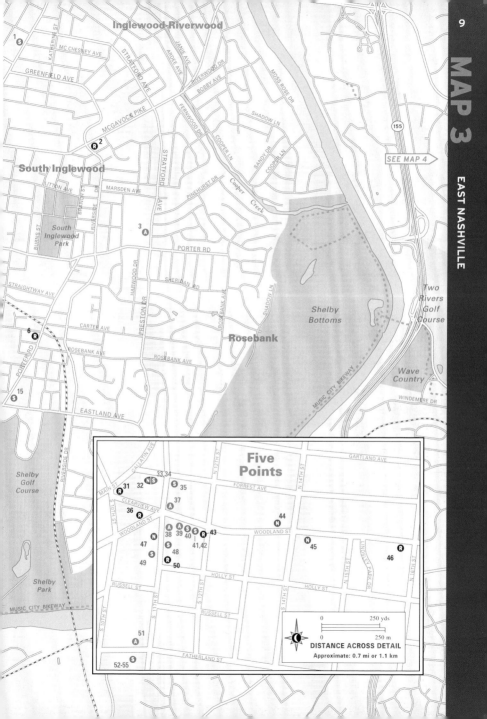

Inglewood-Riverwood

MC CHESNEY AVE

KATHERINE ST

GREENFIELD AVE

STRATFORD AVE

JANIE AVE

ARDEE AVE

RIVERWOOD DR

BOBBY AVE

MOSS ROSE DR

SHADOW LN

SANDY DR

COOPER LN

COOPER LN

155

SEE MAP 4

MCGAVOCK PIKE

FERNWOOD DR

South Inglewood

LITTON AVE

MARSDEN AVE

STRATFORD AVE

PINEHURST DR

Cooper Creek

BURNS ST

BRANCH ST

RIVERSIDE DR

South
Inglewood
Park

3

PORTER RD

HARWOOD DR

SHERIDAN RD

STRAIGHTWAY AVE

PRESTON DR

ROSEBANK AVE

SHADOW LN

Shelby
Bottoms

Two
Rivers
Golf
Course

6

CARTER AVE

ROSEBANK AVE

Rosebank

PORTER RD

15

ROSEBANK AVE

Wave
Country

MUSIC CITY BIKEWAY

WINDEMERE DR

EASTLAND AVE

RIVERSIDE DR

Shelby
Golf
Course

PORTER RD

**Five
Points**

GARTLAND AVE

GALLATIN AVE

MAIN ST

33, 34

N 12TH ST

FORREST AVE

N 14TH ST

31

32

35

CLEARVIEW AVE

36

37

44

WOODLAND ST

Shelby
Park

38

39

40

43

WOODLAND ST

47

41, 42

45

LINDSLEY PARK DR

N 16TH ST

46

48

49

50

RUSSELL ST

HOLLY ST

HOLLY ST

MUSIC CITY BIKEWAY

S 11TH ST

S 12TH ST

N 15TH ST

RUSSELL ST

51

FATHERLAND ST

52-55

0   250 yds

0   250 m

DISTANCE ACROSS DETAIL
Approximate: 0.7 mi or 1.1 km

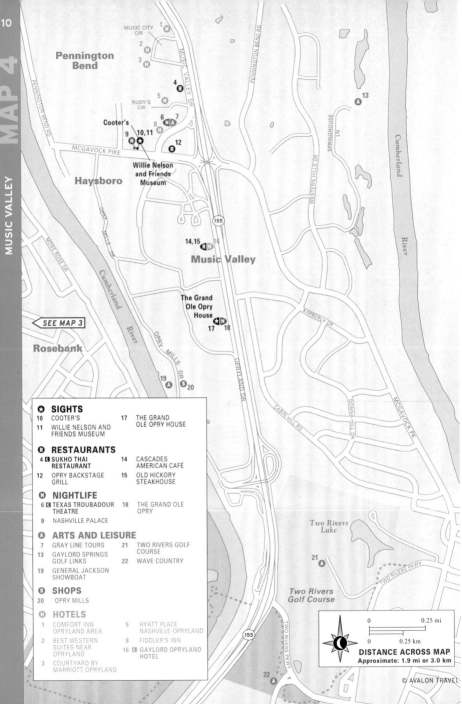

Pennington Bend

MUSIC CITY CIR

RUDY'S CIR

Cooter's

MCGAVOCK PIKE

Willie Nelson and Friends Museum

Haysboro

Music Valley

The Grand Ole Opry House

SEE MAP 3

Rosebank

Cumberland River

Cumberland River

Two Rivers Lake

Two Rivers Golf Course

○ SIGHTS
10 COOTER'S
11 WILLIE NELSON AND FRIENDS MUSEUM
17 THE GRAND OLE OPRY HOUSE

○ RESTAURANTS
4 ○ SUKHO THAI RESTAURANT
12 OPRY BACKSTAGE GRILL
14 CASCADES AMERICAN CAFÉ
15 OLD HICKORY STEAKHOUSE

○ NIGHTLIFE
6 ○ TEXAS TROUBADOUR THEATRE
9 NASHVILLE PALACE
18 THE GRAND OLE OPRY

○ ARTS AND LEISURE
7 GRAY LINE TOURS
13 GAYLORD SPRINGS GOLF LINKS
19 GENERAL JACKSON SHOWBOAT
21 TWO RIVERS GOLF COURSE
22 WAVE COUNTRY

○ SHOPS
20 OPRY MILLS

○ HOTELS
1 COMFORT INN OPRYLAND AREA
2 BEST WESTERN SUITES NEAR OPRYLAND
3 COURTYARD BY MARRIOTT OPRYLAND
5 HYATT PLACE NASHVILLE-OPRYLAND
8 FIDDLER'S INN
16 ○ GAYLORD OPRYLAND HOTEL

DISTANCE ACROSS MAP
Approximate: 1.9 mi or 3.0 km

0   0.25 mi
0   0.25 km

© AVALON TRAVEL

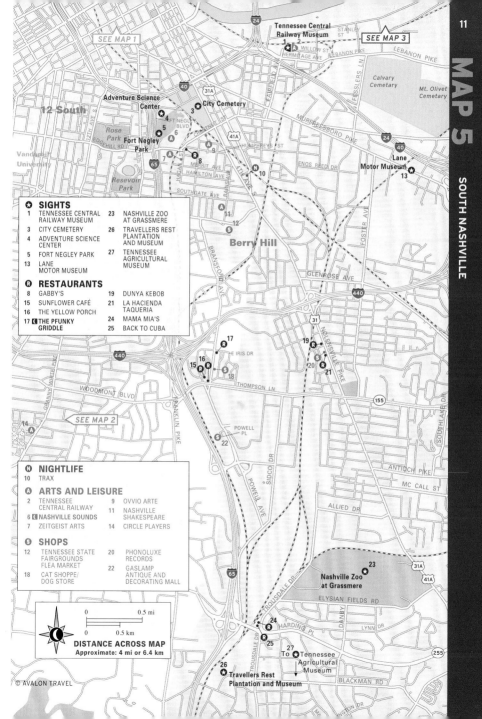

Tennessee Central
Railway Museum

SEE MAP 1

SEE MAP 3

Calvary
Cemetery

Mt. Olivet
Cemetery

12 South

Adventure Science
Center

City Cemetery

MURFREESBORO PIKE

Vanderbilt
University

Rose
Park

Fort Negley
Park

Lane
Motor Museum

Reservoir
Park

Berry Hill

SIGHTS

1	TENNESSEE CENTRAL RAILWAY MUSEUM	23	NASHVILLE ZOO AT GRASSMERE
3	CITY CEMETERY	26	TRAVELLERS REST PLANTATION AND MUSEUM
4	ADVENTURE SCIENCE CENTER		
5	FORT NEGLEY PARK	27	TENNESSEE AGRICULTURAL MUSEUM
13	LANE MOTOR MUSEUM		

RESTAURANTS

8	GABBY'S	19	DUNYA KEBOB
15	SUNFLOWER CAFÉ	21	LA HACIENDA TAQUERIA
16	THE YELLOW PORCH	24	MAMA MIA'S
17	THE PFUNKY GRIDDLE	25	BACK TO CUBA

WOODMONT BLVD

SEE MAP 2

IRIS DR

THOMPSON LN

POWELL PL

NIGHTLIFE
10 TRAX

ARTS AND LEISURE

2	TENNESSEE CENTRAL RAILWAY	9	OVVIO ARTE
6	NASHVILLE SOUNDS	11	NASHVILLE SHAKESPEARE
7	ZEITGEIST ARTS	14	CIRCLE PLAYERS

SHOPS

| 12 | TENNESSEE STATE FAIRGROUNDS FLEA MARKET | 20 | PHONOLUXE RECORDS |
| 18 | CAT SHOPPE/ DOG STORE | 22 | GASLAMP ANTIQUE AND DECORATING MALL |

ALLIED DR

MC CALL ST

ANTIOCH PIKE

Nashville Zoo
at Grassmere

ELYSIAN FIELDS RD

HARDING PL

To Tennessee
Agricultural
Museum

Travellers Rest
Plantation and Museum

BLACKMAN RD

0   0.5 mi
0   0.5 km

DISTANCE ACROSS MAP
Approximate: 4 mi or 6.4 km

© AVALON TRAVEL

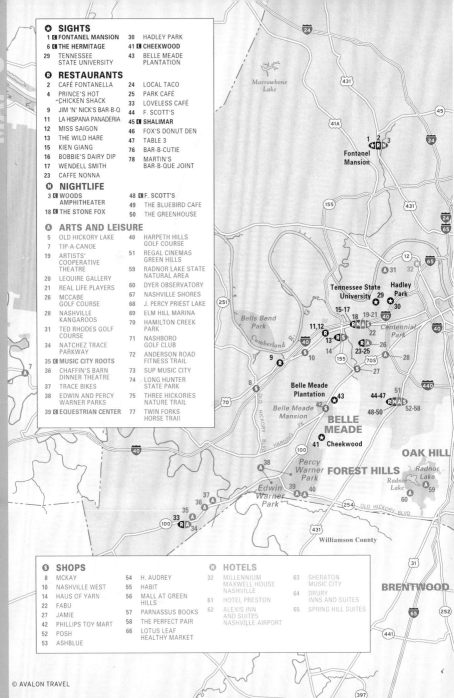

✪ SIGHTS

1	FONTANEL MANSION	30	HADLEY PARK
6	THE HERMITAGE	41	CHEEKWOOD
29	TENNESSEE STATE UNIVERSITY	43	BELLE MEADE PLANTATION

℞ RESTAURANTS

2	CAFÉ FONTANELLA	24	LOCAL TACO
4	PRINCE'S HOT CHICKEN SHACK	25	PARK CAFÉ
9	JIM 'N' NICK'S BAR-B-Q	33	LOVELESS CAFÉ
11	LA HISPANA PANADERIA	44	F. SCOTT'S
12	MISS SAIGON	45	SHALIMAR
13	THE WILD HARE	46	FOX'S DONUT DEN
15	KIEN GIANG	47	TABLE 3
16	BOBBIE'S DAIRY DIP	76	BAR-B-CUTIE
17	WENDELL SMITH	78	MARTIN'S BAR-B-QUE JOINT
23	CAFFE NONNA		

◐ NIGHTLIFE

3	WOODS AMPHITHEATER	48	F. SCOTT'S
18	THE STONE FOX	49	THE BLUEBIRD CAFE
		50	THE GREENHOUSE

⊙ ARTS AND LEISURE

5	OLD HICKORY LAKE	40	HARPETH HILLS GOLF COURSE
7	TIP-A-CANOE	51	REGAL CINEMAS GREEN HILLS
19	ARTISTS' COOPERATIVE THEATRE	59	RADNOR LAKE STATE NATURAL AREA
20	LEQUIRE GALLERY	60	DYER OBSERVATORY
21	REAL LIFE PLAYERS	67	NASHVILLE SHORES
26	MCCABE GOLF COURSE	68	J. PERCY PRIEST LAKE
28	NASHVILLE KANGAROOS	69	ELM HILL MARINA
31	TED RHODES GOLF COURSE	70	HAMILTON CREEK PARK
34	NATCHEZ TRACE PARKWAY	71	NASHBORO GOLF CLUB
35	MUSIC CITY ROOTS	72	ANDERSON ROAD FITNESS TRAIL
36	CHAFFIN'S BARN DINNER THEATRE	73	SUP MUSIC CITY
37	TRACE BIKES	74	LONG HUNTER STATE PARK
38	EDWIN AND PERCY WARNER PARKS	75	THREE HICKORIES NATURE TRAIL
39	EQUESTRIAN CENTER	77	TWIN FORKS HORSE TRAIL

⑤ SHOPS

8	MCKAY	54	H. AUDREY
10	NASHVILLE WEST	55	HABIT
14	HAUS OF YARN	56	MALL AT GREEN HILLS
22	FABU	57	PARNASSUS BOOKS
27	JAMIE	58	THE PERFECT PAIR
42	PHILLIPS TOY MART	66	LOTUS LEAF HEALTHY MARKET
52	POSH		
53	ASHBLUE		

◗ HOTELS

32	MILLENNIUM MAXWELL HOUSE NASHVILLE	63	SHERATON MUSIC CITY
61	HOTEL PRESTON	64	DRURY INNS AND SUITES
62	ALEXIS INN AND SUITES NASHVILLE AIRPORT	65	SPRING HILL SUITES

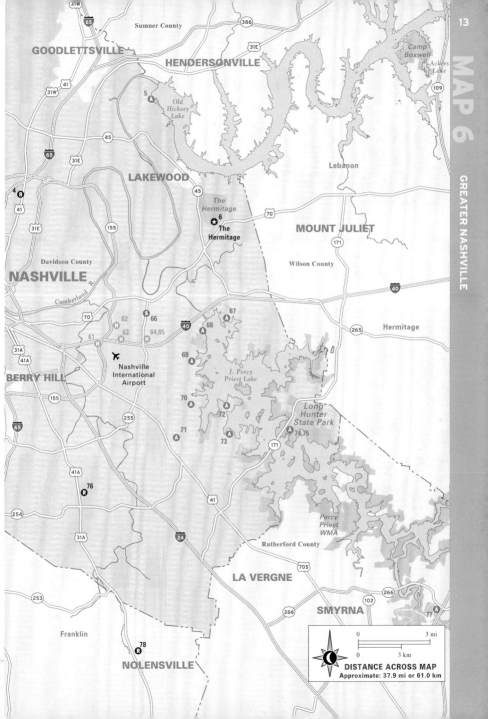

MAP 6

Sumner County

31W

386

GOODLETTSVILLE

31E

Camp
Boxwell

65

HENDERSONVILLE

Ackers
Lake

41

31W

109

5
A

Old
Hickory
Lake

45

LAKEWOOD

65

31E

Lebanon

45

The
Hermitage

70

4
R

6
The
Hermitage

MOUNT JULIET

41

31E

155

171

Davidson County

Wilson County

NASHVILLE

Cumberland R.

40

70

62

5
66

67

265

Hermitage

63

64,65

40

68

61
H

69
A

Nashville
International
Airport

31A

41A

70
A

J. Percy
Priest Lake

BERRY HILL

Long
Hunter
State Park

155

72

65

255

71
A

73

74,75

171

41

76
R

254

31A

24

Percy
Priest
WMA

253

Rutherford County

705

LA VERGNE

Franklin

266

102

266

SMYRNA

77
A

78
R

NOLENSVILLE

DISTANCE ACROSS MAP
Approximate: 37.9 mi or 61.0 km

0 _____ 3 mi

0 _____ 3 km

Discover Nashville

When it comes to creative energy, nowhere compares to Music City. People come here to make their dreams come true. Even before Johnny Cash picked up a guitar or Elvis entered RCA Studio B, this was a city that attracted mavericks and iconoclasts. And whether you have a banjo in that overhead bin or you can't tell a harmony from a melody, it doesn't matter. Because Nashville isn't just about the music. People here are willing to try new things and do things differently.

Creativity of all kinds flows in the veins of folks who call this place home. Nashville is filled with hyphenates like chef-singer-songwriters and artist-poet-hula-hoop-makers. It fosters an entrepreneurial energy that results in funky music clubs for jamming, quirky boutiques for shopping, and one-of-a-kind roadside eateries for... well, eating.

But the "anything can happen" attitude isn't limited just to residents. You don't have to be here more than a day or two to encounter truly talented musicians singing on the curb on Broadway or taste the creative genius emerging from the kitchens of the city's restaurants—both upscale and down home. Whether you're in town for the weekend or for good, take advantage of that optimism, offered with a dash of Southern hospitality. Move to the offbeat and always interesting Nashville beat.

Planning Your Trip

▶ WHERE TO GO

Downtown and Germantown

Downtown is Nashville's economic and tourism hub, not to mention the geographic center of the city. This is the heart of Music City's beat. Lower Broad is lined with honky-tonks with music playing almost any hour of the day. In addition to some of the city's biggest attractions, downtown is home to hotels, restaurants, and a great view of the Cumberland River, not to mention Fort Nashborough, the city's ancestral beginning.

Midtown and 12 South

Midtown is where the work gets done: It's home to Vanderbilt University, one of many institutions in Nashville that educate, populate, and sustain the city, and Music Row, where record deals are signed. 12 South is

more light-hearted: It boasts well-edited boutique shopping, compelling restaurants, and an active nightlife, from live music venues to comedy clubs. The area lends itself to leisurely strolls down neighborhood streets. The Belmont University campus brings youthful energy to the area.

East Nashville

East Nashville has a love-hate relationship with the "hip" moniker it has earned over the years. This gentrifying (or gentrified) neighborhood just east of downtown is home to stylish vintage boutiques and purveyors of handcrafted goods, not to mention the bulk of the city's sleekest restaurants and best watering holes. Football stadium LP Field is nestled on its banks.

Lower Broad

Vanderbilt University in autumn

white tiger at the Nashville Zoo at Grassmere

Music Valley

Close to the airport and the home of the Grand Ole Opry and Opry Mills, Music Valley is designed for tourists. Here you'll find affordable hotels and motels, kitschy attractions, family-friendly restaurants, and a few attractions that even locals secretly love to frequent.

South Nashville

South Nashville doesn't have the cohesive neighborhood that other parts of the city do. As a result, it can be hard to define where one section of South Nashville ends and another neighborhood begins. What the area may lack in clear borders, however, it makes up for in worthy destinations: the Nashville Zoo at Grassmere, the baseball stadium, and the best international cuisine in Nashville.

Greater Nashville

Nashville's outlying areas and suburbs offer compelling reasons to jump in the car and explore. Out the window you'll see Middle Tennessee's rolling hills and the beauty of some of the area's best attractions, including Cheekwood, Belle Meade Plantation, and Andrew Jackson's home, The Hermitage, and the mammoth log cabin Fontanel Mansion, once Barbara Mandrell's home.

Howe Garden at Cheekwood

Gaylord Opryland

▶ WHEN TO GO

There's no "wrong" time to head to Music City; it just depends on your personal preference. Spring and fall are generally mild, filled with pleasant days and crisp nights. Wildflowers bloom in the Greenway, and streets are lined with flowering trees. Weekends are filled with fun events, and hotel rooms are relatively easy to snag.

Summer is high tourist season. Free and paid concerts alike are booked on stages most weekends, and Lower Broadway is filled with folks enjoying the honky-tonks, long summer days, and high-energy atmosphere. The downside of summer is that it will be hot and humid. Even at night. If you are a high-energy, festival-going kind of traveler, come in the summer and pack accordingly. Remember that sweater for overly air-conditioned hotels and restaurants.

Winter in Nashville is mild compared to cities farther north where snow and slush clog the streets. While Music City will get a light dusting of snow, generally winter means grabbing a coat and hat, not a shovel and gloves. Christmastime at Gaylord Opryland is magical for travelers with families, featuring thousands of lights and holiday displays, and annual performances by the famous Radio City Rockettes.

Explore Nashville

▶ THE TWO-DAY BEST OF NASHVILLE

Parts of Nashville are full of 24/7 activity, others are more traditionally Southern, with some businesses closed on Sunday and relatively early on weekday nights. The following itinerary assumes a Saturday-Sunday stay in Music City, although for the most part it can be adjusted for different days of the week (and seasons of the year).

Day 1

▶ Arrive in Nashville. Check early into a historic downtown hotel, such as the Hermitage or Union Station. Allow the exceptional staff to take your bags so you can make the most of your days unencumbered.

▶ Set out on foot to the Civil Rights Room at the Nashville Public Library, where you'll learn about the city's role in the national movement.

▶ From there take in the Tennessee State Capitol and then head down the hill for lunch at one of the many tasty choices at the Nashville Farmer's Market.

▶ You'll need a walk after enjoying wood-oven-fired pizza and butter cake. Take one across the street at Bicentennial Capitol Mall State Park. After hearing the carillon bells play "The Tennessee Waltz," head back downtown.

▶ Spend the afternoon at the Country Music Hall of Fame and RCA Studio B. Head back to the hotel to cleanup for the evening.

▶ Start the night off with a drink in the swanky Oak Bar. It'll be the most refined place you go all evening.

historic RCA Studio B

Carl Van Vechten Gallery, Fisk University

▶ Grab dinner at Jack's Bar-b-que and spend the evening strolling, dancing, and drinking on Lower Broadway's honkytonks. Or, check out the show playing at the Ryman Auditorium. If you're in town between Thanksgiving and New Year's Eve, you'll be able to see the Grand Ole Opry at the Ryman.

Day 2

▶ Grab the car and drive through the historic Fisk University campus. Stop at both the Carl Van Vechten Gallery and the Aaron Douglas Gallery on campus.

▶ Make your way to Arnold's Country Kitchen for a late breakfast.

▶ Sated with biscuits, head to bucolic Centennial Park and the majestic Parthenon. The replica is striking from the outside, but take the time to go inside and see the museum and the striking gold *Athena* sculpture. Grab a snack from one of the many food trucks that gather in Centennial Park.

▶ Drive through Midtown, looking at the Vanderbilt University campus and Music Row, where you might see celebs on their way to meetings with their record label executives.

▶ Shoppers will enjoy strolling the boutiques in Hillsboro Village.

▶ Grab an afternoon pick-me-up from Fido or Hot and Cold.

▶ If the sun is shining, spend the afternoon checking out the museum and gardens at Cheekwood. If not, take shelter in a big pink bus and enjoy the rollicking humor of a Nash Trash Tour.

▶ Cross the bridge into East Nashville for your evening out. Choose to dine early at Holland House Bar and Refuge, where you can have both drinks and dinner in a sleek, modern environment.

▶ Then head across the river to Music Valley,

MUSIC CITY ON A BUDGET

Experience the city for free at events like the Independence Day celebration.

It's Saturday night. You want to go out and hear some of the sound that makes Music City groove, but your wallet is empty. Not a problem! One of Nashville's strengths is that there are so many free and low-budget options to explore.

MUSIC

- All the downtown honky-tonks, including **Tootsie's Orchid Lounge** and **Robert's Western World** are cover-charge free, though you are expected to put money in the (actual) hat when the band passes it.

- **Midnite Jamboree** is an hour-long, always free radio show starting at midnight on Saturday nights. The show doesn't charge for admission or parking, and the caliber of talent that plays is always rich.

CULTURE

- The **Civil Rights Room at the Nashville Public Library** shows the city's essential role in the civil rights movement with the 1960s Nashville sit-ins.

- Want to experience Nashville's amazing downtown? Parking is usually free in Lot R, which is close to **Cumberland Park,** a great place to play and learn about the river's role in the city. Then you can walk across the **Shelby Street Pedestrian Bridge** and explore downtown on foot.

- Many of the city's major attractions, including the **Frist Center for the Visual Arts** and **Cheekwood** offer free days throughout the year. The city is also home to free events like the **East Nashville Tomato Art Festival** and its **Independence Day** celebrations.

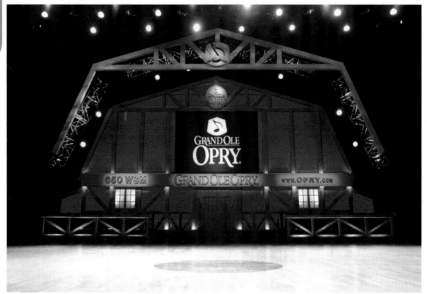

Grand Ole Opry

to catch the Grand Ole Opry in all its grand ole glory.

▶ If you were lucky enough to catch the Opry downtown the night before, then you get a more leisurely night of enjoying East Nashville's cocktails and culinary delights. Spread the love around No. 308, The 5 Spot, and Marché.

▶ FOODIE WEEKEND

The city's kitchens are making one "best of" list after another. To that end, the following itinerary is a foodie's fantasy weekend.

Saturday
BREAKFAST
▶ Start with a well-edited and well-presented continental breakfast at Barista Parlor. The coffee is a work of art, and you'll want a light meal considering what you've got planned for the rest of the day.

LUNCH
▶ Feast on smartly designed cocktails and plates of oysters at The Southern Steak and Oyster.

▶ A mid-afternoon snack should involve some of Nashville's signature hot chicken, served on white bread, either from Bolton's Spicy Chicken & Fish or Prince's Hot Chicken Shack.

DINNER
▶ Do whatever it takes (which means logging on 30 days in advance) to nab one of the coveted 32 seats at acclaimed The Catbird Seat. Your three-hour meal is a culinary performance as much as dinner. The evening includes drink pairings and dessert. Enjoy the experience.

PINT-SIZED NASHVILLE

Hot and Cold serves tasty treats at both ends of the thermometer.

Sure, Nashville is filled with beer, bourbon, and late-night carousing: That's the honky-tonk way. But there's no shortage of things for kids to do, see, and eat.

- Animal lovers will adore the meerkat exhibit at the **Nashville Zoo at Grassmere,** as well as the zoo's Wild Animal Carousel. There's something new going on at the zoo almost every week.

- The **Adventure Science Center** and its **Sudekum Planetarium** offer hands-on exhibits, education disguised as entertainment, and a great option for being indoors on rainy days. Clear nights call for a drive to the **Dyer Observatory.**

- Nashville's many parks and open spaces are perfect for getting kids moving.

The **Centennial Sportsplex** offers ice skating, tennis, and more. Hillsboro Village's **Fannie Mae Dee Park** is known as the dragon park because of a giant dragon sculpture that kids love to climb.

- **Nashville Shores** and **Wave Country** are the go-to places to get wet and cool off in those hot Tennessee summers.

- Hungry after all that play? Berry Hill's **The Pfunky Griddle** lets kids (and their parents) cook their own pancakes on a table-side grill, filling them with M&Ms, blueberries, or other toppings. For sweet treats, head to Hillsboro Village's **Hot and Cold,** where you can grab a **Las Paletas** popsicle dipped in chocolate. That's something grown-ups will savor, too.

GNATURE FLAVORS
GKOK PEANUT
K COFFEE
MBLEBERRY CRISP
N BUTTER ALMOND BRITTLE
RRY LAMBIC SORBET
K CHOCOLATE
AT CHEESE WITH RED CHERRIES
ON FROZEN YOGURT
ACHIO & HONEY

QUEEN CITY CAYENNE
RIESLING POACHED PEAR SORBET
SALTY CARAMEL
THE BUCKEYE STATE
THE MILKIEST CHOCOLATE
IN THE WORLD
UGANDAN VANILLA BEAN
WHISKEY & PECANS
WILDBERRY LAVENDER

PERENNIAL FLAVORS
DOUBLE-TOASTED COCONUT
BANANA CAJETA
ROXBURY ROAD
BLACK CURRANT FROZEN YOGURT
SAVANNAH BUTTERMINT

LIMITED EDITION
YAZOO SUE WITH ROSEMARY BAR NUTS
GUAVA CLOVERTON
THE + MERINGUES
SAFFRON, ORANGE + CARAMEL

CREAM SANDWICHES

SALTY CARAMEL

DOUBLE-TOASTED COCONUT
AND CAJETA

Jeni's Splendid Ice Creams

Sunday

BREAKFAST

▶ East Nashville's Sky Blue is known and be-loved for its brisket bowl, a breakfast treat said to calm even the worst hangover.

LUNCH

▶ The city's movers and shakers diner at Swett's, an old-school-style cafeteria with tasty soul food. The gossip dished up here is a good as the food on the plate.

▶ Afterward, grab a palate-cleansing frozen treat at Las Paletas before moving on to the next meal of the day.

DINNER

▶ Southern ingredients served in decidedly un-Southern ways are on the menu at Husk Nashville.

▶ Save room for dessert because you'll want to swing by Jeni's Splendid Ice Creams, where there's always a line of folks waiting for these seasonal treats.

SIGHTS

Nashville's location, within a day's drive for much of the U.S. population, and its recent popularity thanks to TV shows like ABC's *Nashville,* means it has become the "it" city for weekend getaways. In just two days you can see many of the city's best attractions and catch a show at the Grand Ole Opry. But musical pilgrims, Civil War buffs, shoppers, and outdoorspeople should plan to spend more time in Music City. Even the most disciplined explorers will find themselves happily occupied if they choose to stay a full week—or more.

For a city of its size, Nashville takes up a lot of physical space. In fact, Nashville has the second-largest footprint of any major American city. But don't picture a scene of concrete: Nashville is a leafy, green city. Outside downtown is a patchwork of traffic lights, strip malls, and tree-lined residential neighborhoods, several of which are incorporated towns with their own elected officials, city halls, and police.

Nashville's attractions are spread out among the city's various neighborhoods, and exploring them is part of experiencing Music City's charms. A car is essential to reach some of the best attractions away from downtown. Prepare for traffic during rush hour. All that sprawl means watching the taillights in front of you from time to time. Look to your right or left. That person singing to the radio while in traffic? Next year, you might hear him or her *on* the radio.

COURTESY NASHVILLE CONVENTION & VISITORS CORP.

HIGHLIGHTS

LOOK FOR ◖ TO FIND
RECOMMENDED SIGHTS.

COURTESY OF CHEEKWOOD

Cheekwood's manicured gardens are ripe for strolling.

◖ **Where to Hear the Bells Ring:** Every hour on the hour you can hear "The Tennessee Waltz" (among other songs) played from 95 carillon bells on the north end of **Bicentennial Capitol Mall State Park** (page 27).

◖ **Most Inspiring Place:** In the **Civil Rights Room at the Nashville Public Library,** you can see how a few people changed the world with peaceful contributions to desegregation efforts (page 28).

◖ **First Stop for Getting Up to Speed on the Nashville Sound:** Head directly to the **Country Music Hall of Fame,** where you'll learn about the genre's complex roots and then be ready to explore the city's live music bounty (page 28).

◖ **Best Way to Relive Ancient Greece:** A life-size replica of the Greek wonder, **The Parthenon** is a gathering place, a museum, and one of the reasons Nashville is called "The Athens of the South" (page 35).

◖ **Best Place to See Elvis:** The King's Memphis connections are better-known than his Nashville ones, but Elvis Presley did record at **RCA Studio B** (page 36).

◖ **Best Place to See Art in the Great Outdoors:** The mile-long Carell Woodland Sculpture Trail at **Cheekwood** winds through manicured gardens (page 43).

◖ **Best Celebrity Mansion Tour:** Forget the bus tours of stars' homes in L.A.: Head to **Fontanel Mansion** and get a glimpse of the lifestyle of legend Barbara Mandrell (page 44).

◖ **Best Presidential Home:** The tours of **The Hermitage** home and plantation don't sugarcoat the legacy of the seventh president, Andrew Jackson (page 45).

Downtown and Germantown Map 1

Downtown in general, and Broadway specifically, is the entertainment and retail hub of Nashville. Walk along lower Broad, as the blocks from 5th Avenue to the river are called, and you will pass dozens of different bars (primarily honky-tonks), restaurants, and shops catering to visitors. Second Avenue, near where it crosses Broadway, is a neighborhood where old warehouses have been converted to restaurants, shops, office space, and loft condominiums.

Much of downtown is dominated by large office buildings and federal, state, and city government structures. From Commerce Street northward to the state capitol, you will find historic churches, museums, and hordes of office workers.

THE ARCADE
244 5th Ave. N.
HOURS: Vary by merchant
COST: Free
One of Nashville's most distinctive downtown structures is the covered arcade that runs between 4th and 5th Avenues and parallel to Union Street. The two-story arcade with a gabled glass roof was built in 1903 by developer Daniel Buntin, who was inspired by similar arcades he saw in Europe. It has identical Palladian facades at both entrances, on both 4th and 5th Avenues. From the moment it opened, the Arcade was a bustling center for commerce. Famous for its **Peanut Shop** (19 Arcade, 615/256-3394, www.nashvillenut.com, Mon.-Fri. 9am-5pm, Sat. noon-3pm), the Arcade has also been the location of photo studios, jewelers, and a post office for many years. Today, restaurants—including **Manny's House of Pizza** (15 Arcade, 615/242-7144, www.mannyshouseofpizza.com, Mon.-Fri. 10am-6pm, Sat. 11am-5pm)—crowd the lower level, while art galleries, artists' studios, and professional offices line the 2nd floor. Don't miss the bustling activities here during the **First Saturday Art Crawl** (www.nashvilledowntown.com), held on the first Saturday of the month.

◖ BICENTENNIAL CAPITOL MALL STATE PARK
600 James Robertson Pkwy., 615/741-5280, www.state.tn.us
HOURS: Sunrise-sunset
COST: Free
Tennessee celebrated its 100th anniversary in 1896 with the construction of the beloved Centennial Park, so it made sense to celebrate its 200th anniversary in much the same way. The Bicentennial Capitol Mall State Park occupies 19 acres on the north side of the capitol building. It offers excellent views of the capitol, which towers over the mall. The mall and the capitol are separated by a steep hill and more than 200 steps, which may look daunting but are worth the climb for the views and access to downtown.

The mall has dozens of features that celebrate Tennessee and Tennesseans, including a 200-foot granite map of Tennessee embedded in concrete; a River Wall with 31 fountains, each representing one of Tennessee's rivers; and a timeline with Tennessee events, inscriptions, and notable quotes from 1796 to 1996. A one-mile path that circles the mall's perimeter is popular with walkers and joggers, and a 2,000-seat amphitheater is used for special events. The park may be a civics lesson incarnate, but it is also a pleasant place to pass the time. Ninety-five carillon bells (for the state's 95 counties) play "The Tennessee Waltz," "Rocky Top," and other Tennessee-themed songs every hour on the hour.

To the west of the mall is the amazing **Nashville Farmers' Market** (900 Rosa Parks Blvd., 615/880-2001, www.nashvillefarmersmarket.org, daily 8am-6pm), where you can buy fresh produce, flowers, gourmet breakfasts and lunches, and locally made crafts. Locals often picnic in the mall with goodies from the market. There's plenty of free parking here, but don't speed. Because this is a state park, tickets come from the state police, and they're pricier than metro Nashville tickets.

CIVIL RIGHTS ROOM AT THE NASHVILLE PUBLIC LIBRARY

615 Church St., 615/862-5782,
www.library.nashville.org
HOURS: Mon.-Thurs. 9am-8pm, Fri. 9am-6pm, Sat. 9am-5pm, Sun. 2pm-5pm
COST: Free

The 2nd floor of the main Nashville Public Library houses a powerful freestanding exhibit on the movement for civil rights that took place in Nashville in the 1950s and 1960s. Nashville was the first Southern city to desegregate public services, and it did so relatively peacefully, setting an example for activists throughout the South. This history is an important part of Nashville's legacy. The library is a fitting location for the exhibit, which includes photographs, videos, and displays, because the block below on Church Street was the epicenter of the Nashville sit-ins during 1960.

Inside the room, large-format photographs show school desegregation, sit-ins, and a silent march to the courthouse. A circular table at the center of the room is symbolic of the lunch counters where young students from Fisk, Meharry, American Baptist, and Tennessee A&I sat silently and peacefully at sit-ins. The table is engraved with the 10 rules of conduct set out for sit-in participants, including to be polite and courteous at all times, regardless of how you are treated. A timeline of the national and Nashville civil rights movements is presented above the table. Inside a glass-enclosed viewing room you can choose from six different documentary videos, including an hour-long 1960 NBC news documentary about the Nashville sit-ins. Many of the videos are 30 minutes or longer, so plan on spending several hours here if you are interested in exploring the topics in-depth.

The centerpiece of the Civil Rights Room is a glass inscription by Martin Luther King Jr., who visited the city in 1960 and said, during a speech at Fisk University: "I came to Nashville not to bring inspiration, but to gain inspiration from the great movement that has taken place in this community."

COUNTRY MUSIC HALL OF FAME

222 5th Ave. S., 615/416-2001,
www.countrymusichalloffame.com
HOURS: Jan.-Feb. Wed.-Mon. 9am-5pm, Mar.-Dec. daily 9am-5pm
COST: $20 adults, $18 seniors, $12 children

The distinctive design of the Country Music Hall of Fame and Museum is the first thing you will notice about this monument to country music. Vertical windows at the front and back of the building resemble piano keys; the sweeping arch on the right side of the building portrays a 1950s Cadillac fin; and from above, the building resembles a bass clef. The hall of fame was first established in 1967, and its first inductees were Jimmie Rodgers, Hank Williams, and Fred Rose. The original hall was located on Music Row, but in 2002 it moved to this signature building two blocks off Broadway. Country music fans are drawn by the carload to the hall of fame, where they can pay homage to country's greatest stars, as well as the lesser-known men and women who influenced the music. Those who aren't fans when they walk in generally leave with an appreciation of the genre's varied roots. The hall's slogan is "Honor Thy Music."

The museum is arranged chronologically, beginning with country's roots and ending with displays on some of the genre's hottest stars of today. In between, exhibits detail themes including the rise of bluegrass, honkytonk, and the world-famous Nashville Sound, which introduced country music to the world. There are half a dozen private listening booths where you can hear studio-quality recordings of seminal performances, as well as a special display of a few of the genre's most famous instruments. Here you can see Bill Monroe's mandolin, Maybelle Carter's Gibson, and Johnny Cash's Martin D-355. The hall of fame itself is set in a rotunda in the museum. Brass plaques honor the inductees, and around the room are the words *Will the Circle Be Unbroken,* from the hymn made famous by the Carter family.

The only way to visit Music Row's famous **RCA Studio B** (1611 Roy Acuff Pl.), where Elvis

COURTESY NASHVILLE CONVENTION & VISITORS CORP.

Honor thy music at the Country Music Hall of Fame.

Appleton Potter, it was completed in 1916. Although it is called a customs house, in truth the building served as the center of federal government operations in the city, with government offices, courts, and treasury offices housed in the building. The building houses government offices, so it is open to the public during business hours. But only those who really love the details of iron work and woodwork will want to peruse the interior. Otherwise this landmark's ornate design, including its lovely clock tower and Victorian windows, are easily admired from the outside.

DOWNTOWN PRESBYTERIAN CHURCH
154 5th Ave. N., 615/254-7584, www.dpchurch.com
HOURS: Services Tues. 4:45pm and Sun. 11am
COST: Free

William Strickland, the architect who designed the Tennessee State Capitol, also designed the Downtown Presbyterian Church, now both a place of worship and the holder of a coveted spot on the National Register of Historic Places. Built in 1848 to replace an earlier church destroyed by fire, the church is in the Egyptian revival style that was popular at the time. It is one of only three surviving churches in the country to be built in this style. Downtown Presbyterian was used as a Union hospital during the Civil War, and it is where James K. Polk was inaugurated as Tennessee governor in 1839. Visitors are welcome to come for a self-guided tour (Mon.-Fri. 9am-3pm); groups of five or more should call in advance. The church's **Waffle Shop** brunch, held in December, is a popular local tradition.

once recorded, is to buy your ticket at the museum box office and hop on the hall of fame's guided tour bus. The tour takes about an hour, including the 10-minute drive to Music Row and back. The Studio B tour is an additional fee to your admission, but comes as part of a package ($35 adults, $26 children) with admission to the Country Music Hall of Fame.

CUSTOMS HOUSE
701 Broadway
HOURS: Mon.-Fri. 9am-5pm
COST: Free

Located at 701 Broadway, the old Nashville Customs House is a historic landmark and architectural beauty. Construction on the Customs House began in 1875, and President Rutherford B. Hayes visited Nashville to lay the cornerstone in 1877. The building is an impressive example of the Victorian Gothic style. Designed by Treasury architect William

FORT NASHBOROUGH
170 1st Ave. S., 615/862-8400,
www.nashville.gov/parks
HOURS: Mon.-Sat. 10am-4pm, Sun. 1pm-5pm
COST: Free

Fort Nashborough is a one-quarter-size replica of the fort erected by James Robertson and John Donelson when they first settled what was then called French Lick on Christmas Day 1779. While the replica fort is open, it is mostly left

THE BATTLE OF NASHVILLE

During most of the Civil War, Nashville was occupied by Federal forces. After Fort Donelson, 90 miles northeast of Nashville, fell in mid-February 1862, Nashville was in Union hands. Nashville became an important goods depot for the Northern cause, and the Federalists set strict rules for city residents during the occupation.

As the war drew to a close in late 1864, Nashville was the site of what war historians now say was the last major battle of the Western Theater.

The Battle of Nashville came after a string of defeats for the Confederate army of Tennessee, commanded by John Bell Hood. After his bloody and humiliating losses at Spring Hill and Franklin a few miles south, Hood moved north and set up headquarters at Travellers Rest, the home of John Overton. His plan was to set up his troops in an arc around the southern side of the city. Union Maj. Gen. George H. Thomas did not plan to wait for Hood's attack, however. He devised a plan to attack first and drive the Confederates away from Nashville.

A winter storm and frigid temperatures delayed the battle. For two weeks, from December 2 to 14, 1864, the two armies peered at one another across the no-man's-land between the two lines. Then, at dawn on December 15, 1864, the Union attack began. Union troops on foot and horse, including at least four U.S. Colored Infantry brigades, attacked various Confederate posts around the city. By the close of the first day of fighting, Hood withdrew his troops two miles farther south from the city.

The dawn of the second day of battle augured more losses for the Confederates. Unable to hold their line against the Union assault, they fell back again. As darkness fell, Union Major General Thomas wired Washington to announce his victory. Pursued by a Union cavalry commanded by Maj. Gen. James Wilson, what remained of the Confederate army of Tennessee marched south and, on the day after Christmas, crossed the Tennessee River into Alabama. Four months later, the war was over.

The **Battle of Nashville Preservation Society, Inc.** (www.bonps.org) offers tours of area battlefield sites.

---

unattended, and there is limited educational information here. The interiors of the five cabins have been gated with iron bars, perhaps to prevent vagrants from settling in. Standing on this site, it's easy to understand why Nashville's settlers chose this riverfront property. The spot is fascinating now because it looks so out of place among Nashville's skyscrapers and the Tennessee Titans' stadium, LP Field.

FRIST CENTER FOR THE VISUAL ARTS

919 Broadway, 615/244-3340, www.fristcenter.org
HOURS: Mon.-Wed. and Sat. 10am-5:30pm, Thurs.-Fri. 10am-9pm, Sun. 1pm-5:30pm
COST: $10 adults, $7 seniors and students

Nashville's foremost visual art space is the Frist Center for the Visual Arts. The Frist is located in a stately building that once housed the 1930s downtown post office (and there's still a working post office in the basement). High ceilings, art deco finishes, and unique hardwood tiles distinguish the museum. Look carefully in the hallways, and you can see the indentations in the walls from folks who leaned here waiting for their turn in line at the post office. The Frist has no permanent collection of its own, which is why it is called a visual arts center rather than a museum. The Frist puts on about 12 different major visiting exhibitions annually, many of which have garnered national attention. At any given time, you can see 3-4 different exhibits, many of which are regional or national premieres. There are typically plenty of ongoing educational activities paired with the exhibitions. ArtQuest, a permanent part of the Frist, is an excellent hands-on arts activity room for children and their parents. The **Frist Center Café** serves better-than-expected salads and sandwiches, and has a nice outdoor patio for alfresco dining. There are many free-admission days throughout the year.

HUME FOGG

700 Broadway, 615/291-6300,
www.humefogghs.mnps.org

Located across Broadway from the Customs House is Hume Fogg Magnet School. It sits on land formerly occupied by Hume School, which was Nashville's first public school. The four-story, stone-clad 1912 building was designed by William Ittner of St. Louis in the Norman Gothic style with Tudor Gothic details. Today, it is a public magnet school with a reputation for high academic standards. Hume Fogg is not open to the public, and can only be viewed from the outside.

THE JOHNNY CASH MUSEUM

119 3rd Ave. S., 615/256-1777,
www.johnnycashmuseum.com
HOURS: Mon.-Sun. 11am-7pm
COST: $14

Opened in April 2013, this museum looks like a small storefront with a tiny gift shop. But back behind the cash register is a wealth of information on all things Johnny Cash. The collection was amassed by one fan-turned-collector, and features interactive listening booths, the jumpsuit the Man in Black wore when he flipped the bird in public, and other memorabilia from a varied and lauded career. Locals are crazy for the rebuilt stone wall that was taken from Cash's fire-destroyed suburban home.

MILITARY BRANCH MUSEUM

War Memorial Auditorium, 301 6th Ave. N.,
615/741-2692
HOURS: Tues.-Sat. 10am-5pm
COST: Free

Associated with the **Tennessee State Museum** (505 Deaderick St., 615/741-2692, www.tnmuseum.org), the Military Branch Museum highlights America's overseas conflicts, beginning with the Spanish-American War in 1989, and ending with World War II. The exhibits examine the beginnings of the wars, major battles, and the outcomes. There is a special exhibit about Alvin C. York, the fascinating Tennessee native and World War I hero. The military museum is located in the War Memorial Building on the south side of the capitol.

THE RYMAN AUDITORIUM

116 5th Ave. N., 615/889-3060,
www.ryman.com
HOURS: Daily 9am-4pm
COST: $13 adults, $6.50 children

The historic Ryman Auditorium remains one of the best places in the United States to hear live music. Built in 1892 by Capt. Thomas Ryman, the Union Gospel Tabernacle, as the Ryman was then called, was designed as a venue for the charismatic preaching of Rev. Samuel P. Jones. During the first half of the 20th century, the Ryman began to showcase music and performances. In 1943, the Ryman began hosting a popular barn dance called the Grand Ole Opry. The legacy of this partnership gave the Ryman its place in history as the Mother Church of Country Music. After the Opry left in 1974, the Ryman fell into disrepair and was virtually condemned until Gaylord Entertainment, the same company that owns the Opry, decided to invest in the grand old tabernacle. Today, it is a popular concert venue, booking rock, country, and classical acts, plus comedy and more. Performers like to show the building's acoustics off, playing a number or two without a mic. The Opry returns here during the Christmas season, and in the summer there's a weekly bluegrass series.

Seeing a show at the Ryman is by far the best way to experience this historic venue, but if you can't do that, pay the admission fee to see a short video and explore the auditorium on your own, which includes museum-style exhibits about the musicians who have performed here through the ages. You can sit for a few minutes on the old wooden pews and even climb on stage to be photographed in front of the classic Opry backdrop. A backstage, guided tour ($17 adults, $10.50 children) is available, and isn't just for die-hard fans. It gives lots of insight into how stars behaved when they were behind these famous walls. Plus, you get to walk on the storied stage yourself.

SIGHTS

COURTESY NASHVILLE CONVENTION & VISITORS CORP.

The halls of the Ryman Auditorium are among Music City's most sacred spaces.

SHELBY STREET PEDESTRIAN BRIDGE
Spanning the Cumberland River, one block south of Broadway
COST: Free

Built in 1909, what was once called the Sparkman Street Bridge was slated for demolition in 1998 after inspectors called its condition "poor." But citing the success of the Walnut Street Bridge in revitalizing downtown Chattanooga, advocates succeeded in saving the bridge. The Shelby Street Bridge reopened in 2003 as a pedestrian and bike bridge.

Today, the Shelby Street Bridge connects East Nashville neighborhoods with downtown. It is frequently featured on ABC's *Nashville* because of its great views of the city, and many folks get their iconic Music City photos taken there (including this author). At the base of the east side of the bridge is **Cumberland Park** (592 S. 1st St., 615/862-8508, www.nashville.gov/parks), and by late 2013 there will be easy kayak, canoe, and paddleboard launches, and

the future home of the Cumberland River Compact's River Center.

TENNESSEE SPORTS HALL OF FAME
Bridgestone Arena, 501 Broadway, 615/242-4750, www.tshf.net
HOURS: Tues.-Sat. 10am-5pm
COST: $3

Sports fans of all kinds will enjoy the Tennessee Sports Hall of Fame. Located in a state-of-the-art 7,500-square-foot exhibit space inside Bridgestone Arena, the hall chronicles the history of sports in Tennessee beginning in the 1800s. The hall is chock-full of photos and videos of players through the ages. Athletes honored include Chicago Bear Jay Cutler (a Vanderbilt University graduate) and Peyton Manning. The aim of the museum is to emphasize athletics' high ideals of sportsmanship and teamwork, and to honor the accomplishments of many.

TENNESSEE STATE CAPITOL
Charlotte Ave. between 6th and 7th Aves., 615/741-2692, www.capitol.tn.gov
HOURS: Mon.-Fri. 8am-4pm
COST: Free

Set on the top of a hill and built with the formality and grace of classic Greek architecture, the capitol building of Tennessee strikes a commanding pose overlooking downtown Nashville, and one unlike the traditional domed state capitol buildings. Construction of the capitol began in 1845; it took 14 years to finish the building. The capitol is built of limestone, much of it from a quarry located near present-day Charlotte and 13th Avenues. In the 1950s, extensive renovations were carried out, and some of the original limestone was replaced. The interior marble came from Rogersville and Knoxville, and the gasoliers were ordered from Philadelphia. The capitol was designed by architect William Strickland, who considered it his crowning achievement and is buried in a courtyard on the north end of the capitol. Ask at the information desk for a printed guide that identifies each of the rooms and many of the portraits and sculptures both inside and outside the building. If the legislature is not in session, you can go inside both the House and Senate chambers, which look much as they did back in the 19th century. In the 2nd-floor lobby, you can see two bronze reliefs depicting the 14th and 19th amendments to the U.S. Constitution, both of which were ratified by the State of Tennessee in votes held at the capitol. **Guided tours** (Mon.-Fri. 9am-11am, 1pm-3pm) of the capitol depart hourly. Ask at the information desk inside for further details.

TENNESSEE STATE MUSEUM

505 Deaderick St., 615/741-2692, www.tnmuseum.org
HOURS: Tues.-Sat. 10am-5pm, Sun. 1pm-5pm
COST: Free

The displays at the Tennessee State Museum are largely straightforward combinations of text and images, and they require visitors to read and examine on their own. (There are but a few video presentations.) For patrons with enough patience to give the displays their due, the museum offers an excellent overview of Tennessee history from Native Americans to the New South era of the 1880s. Exhibits detail the state's political development, explore the Revolutionary and Civil Wars, and profile famous Tennesseans including Andrew Jackson and Davy Crockett. They also cast a spotlight on the lifestyles and diversions of Tennesseans of various eras, from the early frontierspeople to a free African American family before emancipation. Special artifacts include the top hat worn by Andrew Jackson at his presidential inauguration, a musket that belonged to Daniel Boone, and the jawbone of a mastodon.

WAR MEMORIAL PLAZA

Charlotte Ave. at 7th Ave. N.

This stone plaza on the south side of the capitol is an open space surrounded by Doric-style columns and tablets inscribed with the names of more than 3,000 Tennesseans who died in World War I. It's a lovely place to people-watch. This is where Occupy Nashville protesters gathered in 2011. A number of state office buildings are nearby, and state employees can be seen walking to and fro, particularly at lunchtime. The famous **War Memorial Auditorium** (301 6th Ave. N., 615/782-4040, www.wmarocks.com) is also located here.

Midtown and 12 South   Map 2

Home to the business end of the country music industry, Music Row can be found along 16th and 17th Avenues, south of where they cross Broadway. While there are few bona fide attractions here, it is worth a jaunt to see the headquarters of both major and independent music labels all in one place (this might be your best chance for a celebrity sighting).

Music Row's most famous, or infamous, landmark is *Musica,* the sculpture at the Music Row traffic circle. The sculpture, by local artist Alan LeQuire, caused a stir when it was unveiled in 2003 for the larger-than-life anatomically correct men and women it depicts. Encompassing the neighborhoods of Elliston Place, Hillsboro Village, and West End, Midtown refers to the parts of Nashville between downtown and the West End, which include Vanderbilt University and its environs.

Adjacent to Midtown, the 12 South neighborhood is quaint, hip, and brimming with student- and local-filled restaurants, bars, and boutiques. The two main sightseeing attractions in this area are on the Belmont University campus.

BELMONT MANSION

1900 Belmont Blvd., 615/460-5459,
www.belmontmansion.com
HOURS: Mon.-Sat. 10am-4pm, Sun. 1pm-4pm
COST: $10 adults, $9 seniors, $3 children ages 6-12

Originally named Belle Monte, this elaborate summer home of Adelicia Acklen was constructed in 1853. Belmont Mansion, as it is known today, is a monument to the glories of the Victorian age. Adelicia was born to a wealthy Nashville family in 1817. When she was 22, she married Isaac Franklin, a wealthy bachelor 28 years her senior. When Franklin died seven years later, Adelicia inherited his substantial wealth. Adelicia remarried to Joseph Acklen, a young lawyer, and together they planned and built Belmont Mansion. The home was built in the Italian style, with touches of Egyptian revival style. The home boasted 36 rooms and 16,000 square feet of space, including a grand gallery where the Acklens hosted elaborate balls and dinner parties. The property included a private art gallery, aviary, zoo, and conservatory, as well as a lake and acres of manicured gardens. After the Civil War, Adelicia traveled to Europe, where she purchased a number of paintings and sculptures that are now on display in her restored mansion. Visitors to the mansion are given a 45-minute guided tour of the property, which includes the downstairs sitting and entertaining rooms and three of the upstairs bedrooms.

BELMONT UNIVERSITY
1900 Belmont Blvd., 615/460-6000, www.belmont.edu
HOURS: Daily 24 horus
COST: Free
The school for girls founded in the Belmont Mansion in 1890 evolved in 1913 to the Ward-Belmont School for Women and in 1951 to coed Belmont College. In 1991 it became Belmont University, a higher-education institution with links to the Tennessee Baptist Convention. Today Belmont is a fast-growing university with highly respected music and music business programs. In 2011 the school opened the first new law school in the state in the last century. Belmont, which hosted one of the 2008 presidential debates, has a student enrollment of 6,400. Campus tours are available twice a day on weekdays. Several Belmont facilities are worth visiting, including the student-run **Buzzy's Candy Store** (2006 Belmont Blvd., 615/460-8561, Mon.-Sat. 11am-8pm) and the **Curb Event Center** (2002 Belmont Blvd., 615/460-8500). The Curb Center hosts sporting events, concerts, and lectures.

FISK UNIVERSITY
1000 17th Ave. N., 615/329-8500, www.fisk.edu
HOURS: Daily 24 hours
COST: Free
Founded in 1866 to educate newly freed slaves, Fisk University has a long and proud history as one of the United States' foremost black colleges. W. E. B. Du Bois attended Fisk, graduating in 1888, and Booker T. Washington married a Fisk alumna and sent his own children to Fisk. In more modern times, Knoxville native and poet Nikki Giovanni attended Fisk. Fisk sits at the corner of Jefferson Street and Dr. D. B. Todd Jr. Boulevard, about 10 blocks west of downtown Nashville. The campus is a collection of elegant redbrick buildings set on wide green lawns, although a few more modern buildings, including the library, break up the classical feel. One of the oldest Fisk buildings is **Jubilee Hall,** on the north end of the campus, which is said to be the first permanent building constructed for the education of African Americans in the country. It was built with money raised by the Fisk Jubilee Singers, who popularized black spirituals during a world tour 1871-1874. Another notable building is the **Fisk Little Theatre,** a white clapboard building that once served as a Union hospital during the Civil War.

The campus is beautiful from many approaches, but is particularly striking if you enter on 17th Avenue North from the south, where you will be greeted by the big iron Fisk University gate. There is some metered and free street parking on the side streets in the neighborhood, and campus lots are well marked for visitors.

MARATHON VILLAGE
Bordered by 12th Ave., Jo Johnston Ave., 16th Ave., and Clinton St., www.marathonvillage.com
This "new" neighborhood is actually one that dates back to 1881. A former auto factory, Marathon Village now houses sleek urban condos, restaurants, the **Corsair Artisan Distillery** (1200 Clinton St., 615/200-0321, www.corsairartisan.com, Wed.-Fri. 4pm-8pm, Sat. 2pm-8pm), **Bang Candy Company** (1300

THE JUBILEE SINGERS

In 1871, Fisk University needed money. Buildings at the school established in old Union army barracks in 1866 were decaying, while more and more African Americans came to seek education.

So, in what might now be considered a very Nashville-style idea, the school choir withdrew all the money from the university's treasury and left on a world tour. The nine singers were Isaac Dickerson, Maggie Porter, Minnie Tate, Jennie Jackson, Benjamin Holmes, Thomas Rutling, Eliza Walker, Green Evans, and Ella Sheppard. Remembering a biblical reference to the Hebrew "year of the jubilee," Fisk treasurer and choir manager George White gave them their name, the Fisk Jubilee Singers.

The choir struggled at first, but before long audiences were singing their praises. They toured first the American South, then the North, and in 1873 sailed to England for a successful British tour. Their audiences included William Lloyd Garrison, Wendell Phillips, Ulysses S. Grant, William Gladstone, Mark Twain, Johann Strauss, and Queen Victoria. Songs like "Swing Low, Sweet Chariot" and "Nobody Knows the Trouble I've Seen" moved audiences to tears. The singers introduced the spiritual to mainstream white audiences and erased negative misconceptions about African Americans and African American education.

In 1874 the singers returned to Nashville. They had raised enough money to pay off Fisk's debts and build the university's first permanent structure, an imposing Victorian Gothic six-story building now called Jubilee Hall. It was the first permanent structure built solely for the education of African Americans in the United States.

Every October 6, the day in 1871 that the singers departed Fisk, the university recalls their struggle and their triumph with a convocation featuring the modern-day Jubilee Singers.

The singers still perform regularly, including on the NPR program *Says You*, when it was in Nashville in 2012. If you have an opportunity to hear them, don't miss it.

Clinton St., 615/587-4819. www.bangcandycompany.com, Tues.-Sat. 10am-5pm), and shops like **Antique Archaeology** (1300 Clinton St., 615/810-9906, www.antiquearchaeology. com, Mon.-Sat. 10am-6pm, Sun. noon-5pm), owned by Mike Wolfe of TV's *American Pickers* fame. Marathon Village's development has been slow, and it still has a ways to go to be a bustling destination. But the 2011 addition of live music venue **Marathon Music Works** (1402 Clinton St., 615/891-1781, www.marathonmusicworks.com, box office Mon.-Fri. noon-1pm) is bringing out the locals, and architecture and history buffs love the buildings' bones.

MEHARRY MEDICAL COLLEGE

1005 Dr. D.B. Todd Jr. Blvd., 615/327-6000, www.mmc.edu

Just across Dr. D. B. Todd Jr. Boulevard from Fisk University is Meharry Medical College, the largest private, comprehensive, historically black institution educating medical professionals. It was founded in 1876 as the Medical Department of the Central Tennessee College of Nashville, under the auspices of the Freeman's Aid Society of the Methodist Episcopal Church. At one time in its history, Meharry was responsible for graduating more than half of all African American doctors and nurses in the United States. Today, it has an enrollment of almost 800 students.

◖ THE PARTHENON

Centennial Park, 2600 West End Ave., 615/862-8431, www.nashville.gov/parthenon

HOURS: June-Aug. Sun. 12:30pm-4:30pm, Sept.-May Tues.-Sat. 9am-4:30pm

COST: $6 adults, $4 seniors and children

In 1893, funds began to be raised for a mighty exposition that would celebrate the 1896 centennial of the state of Tennessee. Though the exposition would start a year late, in 1897, it would exceed all expectations. The old West Side Race Track was converted to a little city

McKISSACK AND McKISSACK ARCHITECTS

The oldest African American architectural firm in Tennessee can trace its roots to Moses McKissack (1790-1865), a member of the West African Ashanti tribe. Sold into slavery to William McKissack of North Carolina and then Middle Tennessee, Moses became a master builder. He passed his knowledge on to his son, Gabriel Moses McKissack, born in 1840. Gabriel Moses passed his knowledge of the building trade to his own son, Moses McKissack III, born in 1879.

Moses McKissack III was born in Pulaski, where he received a basic education in the town's segregated schools. In 1890 he was hired by a local white architect. Until 1905, McKissack designed and built homes throughout the area, including many in Mount Pleasant in Maury County. He developed a reputation as an excellent architect and tradesman.

In 1905 McKissack moved to Nashville, where he started his own construction company. Within a few years, he was working on major projects. He built a home for the dean of architecture and engineering at Vanderbilt University, and the Carnegie Library at Fisk University. In 1922, Moses's brother, Calvin, joined him, and they opened McKissack and McKissack, Tennessee's first black architectural firm.

The McKissacks have continued to distinguish themselves in the building industry, and they have also kept the business in the family. Since 1991 the company has been led by Cheryl McKissack, a fifth-generation McKissack. The firm employs more than 100 people and has corporate offices in Philadelphia and New York City.

with exhibit halls dedicated to transportation, agriculture, machinery, minerals, forestry, and African Americans, among other themes. There were Chinese, Cuban, and Egyptian villages; a midway; and an auditorium. The exposition attracted 1.7 million people between May 1 and October 31.

When the exposition closed in the fall of 1897, all the exhibit halls were torn down except for a life-size replica of the Greek Parthenon, which had housed an art exhibit during the centennial. The exposition grounds were made into a public park, aptly named Centennial Park, and Nashvillians continued to admire their Parthenon.

The Parthenon replica had been built out of wood and plaster, and it was designed only to last through the centennial. Remarkably, it survived well beyond that. But by the 1920s, the Parthenon was crumbling. City officials, responding to public outcry to save the Parthenon, agreed to restore it, and they hired a contractor to rebuild the replica. The contractor did so using tinted concrete. Today the Parthenon remains one of Nashville's most iconic landmarks. It is a monument to the

creativity and energy of the New South, and also to Nashville's distinction as the Athens of the South. You can see and walk around the Parthenon simply by visiting Centennial Park. It is, in many respects, most beautiful from the outside, particularly when lit dramatically at night.

As breathtaking as it is from the exterior, it is worth paying to go inside the Parthenon. The landmark has three gallery spaces; the largest is used to display works from its permanent collection of 63 pieces of American art. The other two galleries host interesting changing exhibits. But upstairs is the remarkable 42-foot statue of Athena, by local sculptor Alan LeQuire. *Athena* is designed as a replica of what the statue would have looked like in ancient Greece, in all her golden glory. In ancient Greece the doors of the Parthenon would have been open, and she would have been seen from a distance. In Nashville her scale and gilded loins are front and center.

◀ RCA STUDIO B
1611 Roy Acuff Pl., 615/416-2001,
www.countrymusichalloffame.com

© NEVENA KOZEKOVA/123RF

The Parthenon earned Nashville its reputation as the "Athens of the South."

HOURS: Tours hourly Sun.-Thurs 10:30am-2:30pm, every half hour Fri.-Sat. 10:30am-2:30pm
COST: $22-33

As a rule, the music labels in Music Row are open for business, not tours. The lone exception is historic RCA Studio B. The RCA studio was the second recording studio in Nashville and the place where artists including the Everly Brothers, Roy Orbison, Dolly Parton, Elvis Presley, and Hank Snow recorded hits. Also called the RCA Victor Studio, this nondescript studio operated from 1957 to 1977. Visitors on the one-hour tour, which departs from the Country Music Hall of Fame downtown, hear anecdotes about recording sessions at the studio and see rare footage of a 1960s Dottie West recording session. Tours can only be purchased in conjunction with admission to the Country Music Hall of Fame.

THE UPPER ROOM

1908 Grand Ave., 615/340-7207, http://chapel.upperroom.org
HOURS: Mon.-Fri. 8am-4:30pm

COST: Free, $4 suggested donation

Three million Christians around the world know the *Upper Room Daily Devotional Guide,* a page-a-day pocket devotional available in 106 countries and 40 languages. Headquartered in Nashville, the Upper Room Ministry has established a bookstore, museum, and chapel to welcome visitors. The Upper Room Chapel and Museum features a small museum of Christian-inspired art, including a wonderful collection of Nativity scenes from around the world made from materials ranging from needlepoint to camel bone. Visitors may also tour the chapel, with its 8- by 20-foot stained-glass window and 8- by 17-foot wood carving of Leonardo da Vinci's *Last Supper.* A 15-minute audio presentation discusses features of the carving and tells the history and mission of the Upper Room.

VANDERBILT UNIVERSITY

2201 West End Ave., 615/322-7311, www.vanderbilt.edu
Named for philanthropist Commodore Cornelius Vanderbilt, who donated $1 million in 1873 to found a university that would

"contribute to strengthening the ties which should exist between all sections of our common country," Vanderbilt University is now one of the region's most respected institutions of higher education. A private research university, Vanderbilt has an enrollment of 6,700 undergraduates and 5,200 graduate students. The university comprises 10 schools, a medical center, public policy center, and The Freedom Forum First Amendment Center. Vanderbilt's campus life is vibrant, and there is a daily roll call of lectures, recitals, exhibits, and other special events for students, locals, and visitors alike. Check http://calendar.vanderbilt.edu for an up-to-date listing of all campus events. Vanderbilt offers a self-guided tour of the campus's trees, which form the Vanderbilt Arboretum. Most trees on the tour are native trees common to Nashville and Middle Tennessee. Download a podcast or print a copy of the tour from the website, or contact the university for more information.

There is designated visitor parking in several lots on the Vanderbilt campus. Look on the eastern edge of the sports facilities parking lot off Natchez Trace, in the Wesley Place parking lot off Scarritt Place, or in the Terrace Place parking lot between 20th and 21st Avenues north of Broadway. Pay attention to the signs, as the university parking monitors do ticket those who park in prohibited areas.

Music Valley   Map 4

A collection of tourist attractions separated from the rest of Nashville by the Cumberland River, Music Valley is most known for being the new home of the Grand Ole Opry. The area was one of those hit hardest by the 2010 flood, leading to some significant improvements and upgrades, and some closures. This strip of motels, restaurants, and country music "museums" is tourist-centric. It is more campy than authentic, although it does offer fun, affordable ways to explore Music City's kitsch, and many locals secretly love to play tourist here.

COOTER'S

2613 McGavock Pike, 615/872-8358,
www.cootersplace.com
HOURS: Mon.-Thurs. 9am-7pm, Fri.-Sat. 9am-8pm,
Sun. 9am-6pm
COST: Free

If you're game for Music Valley's signature camp, head straight for Cooter's, a gift shop and museum dedicated to the *Dukes of Hazzard* television show. The museum features a mind-boggling array of toys, ornaments, and model cars manufactured in the 1970s to profit off the Dukes' wild popularity. You can also see one of the bright-orange Dodge Chargers that became the Dukes'

icon. In the gift shop, buy a pair of "official" Daisy Dukes or any number of General Lee souvenirs. Cooter's is operated by Ben Jones, who played Cooter, the affable sidekick mechanic, in the original television series. In recent years, Jones has been one of the forces behind DukeFest, a wildly popular annual celebration of fast cars and the General Lee held at the Nashville Motor Speedway.

THE GRAND OLE OPRY HOUSE

2802 Opryland Dr., 615/871-6779, www.opry.com
HOURS: Daytime tour: times vary, check website;
post-show backstage tour: Tues. and Fri.-Sat. 9:30pm;
VIP tour: Tues. and Fri.-Sat. 6:30pm
COST: Daytime tour: $18.50 adults, $13.50 children;
post-show backstage tour: $21 adults, $16 children; VIP
tour: $90

Since 1974, the Grand Ole Opry has been most often staged at the specially built Grand Ole Opry House in Music Valley. This is the Opry's sixth regular home, and it was completely renovated after it was shuttered due to the 2010 flood. And while The Opry House may have been closed, the Opry went on. The show still made the airwaves for every single scheduled performance, playing at different venues around town while construction went

George Jones is just one of many stars who has graced the stage of the Grand Ole Opry.

on around the clock. This is a point of pride for Nashvillians and Opry fans alike.

The Opry performs at least two times a week, Friday and Saturday, with additional shows on Tuesday night most weeks. The **Grande Ole Opry Museum** is still shuttered since the flood (it is unclear if it will reopen), but with the renovated Opry came a renovated backstage tour. Daytime tour tickets go on sale two weeks in advance and are generally offered every 15 minutes; if you are buying tickets to a show, you can also purchase a post-concert backstage tour led by docents, where you'll get to see dressing rooms, learn lots of Opry history, and hear plenty of juicy stories about performers and their backstage behavior. One of the highlights of the guided tour is getting to go onstage and have your photo taken under the lights. If you book a post-show tour, you'll see a performer or two.

WILLIE NELSON AND FRIENDS MUSEUM

2613 McGavock Pike, 615/885-1515

HOURS: Mon.-Sat. 8:30am-9pm, Sun. 8:30am-8pm
COST: $10

A few doors down from Cooter's, you will find Willie Nelson and Friends Museum, which looks like a roadside stand in the touristy Music Valley area. It's packed with memorabilia from Nelson's career, showcasing a number of things that once belonged to the artist, including his golf bag, a replica of his tour bus, and the guitar he played during his first performance on the Grand Ole Opry. Many of the Willie Nelson items were purchased by museum operators Jeannie and Frank Oakley at an IRS auction. The gift shop is popular for trip mementos, although few visitors think of this spot as a real "museum." A quick trip here is appreciated by true country fans, but it isn't a go-out-of-your-way destination.

© GRAND OLE OPRY/CHRIS HOLLO

SIGHTS

South Nashville

Map 5

An odd amalgamation of areas, South Nashville lacks the neighborhood feel of Midtown, 12 South, and East Nashville, nor does it have the energy of downtown. What is does have, however, is some of the city's leading attractions, including the zoo, the science museum, and military history.

ADVENTURE SCIENCE CENTER

800 Fort Negley Blvd., 615/862-5160,
www.adventuresci.com
HOURS: Mon.-Sat. 10am-5pm, Sun. 12:30pm-5:30pm
COST: $12 adults, $10 children

Children and grown-ups alike will enjoy the hands-on science education available at the Adventure Science Center. Interactive exhibits explore how the body works, the solar system, and other scientific areas. Perhaps the most popular attraction is the multistory climbing tower in the building's center, which features a giant guitar and other instruments, and is always covered in enthusiastic visitors. The center's **Sudekum Planetarium** (www.sudekumplanetarium.com) is the largest planetarium in Tennessee; it has 164 seats and offers a variety of space-themed shows. There are also star-viewing parties, gravity-suspending rides, and other exhibits about space flight, the moon, the solar system, and other things found in space.

CITY CEMETERY

1001 4th Ave. S., www.thenashvillecitycemetery.org
HOURS: Daily 8am-5pm; guided tours by appointment
COST: Free

Right next to Fort Negley Park, off Chestnut Street, is the old City Cemetery. Opened in 1822, City Cemetery was the final resting place of many of Nashville's most prominent early

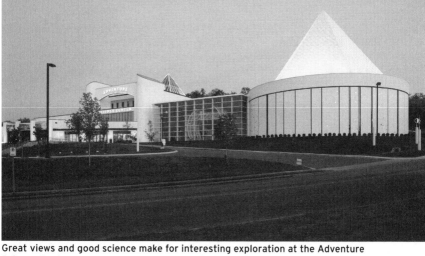

Great views and good science make for interesting exploration at the Adventure Science Center.

COURTESY NASHVILLE CONVENTION & VISITORS CORP.

citizens, including founder James Robertson; William Driver, the U.S. Navy captain who named the flag "Old Glory"; Mabel Lewis Imes and Ella Sheppard, members of the original Fisk Jubilee Singers; and 14 Nashville mayors. During the Civil War, the cemetery was contracted to bury more than 15,000 Union and Confederate dead, although they were later reinterred in different cemeteries.

Consult the information board in the Keeble Building for help with your self-guided tour. Guided tours and special events, such as living history tours, garden tours, and historical lectures, take place on the second Saturday of each month. The events are aimed at telling the history of Nashvillians who are buried at this historical cemetery.

FORT NEGLEY PARK

1100 Fort Negley Blvd., 615/862-8470,
www.nashville.gov
HOURS: Daily dawn-dusk
COST: Free

Early in the Civil War, the Union army determined that taking and holding Nashville was a critical strategic link in their victory. So after Nashville fell in 1862, the Federals wasted no time fortifying the city against attacks. One of the city's forts was Fort Negley, built between August and December 1862 on St. Cloud Hill south of the city center.

Fort Negley owes its existence to the 2,768 men who were enrolled to build it. Most were blacks, some free and some slave who were pressed into service by the Union army. These men felled trees, hauled earth, and cut and laid limestone for the fort. They slept in the open and enjoyed few, if any, comforts while they labored. Between 600 and 800 men died while building the fort, and only 310 received payment.

When it was completed, Fort Negley was the largest inland masonry fortification in North America. It was never challenged. Fort Negley was abandoned by the military after the war, but it remained the cornerstone of one of Nashville's oldest African American communities, now known as Cameron-Trimble.

During the New Deal, the Works Progress Administration rebuilt large sections of the crumbling fort, and it became a public park.

In 2007, the city opened a visitors center (June-Aug. Tues.-Thurs. noon-4pm, Fri.-Sat. 9am-4pm, Sept.-May Tues.-Fri. noon-4pm, Sat. 9am-4pm, free) to tell the story of the fort. It includes a museum about the fort and Nashville's role in the Civil War. There is a short paved loop trail around the base of the fort, plus raised boardwalks through the fortifications themselves. Historical markers tell the story of the fort's construction and detail its military features. Fort Negley is one of the great places to take in a view of Music City.

LANE MOTOR MUSEUM

702 Murfreesboro Pike, 615/742-7445,
www.lanemotormuseum.org
HOURS: Thurs.-Mon. 10am-5pm
COST: $9 adults, $6 seniors, $3 children

Kids and adults alike relish coming to this off-the-beaten-track museum. Here you'll find all manner of automobiles, from early hybrids and steam engines to a car that's so small it can be "reversed" merely by picking it up and putting it down facing the other direction. The museum, based in an old bakery, has the largest European collection of cars and motorcycles in the country.

NASHVILLE ZOO AT GRASSMERE

3777 Nolensville Pike, 615/833-1534,
www.nashvillezoo.org
HOURS: Apr. 1-Oct. 15 daily 9am-6pm, Oct. 16-Mar. 31 daily 9am-4pm
COST: $15 adults, $13 seniors, $10 children ages 3-12, free children under 3, free parking

See familiar and exotic animals at the Nashville Zoo at Grassmere. Many of the zoo's animals live in beautiful habitats like Lorikeet Landing, Gibbon Islands, and Bamboo Trail. The zoo's meerkat exhibit, featuring the famously quizzical and erect animals, is one of its most popular. The Wild Animal Carousel is an old-time carousel with 39 different brightly painted wooden animals.

The zoo is located at Grassmere, the onetime

SIGHTS

© AMIEE STUBBS

The clouded leopard is just one of the animals who calls the Nashville Zoo home.

home and farm of the Croft family. The historic Croft farmhouse has been preserved and is open for guided tours in October and December.

TENNESSEE AGRICULTURAL MUSEUM
440 Hogan Rd., 615/837-5197, www.tnagmuseum.org
HOURS: Mon.-Wed. and Sat. 10am-5:30pm, Thurs.-Fri. 10am-9pm, Sun. 1pm-5:30pm
COST: Self-guided tour free; $10 adults, $7 seniors, students, and military

The Tennessee Agricultural Museum celebrates the ingenuity and dedicated labors of farm life from the 17th to the 20th century. Operated by the Tennessee Department of Agriculture and set on the department's pleasant South Nashville campus, the museum depicts various facets of Tennessee farm life. There are exhibits about clothes washing, blacksmithing, coopering, plowing, weaving, and more. Outside, there is a small kitchen garden with heirloom vegetables, and replicas of a log cabin, one-room school-house, and outdoor kitchen. There is also a short self-guided nature trail illustrating the ways that settlers used various types of native Tennessee

trees. Visitors can always see the historic exhibits on their own in this welcoming and educational space. Hands-on demonstrations are typically only offered on summer Saturdays and by advance appointment. Staff are available to answer any questions.

TENNESSEE CENTRAL RAILWAY MUSEUM
220 Willow St., 615/244-9001, www.tcry.org
HOURS: Tues., Thurs., and Sat. 9am-3pm
COST: Free

Railroad enthusiasts should make a detour to the Tennessee Central Railway Museum. This institution is best known for its special railroad excursions that are part tour, part performance. The museum houses a collection of railroad equipment and paraphernalia. Dedicated volunteers restore and care for the collection and are more than willing to chat about railways with interested visitors. The museum is located in an otherwise industrial area between the interstate and the railroad tracks, one block north of Hermitage Avenue and east of Fairfield

Avenue. It's a quick drive from downtown or East Nashville.

TRAVELLERS REST PLANTATION AND MUSEUM

636 Farrell Pkwy., 615/832-8197,
www.travellersrestplantation.org

HOURS: Tues.-Sat. 10am-4pm, Sun. 1pm-4pm

COST: Ages 12 and older $10, seniors $9, children ages 7-11 $5, children 6 and under free, $5 grounds only

Travellers Rest was the home of John Overton, a Nashville lawyer who helped found Memphis, served on the first Tennessee Supreme Court, and was a trusted advisor to Andrew Jackson, the seventh U.S. president and the first from Tennessee. When workmen were digging the cellar for the original home in 1799, they uncovered Native American skeletons and artifacts—Overton had chosen a Mississipian-era Indian mound for the site of his home. But the archaeological finds did not stop Overton, who initially named his home Golgotha, or hill of skulls. The name did not stick, however; tradition has it that Overton later named the home Travellers Rest because it was his place of rest between long trips as a circuit judge in Middle and East Tennessee. Visitors to Travellers Rest may choose to skip the mansion tour. But to get the real story and flavor of the property, go for the full 45-minute guided tour.

Greater Nashville   Map 6

A car is necessary to reach some of Nashville's farther-flung sights, but it is worth filling up the tank for these attractions.

BELLE MEADE PLANTATION

5025 Harding Pike, 615/356-0501,
www.bellemeadeplantation.com

HOURS: Mon.-Sat. 9am-5pm, Sun. 11am-5pm

COST: $16

The mansion at the former Belle Meade Plantation is the centerpiece of present-day Belle Meade Plantation and one of the finest old homes in the city. Its name means beautiful pasture, and indeed it was Belle Meade's pastures that gave rise to the plantation's fame as the home of a superb stock of horses. Purchased as 250 acres in 1807 by Virginia farmer John Harding and his wife, Susannah, the estate grew to 5,400 acres at its peak in the 1880s and 1890s.

Belle Meade was never a cotton plantation, although small amounts of the cash crop were grown here, along with fruits, vegetables, and tobacco. Instead it was the horses, including the racehorse Iroquois, that made Belle Meade famous. The mansion was built in 1820 and expanded in 1853. Its grand rooms are furnished with period antiques, more than 60 percent of which are original to the house. The estate also includes outbuildings, such as a smokehouse, dairy, and the original log cabin that Harding built for his family when they moved to Belle Meade in 1807.

The plantation also includes a slave cabin, which houses an exhibit on Belle Meade's enslaved population, which numbered more than 160 at its peak. Two of these slaves are described in detail. Susanna Carter was the mansion's housekeeper for more than 30 years, and she remained with the family even after the end of slavery. On her deathbed, Selena Jackson, the mistress of Belle Meade for many years, called Susanna "one of the most faithful and trusted of my friends." The other African American who features prominently at the museum is Bob Green, whose skill and experience as a hostler earned him one of the highest salaries ever paid to a horse hand of the day. Visitors to Belle Meade are given a one-hour guided tour of the mansion and then visit the outbuildings and grounds on their own.

◖ CHEEKWOOD

1200 Forrest Park Dr., 615/356-8000,
www.cheekwood.org

HOURS: Tues.-Sat. 9:30am-4:30pm, Sun. 11am-4:30pm

COST: $12 adults, $10 seniors, $5 students and children, $3 parking

Plan to spend a full morning or afternoon at

COURTESY NASHVILLE CONVENTION & VISITORS CORP.

Belle Meade Plantation was once one of the finest homes in the city.

Cheekwood so you can experience the full scope of this magnificent art museum and botanical garden. Galleries in the Cheekwood mansion house the museum's American and European collections, including an excellent contemporary art collection. Cheekwood has the largest public collection of works by Nashville artist William Edmondson, the sculptor and stoneworker. The museum usually displays items from its permanent collection as well as traveling exhibitions from other museums. Many exhibits have special ties with Nashville.

But Cheekwood is far more than just an art museum. The mansion overlooks hundreds of acres of gardens and woods, and it is easy to forget that you are near a major American city when you're at Cheekwood. Walk the mile-long Carell Woodland Sculpture Trail past works by 15 internationally acclaimed artists, or stroll past the water garden to the Japanese garden. There are dogwood gardens, an herb garden, a delightful boxwood garden, and much more. Wear comfortable shoes and pack a bottle of water so you can enjoy the grounds in comfort.

Cheekwood owes its existence to the success

of the coffee brand Maxwell House. During the 1920s, Leslie Cheek and his wife, Mabel Wood, invested in the new coffee brand being developed by their cousin, Joel Cheek. Maxwell House proved to be a success and earned the Cheeks a fortune, which they used to buy 100 acres of land in West Nashville. The family hired New York residential and landscape architect Bryant Fleming to create a 30,000-square-foot mansion and neighboring gardens. Cheekwood was completed in 1933.

Leslie Cheek lived in the mansion just two years before he died, and Mabel lived there for another decade before deeding it to her daughter and son-in-law, who later offered it as a site for a museum and garden. Cheekwood opened to the public in 1960.

◖ FONTANEL MANSION

4225 Whites Creek Pike, 615/727-0304, www.fontanelmansion.com
HOURS: Daily 9am-3pm
COST: $22 adults, $20 seniors, $12 children
The former estate of country music icon Barbara Mandrell, Fontanel Mansion has become a

COURTESY NASHVILLE CONVENTION & VISITORS CORP.

Fontanel Mansion is the former home of country icon Barbara Mandrell.

surprising draw for locals and tourists alike since it opened in 2010. These 136 acres include walking trails, an outdoor live music venue, a restaurant with its own live music, an art gallery, and a gift shop. But the main attraction is the mansion, a 27,000-square-foot log cabin, which is the city's only country music mansion tour.

Fans get to see how the most famous of the Mandrell sisters lived before her retirement. Tours are sometimes given by Mandrell's daughter, who throws in lots of personal tidbits (such as stories of her brothers jumping from the second story into the pool). Even those who don't love "I Was Country When Country Wasn't Cool" will appreciate the music history, artifacts such as Gretchen Wilson's "Redneck Woman" Jeep, the former indoor shooting range, and the bucolic scenery and impressive architecture.

HADLEY PARK

1037 28th Ave. N., 615/862-8451
HOURS: Mon.-Thurs. 6am-8:30pm, Fri. 6am-7:30pm, Sat. 8am-noon
COST: $3 adults, $1.50 seniors and children
Founded in 1912, Hadley Park is believed to

be the oldest public park developed for African Americans in the South and, most likely, the United States. The park got its start when Fisk University president George Gates requested that the city buy land and create a park for its black citizens. This was in the era of segregation, so other city parks were not open to blacks. The request was granted, and the park opened in July 1912. An old farmhouse was converted into a community center, and benches and a playground were installed. It is now home to a state-of-the-art gym and fitness center, computer labs, meeting rooms, and tennis courts.

◀ THE HERMITAGE

4580 Rachel's Ln., 615/889-2941,
www.thehermitage.com
HOURS: Daily 9am-5pm
COST: $19 adults, $16 seniors, $14 students, $9 children
Andrew Jackson's plantation and home is Nashville's best historical tourist attraction, even though it's technically 16 miles east of the city. The Hermitage is where Jackson

OLD HICKORY

Andrew Jackson was born in 1767 on the South Carolina frontier. His father, an immigrant from Northern Ireland, died before Jackson was born. Jackson's two brothers, Hugh and Robert, died during the Revolutionary War. His mother, Elizabeth, died of smallpox in 1781. At 14 years old, Jackson was alone in the world.

Remarkably, he flourished. In 1784 he moved to Salisbury, North Carolina, where he studied law. In 1787 he became a lawyer and moved to Washington County, now part of Tennessee. In 1788 he was appointed the district attorney for the Mero District, now Middle Tennessee.

In Nashville, Jackson met Rachel Donelson, the daughter of John Donelson, one of the founding fathers of Nashville. Jackson fell in love with Rachel and in 1791 they were married. Later, when they learned that Rachel's earlier, unhappy marriage to Lewis Robards of Kentucky was not legally dissolved, they remarried in 1794.

Jackson practiced law, speculated in land, and dabbled in politics. They bought farmland in Davidson County, where they built The Hermitage, which would be the Jacksons' home for the rest of their lives. The couple never had children of their own, but they adopted a nephew, who was known as Andrew Jackson Jr., and reared several Indian orphans.

By 1798, Jackson was a circuit-riding judge on the Tennessee Superior Court. He had a reputation for violence. He brawled, killed a man in a duel, caned another, and ran a sword through a third. In 1803 he quarreled publicly with Governor John Sevier and nearly dueled him as well.

Jackson's violent temper was better suited for the battlefield. In 1802 he was elected Major General of the Tennessee militia, and with the outbreak of war in 1812, his leadership was required. Jackson earned the nickname "Old Hickory" in 1812 when he disobeyed orders and refused to dismiss his Tennessee soldiers in Natchez, Mississippi, marching them back to Tennessee under great hardship instead. He earned national fame three years later when he marched his men from Florida to New Orleans, where he resoundingly defeated the British. The American public was so pleased with their new war hero that they did not mind when they learned the British had actually surrendered two weeks earlier. Neither did they mind some of his tactics: military executions, imposition of martial law, suspension of habeas corpus, and defiance of a federal court order.

In the succeeding years, Jackson fought battles with Native American tribes and negotiated land treaties with them. By 1821, he quit his post as Major General and came home to the Hermitage for a short retirement.

In 1822 the Tennessee state legislature nominated Jackson for U.S. president. In the 1824 contest, Jackson received more votes than any other contender in the crowded field. But when the U.S. House of Representatives gave the presidency to John Quincy Adams, Jackson called the decision a "corrupt bargain" that violated the will of the voters. His 1828 presidential campaign had begun.

The campaign was spirited and dirty, and historians would point to this as a turning point in American elections. Opponents found seemingly countless stories of Jackson's indiscretions. When Rachel Jackson died on December 22, 1828, Jackson accused his opponents of hastening her death by slander.

Jackson was raised as a Presbyterian and held strong religious beliefs throughout his life. He resisted Rachel Jackson's encouragement to formally join a church, fearing the charge of hypocrisy could be leveled against him as a public churchgoer. Jackson promised Rachel that when he left public life he would join the church, and he was true to his word. In July 1838, Jackson joined the church.

During his two terms as president, Jackson enraged his opponents and delighted supporters. He took unprecedented actions in the name of reform, including several controversial banking decisions. He believed in a strong federal government and stood in the way of state nullification of federal laws. By the end of his eight years in the White House, Jackson was known by his opponents as "King Andrew," while his supporters still saw him as a spokesman of the common man.

Jackson, who never remarried, spent the remaining eight years of his life at The Hermitage. In 1845, at age 78, he died and was buried in the Hermitage garden, next to his beloved Rachel.

retired following his two terms as president of the United States, and it is where he and his beloved wife, Rachel, are buried. Following President Jackson's death, The Hermitage remained in family hands until 1853, when it was sold to the State of Tennessee to pay off the family's debts. It opened as a museum in 1889 and was restored largely due to the persistence of the Ladies Hermitage Association. Because the property never left family hands before it was sold to the state, many of the furnishings are original, and even the wallpaper in several rooms dates back to the years when Andrew Jackson called it home.

The Hermitage tour and museum focuses not only on Jackson and the construction and decoration of the mansion, but also the African American slaves who worked at The Hermitage plantation. It makes no effort to gloss over some of Jackson's less favorable legacies. Curators and archaeologists have studied The Hermitage to learn about the hundreds of men and women who made The Hermitage profitable and successful for so many years. The tour of the grounds takes visitors to Alfred's Cabin, a slave cabin occupied until 1901 by former Hermitage slave Alfred Jackson. You also learn about the agriculture that took place on The Hermitage, and can see cotton being cultivated during the summer months. To learn even more about The Hermitage's slaves, take an add-on **wagon tour** (Apr.-Oct., $10). Visitors to The Hermitage first watch a video

about Andrew Jackson and The Hermitage, then can continue on to a museum. Even if you are not typically an audio-tour-type person, consider the one of the grounds, which includes a kids' version narrated by Jackson's pet parrot. Guided tours of the mansion are offered. Plan on spending at least three hours here to make the most of your visit. Try to come when the weather is good, so you can take in the grounds and not just the mansion.

TENNESSEE STATE UNIVERSITY

3500 John A. Merritt Blvd., 615/963-5000, www.tnstate.edu

HOURS: Daily 24 hours; campus tours June-July Mon.-Wed. 10am, Aug.-May Mon.-Fri. 10am and 2pm

COST: Free

Founded in 1912 as the Agricultural and Industrial State Normal College for black students, Tennessee State University is now a comprehensive university with more than 9,000 students. In 1979, as a result of a court order to desegregate the state's universities, TSU merged with the Nashville campus of the University of Tennessee. Today, TSU's student body is 75 percent African American.

Walking through the leafy, brick-building campus, which takes up more than 500 acres in North Nashville, you'll pass the historic President's Residence, the columned McWherter Administration Building and the modern Lawson Hall. Campus tours are offered twice daily during the school year.

RESTAURANTS

In recent years, as Music City has become the "it" city, its culinary reputation has grown. Today you can find anything you want to eat here, and, in many cases, some of the best chefs in the country are testing inventive menus on willing diners. The Catbird Seat has consistently been named one of the nation's best dining experiences. Farm-to-fork, Southern, Vietnamese, and other cuisines shine here, too.

You can eat in a different restaurant each day in Nashville and never get bored. Southern cooking stars at meat-and-three diners and barbecue joints, fine-dining restaurants cater to the well-heeled, and international eateries reflect the city's surprising diversity.

Certain neighborhoods have their strengths and weaknesses. You're likely to have a more traditionally touristy experience in Music Valley or downtown, while the best ethnic eats are along Nolensville Pike and Charlotte Pike. East Nashville and Germantown have more than their fair share of chef-driven, small restaurants with seasonal menus. Because many of these spots have a limited number of tables, be flexible about your reservation time.

For all its culinary strengths, Nashville is still a laid-back town, and that often means the service isn't to the level of the food, even in the fine-dining establishments. But remember to tip well: In all likelihood your server is an aspiring singer-songwriter.

COURTESY OF THE CATBIRD SEAT

HIGHLIGHTS

LOOK FOR **◖** TO FIND
RECOMMENDED RESTAURANTS.

© MARGARET LITTMAN

Diana's Sweet Shop

◖ Best Relocated Eatery: Quirky **Diana's Sweet Shop** was moved to Music City from Port Huron, Michigan (page 53).

◖ Most Theatrical Dining Experience: Acclaimed spot **The Catbird Seat** offers a select few diners a three-hour meal, complete with paired wines and a view of the chefs (page 57).

◖ Best Hamburger: The secret to **Rotier's** better-than-anywhere burger is that it's served on French bread (page 60).

◖ Place to Go-Kart after Your Meal: Music Valley's **Sukho Thai Restaurant** is a serene place to eat, but right outside the door is a family-friendly go-kart track (page 68).

◖ Best Place to Cook Your Own Meal: At **The Pfunky Griddle** you flip your own slapjacks. Luckily, they provide the batter—and the cleanup (page 68).

◖ Best Signage: The sweets are good, but it's the neon that steals the show at **Fox's Donut Den** (page 71).

◖ Best First Date Spot: Sylvan Park Italian joint **Caffe Nonna** is small enough to converse with your date, but not so intimate as to feel awkward if things don't get amorous (page 72).

Downtown and Germantown

Map 1

Like any city's downtown, Nashville's main business district has its upsides and downsides. Because this is Music City's financial center, there are banks and law offices with lots of office workers who need to eat lunch. So the lunch options are diverse and affordable and fast, and there are alternatives to chains. At dinner, particularly before a show at the Ryman or Bridgestone Arena, things can be trickier. There are high-end places and quick bites, but not a lot in the middle. Expect downtown dinner dining to be pricey.

BARBECUE

JACK'S BAR-B-QUE **❺**

416 Broadway, 615/254-5715, www.jacksbarbque.com
HOURS: Mon.-Wed. 10:30am-8pm, Thurs. 10:30am-9pm, Fri.-Sat. 10:30am-10pm, hours may be extended during the summer

If you are downtown and craving barbecue, Jack's is your best option. It isn't the best in the city, but the location can't be beat. Choose from barbecue pork shoulder, brisket, turkey, ribs, or sausage, and pair it with classic Southern sides like green beans, macaroni and cheese, and fried apples. Jack's serves five types of barbecue sauce, including

RESTAURANTS

PRICE KEY

$ Entrées less than $10

$$ Entrées $10-20

$$$ Entrées more than $20

classic Tennessee, Texas, and Kansas City. Adding to the appeal of the decent, affordable food is the fact that Jack's service is fast and friendly. There's a second location (334 W. Trinity Lane, 615/228-9888, Mon.-Thurs. 10:30am-8pm, Fri.-Sat. 10:30am-9pm, Sun. 11am-7pm) near East Nashville.

MARY'S OLD FASHIONED PIT BAR-B-QUE $

1106 Jefferson St., 615/256-7696

HOURS: Mon.-Sat. 10am-midnight

When is the last time you were handed your food through a hole cut in the wall? That's the case at Mary's, a Memphis-style barbecue place that is long on flavor, but short on atmosphere. The pulled pork and ribs are locals' favorites, though there isn't much on the menu that isn't tasty. Mary's is best as a takeout stop, perhaps on your way to tour Fisk University, rather than a dine-in destination.

CONTEMPORARY

CAPITOL GRILLE $$$

The Hermitage Hotel, 231 6th Ave. N., 615/345-7116, www.capitolgrillenashville.com

HOURS: Daily 6:30am-11am, 11:30am-2pm, 5:30pm-10pm

Rub elbows with legislators, lobbyists, and other members of the Music City jet set at the Capitol Grille. Located in the ground floor of the elegant Hermitage Hotel and set a stone's throw from the Tennessee State Capitol, this is the sort of restaurant where marriages are proposed and deals are done. The menu is fine dining at its best: choice cuts of meat prepared with exacting care and local ingredients. In fact, the ingredients are grown at the nearby Farm at Glen Leven, and this connection to the land has made the restaurant one of the leaders in the farm-to-fork movement. Dinner features rack of elk, sea bass, and pork chops; the provenience of each is noted on the menu. The lunch menu is more modest, including the Capitol Grille burger, a grilled pimento cheese sandwich, and meat entrées. Breakfast may be the most decadent of all, with cinnamon-swirl French toast, eggs Benedict, lobster and shirred eggs, and an array of fresh pastries and fruit. Adjacent to the Capitol Grille is the old-school **Oak Bar** (Mon.-Sat. 11:30am-close, Sun. noon-close), a wood-paneled and intimate bar for pre- or post-dinner drinks and conversation.

ETCH $$$

303 Demonbreun St., 615/522-0685, http://etchrestaurant.com

HOURS: Mon.-Thurs. 11am-2pm and 5pm-10pm, Fri. 11am-2pm and 5pm-11pm, Sat. 5pm-11pm

Chef Deb Paquette was at several of Music City's most-beloved restaurants before she opened Etch. On the ground floor of the Encore tower downtown, Etch has a minimalist, urban vibe. The small dining room has a big-city feel, and the menu is sophisticated—albeit a little offbeat—to match. Try the ginger grits or pork tenderloin with manchego cheese for examples of Paquette's signature taste. There's a decent happy-hour menu, as well as cocktail, beer, and wine lists.

FLYTE $$$

718 Division St., 615/255-6200, www.flytenashville.com

HOURS: Tues.-Thurs. 5pm-9pm, Fri.-Sat. 5pm-10pm

Flyte is not a newcomer to the Nashville dining scene. But a 2012 change in the kitchen brought new inspiration to what has long been a solid wine bar and restaurant. Flyte serves contemporary dishes with a Southern influence. They place an emphasis on local ingredients when possible, featuring seasonal dishes like duck leg or steelhead trout. One dessert specialty is a smoked bourbon chocolate dish. Flyte is slightly off the beaten track, but close enough to downtown to attract visitors, convention-goers, and business diners.

COURTESY OF ETCH RESTAURANT

Even the cheesecake is sophisticated at Etch.

Because of the wine pairings—with grapes from around the globe—a meal at Flyte is leisurely. If you are in a hurry, try their lounge (Tues.-Thurs. 4:30pm-11pm, Fri.-Sat. 4:30pm-midnight) instead.

GERMANTOWN CAFÉ ⑤⑤
1200 5th Ave. N., 615/242-3226,
www.germantowncafe.com
HOURS: Mon.-Fri. 11am-3pm and 5pm-close, Sat.-Sun. 10:30am-2pm and 5pm-close

One of the first restaurants to embrace what eventually became the gentrified Germantown neighborhood, Germantown Café is as close to a patriarch as the area has. Some longtime residents complain that the menu hasn't changed in years and years. But others like that consistency. The menu is small but solid, with squash fritters, crab cakes, and salmon. Sunday brunch is very popular, particularly on holidays like Mother's Day. The lunch crowd tends to be spillover business folks from downtown. There's free valet parking at night; street parking is easy enough during the day.

HUSK NASHVILLE ⑤⑤⑤
37 Rutledge St., 615/256-6565,
www.husknashville.com
HOURS: Mon.-Thurs. 11:30am-2pm and 5pm-10pm, Fri. 11:30am-2pm and 5pm-11pm, Sat. 10am-2pm and 5pm-11pm, Sun. 10am-2pm

Nestled in Rutledge Hill, in a historic former mayoral home, Husk Nashville was one of the most anticipated restaurants to open in 2013. Owned by chef Sean Brock, Husk relies on Southern ingredients, but not necessarily traditional Southern recipes. The menu changes daily, based on what is available locally, and even from the restaurant's own garden. Attention to detail is tantamount at Husk: Order a steak and choose your own handcrafted knife; signage in front lists the source of ingredients. Service is attentive and the ambience welcoming.

MAD PLATTER ⑤⑤
1239 6th Ave. N., 615/242-2563,
www.themadplatterrestaurant.com
HOURS: Mon.-Tues. 11am-2pm, Wed.-Thurs. 11am-2pm

and 5:30pm-10pm, Fri. 11am-2pm and 5:30pm-11pm, Sat. 5:30pm-11pm, Sun. 5pm-9pm

The thoughtful menu and careful preparations at the Mad Platter made it one of Nashville's favorite "nice" restaurants long before everyone else was talking about local ingredients. Located among restored town houses in the quaint Germantown neighborhood, just north of the Bicentennial Mall, the Mad Platter's signature entrées include the Mad Platter rack of lamb, which is tender and juicy, and the porcini-dusted shrimp. For a special occasion, or just to enjoy one of the city's best dining deals, choose the five-course special. The chicken salad is sweet and tangy, and comes with fresh banana bread. Reservations are advisable at dinner because the space is small; at lunch, come early to head off the business crowd.

MERCHANT'S ❸❸❸

401 Broadway, 615/254-1892,
www.merchantsrestaurant.com
HOURS: Downstairs Sun.-Thurs. 11am-11pm, Fri.-Sat. 11am-1am, upstairs daily 5pm-10pm

Since 1892, Merchant's has been a fixture in downtown Nashville, first as a hotel and then, beginning in 1988, as a restaurant. In the 1990s it was the go-to place for proms and parents' weekends. New owners—the folks behind The Catbird Seat, Patterson House, and others—revitalized the joint. Now it is two distinct spaces, one upstairs, one down, that appeal to business diners, visitors, and the special-occasion crowd. Expect classic Cobb salads, burgers, fried green tomatoes, pork osso buco, and more.

ROLF & DAUGHTERS ❸❸

700 Taylor St., 615/866-9897,
http://rolfanddaughters.com
HOURS: Daily 5:30pm-10pm

One of several farm-to-fork-focused restaurants in Germantown, Rolf & Daughters is a pasta-centric, rustic, contemporary restaurant with a killer cocktail list. The tables are communal, so you'll get to meet your neighbors as you sample from a menu that changes with the seasons. In

addition to the pasta, the pâté is a local favorite, although some gripe about the small serving of bread that accompanies it (and an upcharge to receive more bread). The restaurant is located in the century-old Werthan Factory building; parking is not an issue when you dine here. Deciding what tasty treat you want to order is.

SILO ❸❸❸

1121 5th Ave. N., 615/750-2912, www.silotn.com
HOURS: Tues.-Sat. 4pm-11pm, Sun. 10:30am-2pm and 4pm-11pm

This Germantown restaurant takes advantage of interest in farm-to-fork dining with a menu that uses lots of local and regional ingredients. Silo's contemporary menu builds on Southern tastes, thanks to its reliance on local ingredients. Menu items may include chicken-fried local rabbit with red bliss mashed potatoes, rabbit jus, mini biscuits, and pepper jelly; and hanger steak, red potatoes, wild North Carolina ramps, shiitake mushrooms, and hollandaise sauce. The sleek interior space uses barn wood and other elements in a modern way, resulting in a cozy, yet minimalist feel. Silo is not a budget meal: This is somewhere to go when you want a special night out and have the cash and the time to enjoy it. The wine and cocktail list is impressive, but the service can be spotty.

WATERMARK ❸❸❸

507 12th Ave. S., 615/254-2000,
http://watermark-restaurant.com
HOURS: Mon.-Thurs. 5:30pm-9:30pm, Fri.-Sat. 5:30pm-10pm

With one of the first "modern Southern" menus in town, Watermark ushered in a new dining scene to Nashville. There have been many (many) new restaurants come (and go) in Music City since, but Watermark has remained at the top of the culinary scene. Located in The Gulch, Watermark creates European-influenced Southern dishes, with cream sauces and deconstructed approaches to traditional recipes. The wine list is ample. Service is professional and befitting of a fine-dining establishment.

COURTESY OF M STREET ENTERTAINMENT GROUP

A good menu attracts a crowd at Whiskey Kitchen.

WHISKEY KITCHEN 💲💲

118 12th Ave. S., 615/254-3029,
mstreetnashville.com/whiskey-kitchen
HOURS: Daily 11am-3am

This restaurant/bar is one of The Gulch's see-and-be-seen spots. Starting as soon as the office crowd shuts down their laptops, Whiskey Kitchen has a happening bar scene, with both indoor and outdoor space. The outdoor patios are heated so that they can corral the crowds even in cold-weather months. The menu is better-than-bar food, with good burgers, a variation of Nashville hot chicken, and lots of dishes made with, you guessed it, whiskey. The wine and cocktail list is creative.

DINERS AND COFFEE SHOPS

COPPER KETTLE 💲

94 Peabody St., 615/742-5545,
www.copperkettlenashville.com
HOURS: Mon.-Fri. 10:30am-3pm, Sun. 10am-2pm

Locals love this cafeteria-style eatery because it is efficient, casual, and tasty, without being low-brow. The menu is heavy on Southern staples, but there are also plenty of vegetarian and healthier options. This is a something-for-everyone kind of place. Sunday brunches are particularly popular. There are great views of the city and easy, free parking, but it is a bit of a walk from most downtown attractions. There's another location (4004 Granny White Pike, 615/383-7242, Mon.-Fri. 11am-8pm, Sun. 10am-2pm) near Lipscomb University.

🄲 DIANA'S SWEET SHOP 💲

318 Broadway, 615/242-5397,
www.dianasnashville.com
HOURS: Sun.-Thurs. 10:30am-8pm, Fri.-Sat. 10:30am-9pm

This quirky diner and sweet shop has been around since 1926, albeit not in Nashville. The owners (who happen to be the folks behind Gibson Guitar) packed up a shop that was closing in Port Huron, Michigan, and moved it to Nashville, player piano and all, in 2010. Menu items include the standards, such as grilled cheese, club sandwiches, and burgers, but the real draws are the classic candies, fudge, and ice cream concoctions.

FRIST CENTER CAFÉ $

919 Broadway, 616/744-3974, www.fristcenter.org
HOURS: Mon.-Wed. and Sat. 10am-5:30pm, Thurs.-Fri. 10am-9pm, Sun. noon-5pm

Much more than the typical museum snack shop, the Frist Center Café is popular with downtown office workers and others for its fresh salads, wraps, and sandwiches. The restaurant is located at the rear of the Frist Center for the Visual Arts and has lovely outdoor seating in the warm-weather months. Sandwiches are available whole or half, and you can add a soup, salad, or fries for a well-rounded lunch. The café also has daily hot lunch entrées, plus a case of tempting desserts.

PROVENCE $$

601 Church St., 615/664-1150,
www.provencebreads.com
HOURS: Mon.-Fri. 7am-6pm, Sat. 8am-5pm

Provence, located inside the Nashville Public Library, serves excellent European-style pastries, breads, and salads, as well as coffee. Provence's signature sandwiches include creamy chicken salad and turkey and Brie. Or you can try a sampler of the café's salads, including roasted-vegetable salad, Parmesan potato salad, or creamy penne pasta. Save room for a decadent pastry, or at least a cookie, which come in varieties like raspberry hazelnut, chocolate espresso, and ginger molasses. For breakfast, nothing beats a buttery croissant spread with jam. Provence also has locations at Iris Café at the Peabody College Library (1210 21st Ave. S., 615/322-8887, Mon.-Fri. 7:30am-5pm) and in Hillsboro Village (1705 21st Ave. S., 615/386-0363, Mon.-Fri. 7am-8pm, Sat. 8am-8pm, Sun. 8am-6pm).

GREEK
THE GREEK TOUCH $

13 Arcade, 615/259-9493
HOURS: Mon.-Fri. 10am-2:30pm

This small Greek eatery in the Arcade is a great Nashville find: It has relatively authentic Mediterranean food combined with that famous Southern hospitality. The food isn't anything unusual: spanakopita (spinach pie), baklava, gyros, and a Greek salad, plus specialties like a slow-cooked pork chop. The Greek Touch is a good choice for a quick, affordable meal downtown, plus an option for takeout.

SANTORINI $

210 4th Ave. N., 615/254-4524
HOURS: Mon.-Sat. 9am-4pm, Sun. 11am-6pm

There are several Greek restaurants amid Nashville's office towers and state buildings. One of the best is Santorini. Choose from falafel, gyro, chicken, or spinach pie, served as a plate (with rice, salad, and pita), salad (with pita, tabbouleh, and salad), or meal (with fries). The food is fresh and well prepared, and the premises are neat and clean.

ITALIAN
CITY HOUSE $$

1222 4th Ave. N., 615/736-5838,
http://cityhousenashville.com
HOURS: Mon. and Wed.-Sat. 5pm-10pm, Sun. 5pm-9pm

One of Nashville's most acclaimed restaurants, City House is nestled in a brick building on an unassuming block of Germantown. Chef Tandy Wilson has received many of the nation's important culinary accolades, including being named one of the best chefs in the South by the James Beard Foundation. The menu is modern Italian, often heavy on the pork, with inventive pizzas and cocktails. Service can be slow, particularly if you come with large groups, and the space is loud, so don't expect an intimate conversation. It is always an option to eat at the bar, which is a fun choice if you want to chat with locals.

PIZZA
MANNY'S HOUSE OF PIZZA $

15 Arcade, 615/242-7144,
www.mannyshouseofpizza.com
HOURS: Mon.-Fri. 10am-6pm, Sat. 11am-5pm

Located in the lower level of the downtown Arcade, Manny's House of Pizza serves up

COURTESY OF MONELL'S

Monell's is a landmark family-style restaurant in Germantown.

RESTAURANTS

"vegetables." Choose a vegetable plate, with either three or four vegetables, or a meat-and-three for just about a buck more. Meals come with your choice of pillowy yeast rolls or corn bread. The full lunch, plus a drink, will run you under $10.

KATIE'S MEAT & THREE $

10 Arcade, 615/256-1055
HOURS: Daily 7am-4pm
As its name suggests, Katie's is a classic Nashville meat-and-three. Choose from four different meat specials daily, with sides such as turnip greens, mashed potatoes, and white beans. Or you can forgo the meat altogether and go for the four sides. Katie's is one of the eateries in the Arcade, which means it caters to the downtown crowd. Seating is at a premium, and most of the business is to-go orders.

MONELL'S $$

1235 6th Ave. N., 615/248-4747, www.monellstn.com
HOURS: Mon. 10:30am-2pm, Tues.-Fri. 10:30am-2pm and 5pm-8:30pm, Sat. 8:30am-3pm and 5pm-8:30pm, Sun. 8:30am-4pm
Family-style dining is not for everyone. But if you know that your party wants to share platters of fried chicken and country ham, then you ought to consider doing so at Monell's. Located in a brick house in Germantown (with several other locations across the city), Monell's is the local's go-to for family brunch or celebratory Southern dinner out. Everything is all you can eat, and the menu changes based on the day of the week. Contributing to its family-friendly appeal: Kids under 3 eat free and children 4-10 dine at a reduced price.

PUCKETT'S GROCERY & RESTAURANT $$

500 Church St., 615/770-2772, www.puckettsgrocery.com
HOURS: Mon.-Thurs. 7am-10pm, Fri.-Sat. 7am-11pm, Sun. 7am-4pm
There's no shortage of fried chicken south of the Mason-Dixon. Even so, people often throng to one of Puckett's three locations for some of what folks say is among the area's best

thick- and thin-crust varieties (both full pies and by the slice), massive stromboli, mighty lasagna, and huge meatball subs. The restaurant is small; eating in can be a challenge, particularly because Nashvillians flock here for the best slice in town. Manny's stays open later on the first Saturday of the month to accommodate hungry crowds at the downtown Art Crawl.

SOUTHERN

ARNOLD'S COUNTRY KITCHEN $

605 8th Ave. S., 615/256-4455
HOURS: Mon.-Fri. 10:30am-2:45pm
Set in a red cinder-block building on the southern edge of downtown, Arnold's is a food-lover's dream. No haute or fusion cuisine here—this is real food. It's set up cafeteria-style, so grab a tray while you peer at the wonders before you: chocolate pie, congealed salad (that's Jell-O to those who don't know), juicy sliced tomatoes, turnip greens, mashed potatoes, squash casserole, macaroni and cheese—and that's just the

fried chicken. The downtown outpost of this regional mainstay has classic Southern food (don't skip the fried green beans) in a casual, often crowded environment. There's live music many nights and a full bar, but the real appeal is stick-to-your-ribs comfort food in a restaurant that will get you in and out in time to see a show at the Ryman.

THE SOUTHERN STEAK AND OYSTER ❶❷❸
150 3rd Ave. S., 615/724-1762,
www.thesouthernnashville.com
HOURS: Mon.-Thurs. 7:30am-10pm, Fri.
7:30am-midnight, Sat. 10am-midnight, Sun. 10am-10pm
When The Southern (as locals call it) opened, it was as if a void was filled. A void perhaps few realized existed before it was filled. Nevertheless, locals and visitors alike flocked to this sleek, welcoming downtown bar and restaurant to eat oysters the likes of which are not typically found outside of the coasts. In addition to the oysters, The Southern has a fun take on the classic Nashville hot chicken, gumbo, and an impressive cocktail list. Its location makes it a madhouse before the symphony or during conventions, but that buzz is part of its appeal.

THE STANDARD ❶❷❸
167 Rosa L. Parks Blvd., 615/254-1277,
www.smithhousenashville.com
HOURS: Tues.-Sat. 5pm-9pm
Located in the historic Smith house, The Standard is a restaurant of ages gone by. The

© RON MANVILLE

The Southern Steak and Oyster

service is to the standards (pun intended) of this Victorian home. You'll feel like a guest on *Downton Abbey* as your every need is attended to. Menu items include wedge salads, crab bisque, and, yes, "bacon-wrapped-bacon" (that's a pork chop wrapped in bacon). You'll need to forget your diet and bring a credit card, as dining at The Standard is neither healthy nor inexpensive. But it is a night on the town unlike any you've had in decades.

Midtown and 12 South   Map 2

The area around the Vanderbilt campus, just west of downtown, includes almost any dining experience you could want. There are more quick, student-friendly bites than you could ever try, as well as plenty of spots to go out on the town. There are fine-dining options for parents' weekend, as well as for business travelers.

The residential neighborhoods of 12 South and Belmont are prime candidates for eating out, with more than their share of good restaurants. Thanks to the Vanderbilt and Belmont crowds, plus the affluent local residents, there are plenty of cute coffee shops, upscale eateries, and places to grab a beer with your meal.

ASIAN
PM ⬤⬤

2017 Belmont Blvd., 615/297-2070,
www.pmnashville.com
HOURS: Mon.-Sat. 11am-1am, Sun. 4pm-1am
One of the restaurants owned by *Top Chef* contestant and local celeb Arnold Myint, PM is a fun Asian eatery with an indulgent cocktail and sake list. The restaurant knows its audience, as it is smack-dab in the center of the Belmont University neighborhood. The staff is fun and energetic and knows it will see most of its clients the later it gets at night. Parking can be tricky depending on the day and time you are trying to dine.

BARBECUE
HOG HEAVEN ⬤

115 27th Ave. N., 615/329-1234,
www.hogheavenbbq.com
HOURS: Mon.-Sat. 10am-7pm
Near Centennial Park and the Vanderbilt campus, Hog Heaven is a nondescript yet well-known landmark for barbecue. Pulled-pork sandwiches and beef brisket are among the most popular menu items at this mostly takeout eatery. What distinguishes it from other barbecue spots is a good cross section of non-pork offerings. Locals like the

Alabama-style white barbecue sauce. Seating is essentially in a screened-in porch: Don't expect climate control.

CHINESE
SUZY WONG'S HOUSE OF YUM ⬤⬤

1515 Church St., 615/329-2913,
www.suzywongsnashville.com
HOURS: Sun.-Thurs. 5pm-11pm, Fri.-Sat. 5pm-1am
The name of this restaurant reveals that it is not your average Chinese food joint. Owned by *Top Chef* alum Arnold Myint, Suzy Wong's has a menu of shared plates with an Asian fusion spirit. Combined with an inventive cocktail menu and a high-energy soundtrack, this is a great place to go and paint the town red with friends. The food is fun—think Asian nachos—rather than authentic, and this is not a place for kids or those who don't want to have to speak over a din. There are plenty of vegetarian and gluten-free options on the menu, too.

CONTEMPORARY
BURGER UP ⬤⬤

2901 12th Ave. S., 615/279-3767, www.burger-up.com
HOURS: Sun.-Thurs. 11am-10pm, Fri.-Sat. 11am-11pm
You might be thinking: I didn't come to explore the Music City food scene to just have a burger. Well, Burger Up is not just any burger. There are lamb, bison, and bacon burgers, plus all manner of other combinations with different toppings. Of course there are fries, too, including a sweet potato version, and homemade ketchup. The space has floor-to-ceiling windows that look out on 12th Avenue South, great for people-watching.

◖ THE CATBIRD SEAT ⬤⬤⬤

1711 Division St., www.thecatbirdseatrestaurant.com
HOURS: Wed.-Sat. 5:45pm-9:45pm
To describe The Catbird Seat as a restaurant is a bit of a misnomer. It is a culinary performance that happens to include dinner. There are just 32 seats in this U-shaped space. Once you get a coveted reservation (available online only),

you'll be treated to three hours of wines paired with a seasonal meal, made before your eyes. Some of the ingredients don't sound great—hay-infused yogurt, for example—but most of them will blow your mind. Reservations are opened 30 days in advance. The seven-course tasting menu is $100 without drinks. The non-alcoholic pairings are as inventive as the wines.

A MATTER OF TASTE $

2401 Franklin Pike, 615/866-8144, www.amatteroftastetakeout.com
HOURS: Mon.-Fri. 11am-3pm
You're likely to miss this tiny café when you drive by. Next to a liquor store, A Matter of Taste does a brisk takeout business with just a few tables and chairs for the eat-in crowd. But don't let the size fool you. A Matter of Taste has some of the largest selection of gluten-free foods in the city, with a soup, salad, and sandwich menu that everyone will enjoy, not just those on a restricted diet. The food is largely classic luncheon dishes, perfect for a picnic at one of Nashville's great parks.

SLOCO $

2905 12th Ave. S., 615/499-4793, www.slocolocal.com
HOURS: Daily 9am-5pm
Founded by Jeremy Barlow, owner of the now-shuttered Tayst restaurant, Sloco is a little sandwich shop with a big idea. This is a sustainable sandwich shop, meaning ingredients are local and seasonal. If you visit Nashville in December, you won't find a tomato on your sandwich here. A percentage of proceeds are donated to local food charities. Because of the ingredients and concept, prices are higher than your typical sandwich shop.

SUNSET GRILL $$$

2001 Belcourt Ave., 615/386-3663, www.sunsetgrill.com
HOURS: Tues.-Wed. 11am-10pm, Thurs.-Fri. 11am-midnight, Sat.-Sun. 4:30pm-midnight
A favorite for Music Row power lunches, special occasions, and late-night bar food is Sunset Grill. Dinner favorites include Voodoo Pasta, a spicy pasta dish with shrimp and andouille

sausage, and the grilled beef tenderloin. At lunch, when most choices are less than $12, you can order salads, sandwiches, and pasta. The Cobb salad and chicken-salad sandwiches are always popular. Food here is prepared with care, often using organic and locally produced ingredients. The outdoor patio is popular during warm weather, and it is a great place to people-watch.

TAVERN MIDTOWN $$

1904 Broadway, 615/320-8580, http://mstreetnashville.com/tavern
HOURS: Mon.-Thurs. 11am-midnight, Fri. 11am-3am, Sat. 10am-3am, Sun. 10am-midnight
This eatery near the Vanderbilt campus is the mecca of see-and-be-seen for Nashville's under-30 set. It isn't the East Nashville hipster crowd, but more the Music City beautiful people crowd. You're likely to see big groups of people going out on a night on the town here, and that can mean a wait for your table. The food is a nice twist on the unusual, with dishes like a kale salad and a red velvet waffle. Don't skip the cocktail list.

TIN ANGEL $$

3201 West End Ave., 615/298-3444, www.tinangel.net
HOURS: Mon.-Fri. 11am-10pm, Sat. 5pm-10pm, Sun. 11am-3pm
A neighborhood joint near the Vanderbilt campus, Tin Angel is housed in a historic building with, appropriately, tin ceilings. Described as an "American bistro," Tin Angel has solid soups, salads, and entrées, including some that are inspired by other now-shuttered favorite Nashville restaurants. Popular menu items include crab cakes, duck breast, and pasta. The bar is hopping in the evenings.

SWEETS

HOT AND COLD $

1804 21st Ave. S., 615/767-5468, www.bongojava.com
HOURS: Mon.-Thurs. 10am-10pm, Fri. 10am-11pm, Sat. 9am-11pm, Sun. 9am-10pm
Las Paletas (2905 12th Ave. S., 615/386-2101, Tues.-Sun. 11am-8pm), the 12 South mainstay for flavorful popsicles, has an outpost

in Hillsboro Village called Hot and Cold. Its name comes from the fact that you can get warming coffee drinks in addition to cold ice cream treats, so no matter the time of year, you can find something to tempt the sweet tooth. Frozen options include popsicles dipped in chocolate and ice cream from Ohio favorite **Jeni's Splendid Ice Creams** (1892 Eastland Ave., 615/262-8611, www.jenis.com, Sun.-Thurs. noon-10pm, Fri.-Sat. noon-11pm).

LAS PALETAS ⑤
2905 12th Ave. S., 615/386-2101
HOURS: Tues.-Sun. 11am-8pm
For years there was no sign on the door, and the only way to find Las Paletas's amazing, inventive popsicles was to follow the long line of people waiting to get in the door. There is now a sign (and posted hours) and, of course, still lines of locals waiting to get a perfect grapefruit *paleta* to cool the heat of summer, or a tasty Mexican caramel treat after lunch at **Burger Up** (2901 12th Ave. S., 615/279-3767, www.burger-up.com, Sun.-Thurs. 11am-10pm, Fri.-Sat. 11am-11pm). The frozen treats are now sold a few other places around town, including **Bongo Java** (107 S. 11th St., 615/777-3278, www.bongojava.com, Mon.-Fri. 6:30am-6pm, Sat.-Sun 7am-6pm) in East Nashville and **Hot and Cold** (1804 21st Ave. S., 615/767-5468, www.bongojava.com, Mon.-Thurs. 10am-10pm, Fri. 10am-11pm, Sat. 9am-11pm, Sun. 9am-10pm) in Hillsboro Village.

DINERS AND COFFEE SHOPS
ATHENS FAMILY ⑤⑤
2526 Franklin Pike, 615/383-2848,
www.athensfamilyrestaurant.com
HOURS: Mon.-Wed. 7am-10pm, Thurs.-Sat. 24 hours, Sun. midnight-10pm
In cities like Chicago, Greek diners like this are a dime a dozen. In Nashville, Athens is one of the only 24-hour (at least on weekends) places to get an omelet after your late-night honky-tonking. All the classic diner dishes are served here, in a bright, clean space with friendly servers. There's ample parking, and prices are decent. Come on a weekend morning and expect

a wait. The bacon lamb burger has been featured on national TV and is a local legend.

BONGO JAVA ⑤
2007 Belmont Blvd., 615/385-5282,
www.bongojava.com
HOURS: Daily 7am-10pm
Nashville's original coffee shop, Bongo Java, is still one of its most popular. Located near Belmont University, Bongo Java is regularly full of students chatting, texting, and surfing the Web thanks to free wireless Internet. Set in an old house with a huge front porch, Bongo feels homey and welcoming, and perhaps a bit more on the hippie side than other Nashville coffee shops. Breakfast, including Bongo French toast, is served all day. There are other Bonga Java locations, including one in East Nashville (107 S. 11th St., 615/777-3278, Mon.-Fri. 6:30am-6pm, Sat.-Sun 7am-6pm).

ELLISTON PLACE SODA SHOP ⑤
2111 Elliston Pl., 615/327-1090
HOURS: Mon.-Fri. 7am-7pm, Sat. 7am-5pm
In today's retro-happy world, it isn't too hard to find an old-fashioned soda shop. But how many of them are the real thing? Elliston Place Soda Shop, near Centennial Park and Vanderbilt, is one of those rare holdovers from the past, and it's proud of it. The black-and-white tile floors, lunch counter, and Purity Milk advertisements may have been here for decades, but the food is consistently fresh and good. Choose between a sandwich or a plate lunch, but be sure to save room for a classic milk shake or slice of hot pie with ice cream on top. In 2011 the shop threatened to close, citing sluggish sales and increasing rent, but public outcry convinced the owners to renew the lease for five more years.

FIDO ⑤
1812 21st Ave. S., 615/777-3436
HOURS: Mon.-Fri. 7am-11pm, Sat. 8am-midnight, Sun. 8am-11pm
As Bongo Java's big brother, Fido is more than a coffee shop. It is a place to get work done, watch deals being made, and see and be seen. Take a seat along the front plate-glass windows to

watch the pretty people as they stroll between the Sunset Grill and Posh, one of Nashville's most upscale clothing boutiques. In addition to coffee, the menu also features sandwiches, salads, and baked goods.

NOSHVILLE ⑤

1918 Broadway, 615/329-6674, www.noshville.com
HOURS: Mon. 6:30am-2:30pm, Tues.-Thurs. 6:30am-9pm, Fri. 6:30am-10:30pm, Sat. 7:30am-10:30pm, Sun. 7:30am-9pm

When Nashvillians are in the mood for a hearty deli sandwich, they head to Noshville, which is as close to a genuine New York delicatessen as you'll find in this southern town. Lox and bagels, oatmeal, and a variety of egg dishes are popular at breakfast. At lunch and supper, choose from a variety of sandwiches, all served double-stacked, which means it's really more than any one person should eat. To find Noshville, look for the miniature statue of Lady Liberty on the roof. There is another location in Green Hills (4014 Hillsboro Circle, 615/269-3535, Mon.-Fri. 6:30am-2:30pm, Sat.-Sun. 7:30am-3pm), and yet another at the airport (1 Terminal Dr., Terminal A/B, 615/275-6674, daily 5am-close).

PANCAKE PANTRY ⑤

1796 21st Ave. S., 615/383-9333
HOURS: Mon.-Fri. 6am-3pm, Sat.-Sun. 6am-4pm

There's a lot of hype surrounding Nashville's favorite breakfast restaurant, the Pancake Pantry. Founded in 1961 and still family owned, the Pantry serves some of the best pancakes in the city. Owner David Baldwin says that the secret is in the ingredients, which are fresh and homemade. Many of the flours come from Tennessee, and the syrup is made right at the restaurant. The Pantry proves that a pancake can be much more than plain. The menu offers no fewer than 21 varieties, and that doesn't include the waffles. Try the fluffy buckwheat cakes, savory cornmeal cakes, sweet blintzes, or the old standby buttermilk pancakes. And if you decide to order eggs instead, the good news is that most of the

other breakfast platters on offer come with a short stack of pancakes, too. The Pantry offers egg-white omelets for the health conscious, and it's very kid-friendly as well, except for the fact that on weekend mornings, and many weekdays, the line for a seat at the Pantry goes out the door.

◖ ROTIER'S ⑤

2413 Elliston Pl., 615/327-9892
HOURS: Mon.-Tues. 10:30am-9:30pm, Wed.-Fri. 10:30am-10pm, Sat. 9am-10pm

Said to have the best burger in Nashville, Rotier's is also a respected meat-and-three diner. It may look like a dive (okay, maybe it is a dive), but the food lives up to the hype. Choose from classic sandwiches or comfort-food dinners. The Saturday breakfast will fuel you all day long. Ask about the milk shake, a city favorite that appears nowhere on the menu. Whatever you order, don't miss the hash brown casserole.

While the food is tasty, one of the best things about Rotier's is that it is one of the few places in Nashville where everyone goes. City politicians, Vanderbilt professors, music stars, tourists, and locals all come here for a burger, a bargain, and a blast from the past.

INTERNATIONAL
INTERNATIONAL MARKET AND RESTAURANT ⑤

2010 Belmont Blvd., 615/297-4453
HOURS: Daily 10:30am-9pm

The venerable International Market and Restaurant, near Belmont University and Hillsboro Village, is a time-honored choice for a cheap lunch in Nashville. The cafeteria serves lots of vegetable, noodle, and rice dishes, many of them Thai in origin, at prices that seem not to have risen much since the restaurant was established in 1975. If you want to splurge, order a "from the kitchen" special of pad Thai or another dish, which will be made from scratch just for you. Owner Patti Myint is the mother of *Top Chef* contestant and local restaurateur Arnold Myint.

MEXICAN
SAN ANTONIO TACO CO. $

416 21st Ave. S., 615/256-6142, www.thesatco.com
HOURS: Sun.-Wed. 11am-11pm, Thurs.-Sat.
11am-midnight

This Tex-Mex joint has an obsessive fan base among Vanderbilt students and alumni, who spend hours here downing tacos, soda, and oddly addictive queso cheese dip served with light, crunchy chips. The soundtrack has literally not changed in 25 years, nor has the decor. But the real appeal of SATCO, as locals call it, is the deck, which is perfect for people-watching while drinking from a bucket of beer. There's another SATCO location downtown (208 Commerce St., 615/259-4413), if you are craving queso, but without the deck, it just isn't the same. SATCO's hours may be shorter in winter and when school is not in session.

PIZZA
MAFIAOZA'S PIZZERIA AND NEIGHBORHOOD PUB $$

2400 12th Ave. S., 615/269-4646, www.mafiaozas.com
HOURS: Tues.-Fri. 4pm-3am, Sat.-Sun. 11am-3am

This is a busy pizza spot with beer on tap and an open kitchen where you can see your pizza slide into the oven. In an effort to keep little ones entertained, kids are welcome to roll out their own dough at the counter, then their pizzas are put in the oven first, while mom and dad have a drink or an appetizer and everyone is happy. The patio is popular on warm summer nights. Some people quibble that the pizza is not New York-style authentic.

SOUTHERN
SWETT'S $$

2725 Clifton Ave., 615/329-4418,
www.swettsrestaurant.com
HOURS: Daily 11am-8pm

One of Nashville's most beloved meat-and-threes is Swett's, family owned and operated since 1954. People come from all over the city to eat at this Nashville institution, which combines soul food and Southern cooking with great results (and, in 2012, they added barbecue to their offerings). The food here is homemade and authentic, down to the real mashed potatoes, the vinegary greens, and the yeast rolls. Swett's is set up cafeteria-style. Start by grabbing dessert—the pies are excellent—and then move on to the good stuff: Country-fried steak, pork chops, meat loaf, fried catfish, and ham are a few of the usual suspects. A standard plate comes with one meat, two sides, and a serving of either yeast roll or corn bread, but you can add more sides if you like. Draw your own iced tea—sweet or unsweet—at the end, and then find a seat if you can.

STEAK HOUSES
JIMMY KELLY'S $$$

217 Louise Ave., 615/329-4349,
www.jimmykellys.com
HOURS: Mon.-Sat. 5pm-midnight

Jimmy Kelly's is a family-run old-school steak house. Set in an old Victorian mansion a few blocks from Centennial Park and Vanderbilt, Jimmy Kelly's has been operated by the Kelly family since 1934. During its lifetime, food fads have come and gone, but Jimmy Kelly's has continued to serve excellent steaks and other grill foods. Dinner begins with irresistible corn cakes and continues with classic appetizers like crab cakes or fried calamari. Entrée choices include a half dozen different steaks, lamb, grilled chicken, and seafood, including the best blackened catfish in the city. Jimmy Kelly's offers low lighting, wood paneling, and attentive, but not fussy, service. Tables are set throughout what were once parlors, bedrooms, and porches in the old home, giving diners a feeling of homey intimacy.

RESTAURANTS

East Nashville Map 3

Just on the other side of the river from downtown, East Nashville has the reputation as the place where the hipsters hang out. This neighborhood began gentrifying after a 1998 tornado, and even when folks on the other side of town considered it unsafe, they'd still venture over to try one if its great restaurants. Most East Nashville eateries have a neighborhoody vibe.

CONTEMPORARY

EASTLAND CAFÉ ⓢⓢ
97 Chapel Ave., 615/627-1088,
www.eastlandcafe.com
HOURS: Mon.-Thurs. 5pm-10pm, Fri.-Sat. 5pm-11pm

Eastland was one of East Nashville's stalwart upscale dining spots before anyone else bothered to try to put a good restaurant on this side of the river. The place remains solid and cozy, with a nice menu of fish, pasta, and meat. The patio is romantic and comfortable in the summer. But it is the impressive happy hour, with specials on both food and drinks, that draws in the locals.

THE FAMILY WASH ⓢⓢ
2038 Greenwood Ave., 615/226-6070,
www.familywash.com
HOURS: Tues.-Sat. 6pm-midnight

Housed in a former Laundromat, The Family Wash is classic Nashville. Part live music listening room, part bar, part restaurant, part neighborhood gathering place, The Family Wash captures the offbeat energy that so well defines Nashville. Come here to hear local musicians of all stripes (definitely not just country) and eat supper that is better than average bar food. Locals love the shepherd's pie. Reservations are accepted, and they're recommended, as the space isn't large and friends of the band may pack the place when favorites take the small stage.

HOLLAND HOUSE BAR AND REFUGE ⓢⓢⓢ
935 W. Eastland Ave., 615/262-4190,
www.hollandhousebarandrefuge.com
HOURS: Mon.-Thurs. 5pm-midnight, Fri.-Sat. 5pm-2am, Sun. 11am-2pm

There's something about a place that pays attention to the details, and Holland House Bar and Refuge is one of those spots. This East Nashville hideaway is exactly as its name suggests: a refuge from louder restaurants and more frantically paced bars. The impressive cocktail and food menus change seasonally, and the bartender will craft your drink with precision, so expect to wait for that perfectly sized ginger ice cube or muddle mint (try the truffled popcorn while you wait). The food menu isn't as extensive as the cocktail menu, but everything is made with local and seasonal ingredients, ranging from duck to catfish. Locals like Monday night's happy hour and its burger special. This is not a place to bring little ones—it is a bar as much as a restaurant.

MARCHÉ ARTISAN FOODS ⓢⓢ
1000 Main St., 615/262-5346,
www.marcheartisanfoods.com
HOURS: Tues.-Fri. 8am-9pm, Sat. 8am-4pm, Sun. 9am-4pm

Known mostly as a brunch place, Marché is a solid East Nashville brunch, lunch, and dinner joint, with a tiny grocery section to boot. The menu is bistro-inspired, with seasonal salads and entrées, plus homemade baked goods and a decent wine list. The window-filled room looks out on busy Gallatin Pike and during the day is buzzing with good energy. You are guaranteed a long wait for weekend brunches, but hardly anyone comes here for the tasty dinners. The dinner menu is slightly more expensive than the rest of the day, but it is worth it for the extra elbow room.

MARGOT CAFÉ ⬤⬤⬤

1017 Woodland St., 615/227-4668,
www.margotcafe.com
HOURS: Tues.-Sat. 6pm-10pm, Sun. 11am-2pm

This small East Nashville bistro has been serving European-style food for special-occasion diners since before the neighborhood was hip. Other restaurants have more notoriety these days (and many of Margot Café's alums have gone on to helm other restaurants), but Margot Café is still a reliable option for a nice dinner out. The menu is well edited, the service attentive, and the space cozy. The Sunday brunch, with options such as eggs and duck hash, is popular and crowded.

THE PHARMACY BURGER PARLOR & BEER GARDEN ⬤

731 McFerrin Ave., 615/712-9527,
www.thepharmacynashville.com
HOURS: Sun.-Thurs. 11am-10pm, Fri.-Sat. 11am-11pm

The folks behind Holland House opened The Pharmacy, a beer garden and burger joint that has been popular beyond anyone's expectations. In addition to an in-depth beer and burger menu, the team at The Pharmacy makes sodas by hand. The killer grassy backyard beer garden is big and packed anytime the outdoor temperatures rise. Expect long waits on weekend nights, and pay attention to your surroundings when you park. This is a rougher section of East Nashville, and crimes like car break-ins do take place.

RUMOUR'S EAST ⬤⬤

1112 Woodland St., 615/262-5346,
http://rumourseast.com
HOURS: Tues.-Sun. 5pm-midnight

Situated in an old house in the heart of East Nashville, Rumour's East is a cozy local eatery with a decent fresh menu and an impressive wine list. Dishes change seasonally, but are likely to include a vegetarian option or two, salads, pizza, and entrées like meatballs or a grilled fish. Don't miss taking a peek at the beautiful curved wooden bar, even if you are seated in another room. The patio is a lovely place for alfresco dining.

SILLY GOOSE ⬤⬤⬤

1888 Eastland Ave., 615/915-0757,
http://sillygoosenashville.com
HOURS: Tues.-Thurs. 11am-9pm, Fri.-Sat. 11am-10pm

Silly Goose is famous for its couscous. That's not a sentence you get to read often about restaurants. But Silly Goose is a little offbeat. Its menu, with couscous, salads, and rosemary-infused lemonade, makes it sound less interesting than it is. Everything is flavorful, with a few surprises, such as pumpkin seeds in the salads. Seating is limited, and there can be long lines, both for lunch and dinner. A bonus of Silly Goose's location is that it is next door to **Jeni's Splendid Ice Creams** (1892 Eastland Ave., 615/262-8611, www.jenis.com, Sun.-Thurs. noon-10pm, Fri.-Sat. noon-11pm), an Ohio-based gourmet ice cream shop with lines no matter the season.

SKY BLUE ⬤

700 Fatherland St., 615/770-7097,
www.skybluecoffee.com
HOURS: Sun.-Mon. 7am-3pm, Tues.-Sat. 7am-10pm

Sky Blue looks like a coffee shop, and the coffee and bagels are good, but this restaurant is a full-service option for breakfast, lunch, and dinner. Breakfast is served all day, and is one of the reasons locals love it here, particularly the biscuit bowl, with eggs and brisket. The armadillo grilled cheese sandwich has cheese on both the outside and the inside. The space is sweet and cozy, with vintage tablecloths on each table and the work of local artists on the walls.

DINERS AND COFFEE SHOPS
BAGEL FACE ⬤

700 Main St., 615/730-8840,
www.bagelfacebakery.com
HOURS: Tues.-Sat. 7am-1:30pm

People are particular about bagels. A "real" bagel is hand-rolled and boiled. And Bagel Face is your best bet for a real bagel in Nashville. Varieties available vary by the day, but there are always classics such as poppy seed and onion. Sandwiches served on bagels are tasty and affordable. The space is large with plenty of extra

© ANDY MUMMA

Coffee-making is an art at Barista Parlor.

room and parking, but not particularly cozy. The staff couldn't be friendlier. Bagel Face bagels are also sold at coffee shops around the city.

BARISTA PARLOR $

519B Gallatin Ave., 615/712-9766, www.baristaparlor.com
HOURS: Mon.-Fri. 7am-6pm, Sat.-Sun. 8am-6pm
To call Barista Parlor a coffee shop is a gross understatement. It is more an art gallery where the coffee is the star. A renovated auto shop, this is a big, well-designed space with great signage from local artists, uniforms from local designers, interesting furniture, and attentive servers. They take coffee very seriously here and are happy to answer your questions about their pour-over style and different blends. Be patient as your caffeine fix is prepared.

FOOD STANDS
I DREAM OF WEENIE $

113 S. 11th St., 615/226-2622
HOURS: Mon.-Fri. 11am-3pm, Sat. 10:30am-5pm, Sun. 10:30am-3pm, hours vary seasonally
Several years ago this hot dog stand, based in a renovated VW bus, closed its (car) doors. But customer outcry was so loud that new owners bought it and moved it around the corner. Now the lines are back, with people waiting for specialty hot dogs, chips, and drinks. There are a number of hot dog varieties offered on a regular basis, such as the Kraut Dog (served with sauerkraut), as well as some that are offered as specials, such as the Pizza Dog. There is a grassy area where you can sit and eat your dog, but most people take their dogs to go.

ITALIAN
POMODORO EAST $$

701 Porter Rd., 615/873-4978, www.pomodoroeast.com
HOURS: Mon.-Sat. 4:30pm-10pm, Sun. 4:30pm-9pm
Driving up to this Italian restaurant, the first thing you'll notice is a large deck space looking out on the Eastland/Porter intersection. It makes a great place to dine outside when the weather is good. The interior space is more crowded, which can lead to slow service and bumping elbows. The happy-hour specials are worth checking out, with great deals on drinks,

Specialty hot dogs are served from a VW bus at I Dream of Weenie.

pizzas, and Italian appetizers. Dining at the bar can be enjoyable.

MEXICAN
MAS TACOS ❸

732 McFerrin Ave., 615/543-6271

HOURS: Tues.-Thurs. 11am-4pm, Fri. 11am-9pm, Sat. 9am-3pm

Mas Tacos is known and loved for its food truck, but it also has a physical shop where fans can go for the tasty tacos, soups, and other Mexican delights. The menu is bigger than seems possible given the tiny kitchen, and specials change throughout the week. You order at a window, so there's almost always a line, but it moves quickly. Your food will be delivered to you at one of the few tables indoors or out.

SANDWICHES
MITCHELL'S DELICATESSEN ❸

1402 McGavock Pike, 615/262-9862

HOURS: Tues.-Sat. 7am-7pm, Sun. 7am-4pm

Not a deli in the traditional sense, Mitchell's Delicatessen is one of the most creative sandwich shops in town. Order the roasted lamb and *raita;* a Vietnamese-style creation with pork, liver pâté, and veggies; or a BLT fit for a king. Breakfast is served until 11am, and there is also a daily menu of soups and hot plate specials. Stop here for top-notch bread, cheese, and meats for your own sandwiches, too.

SOUTHERN
BOLTON'S SPICY CHICKEN & FISH ❸

624 Main St., 615/254-8015

HOURS: Mon.-Sat. 11am-9pm

Hot chicken is one of Nashville's true culinary specialties. Bolton's is one of the best places to try this local delicacy. In fact, it is a big debate whether it is Prince's or Bolton's that is the city's best. Hot chicken is served bone-in, on a piece of white bread (soaking up the heat), with a pickle on top. And it is spicy. For real. It is made to order, and panfrying takes time, so plan a 20-minute wait into your visit. As its name suggests, Bolton's also serves spicy fish. Bolton's has a second location (2309A Franklin Pike, 615/383-1421).

FOOD TRUCKS

COURTESY OF MAS TACOS POR FAVOR

Food trucks bring new flavors to all corners of the city.

Like every big city with a hipster population worth its salt, Nashville has scores of food trucks driving to and fro, selling gourmet delicacies from their wheel-based restaurants. These snack-masters tend to show up at places with big lunch crowds, late-night after concerts, and large public events, so you may just run into them.

The website for **Nashville Food Trucks** (http://nashfoodtrucks.com) lists menus and upcoming planned stops for more than 25 trucks. If you prefer your meals alfresco, check out this list.

- One of Nashville's first food trucks, **The Grilled Cheeserie** (http://thegrilled-cheeserietruck.com) serves delicious grilled cheese sandwiches and tomato soup. It travels all over the city, particularly at farmers markets in the summer. Track it via Twitter (@GrilldCheeserie), or text CHEESE in a message to 88000.

- It is hard to miss the bright pink presence that is **Barbie Burgers.** To find their tasty burgers and sweet potato fries, follow them on Twitter (@BarbieBurgers).

- Ice cream sandwiches, strawberry shortcake, and other classic desserts are the fuel that keeps **Tin Can Treats** going. Their Twitter handle is @tincantreats.

- Locals loved the Mexican cuisine served out of the **Mas Tacos** truck so much that they were forced to open an East Nashville shop, too (732 McFerrin Ave., 615/543-6271, Tues.-Thurs. 11am-4pm, Fri. 11am-9pm, Sat. 9am-3pm). The mobile option can be tracked down via Twitter (@mastacos).

- **Riff's Fine Street Food** serves a changing menu of sandwiches, salads, and treats like brisket tacos. A handy calendar (www.riffstruck.com) makes this brightly colored truck easy to find.

LOCKELAND TABLE $$

1520 Woodland St., 615/228-4864,
http://lockelandtable.com

HOURS: Mon.-Sat. 5pm-10pm

Lockeland Table is one of several small farm-to-fork restaurants located in Nashville's neighborhoods. The cozy eatery is great for dining with friends or on a date, and the menu takes a creative direction on Southern specialties. Check out the deviled eggs, chow chow, mac and cheese, and the fried green tomato salad. The space itself has a city-meets-farm vibe, and is small and therefore often crowded. Make reservations before you head over.

SWEETS

JENI'S SPLENDID ICE CREAMS $

1892 Eastland Ave., 615/262-8611, www.jenis.com

HOURS: Sun.-Thurs. noon-10pm, Fri.-Sat. noon-11pm

When Jeni's opened its first scoop shop outside of Ohio in East Nashville, you'd have thought no one in Music City had ever eaten ice cream before. Lines flowed out the door—literally—no matter the weather or time of day. Years later, people are still clamoring for these gourmet frozen treats, which change by the season. Several flavors use local ingredients, such as Yazoo beer. Samples are offered freely. Jeni's also sells pints to go as well as ice cream sandwiches, sundaes, and shakes.

RESTAURANTS

Music Valley
Map 4

With its concentration of tourist attractions and budget hotels, the Music Valley area isn't known for its fine cuisine. But there are some better-than-average options for eating out, whether you're in town for a convention or sightseeing with the family. Many of the restaurants in the Gaylord Opryland resort are tasty, although they do come with resort prices.

CONTEMPORARY

CASCADES AMERICAN CAFÉ $$

2800 Opryland Dr., 615/458-6848

HOURS: Daily 7am-11am, 11:30am-3pm, and 5pm-11pm

One of a number of restaurants inside the Opryland resort, Cascades is situated in the atrium, alongside an indoor waterfall (hence the name). The menu is heavy on the seafood, with Gulf fish, crab cakes, and other specialties, but there are also plenty of vegetarian options. Some decently priced lunch combos are offered, too. Breakfast is ordinary and expensive, not the restaurant's strong suit.

SOUTHERN

OPRY BACKSTAGE GRILL $$

2401 Music Valley Dr., 615/231-8854,
www.opry.com/backstagegrill

HOURS: Sun.-Thurs. 6:30am-10am, 11am-3pm, 4pm-10:30pm, Fri.-Sat. 6:30am-10am, 11am-3pm, 4pm-11:30pm

Located at the Inn at Opryland hotel, Opry Backstage Grill is the first of what may or may not become a chain of Opry-themed restaurants. The menu is filled with family-friendly Southern dishes, such as brisket sliders, fried green tomatoes, and pimento cheese. There are more authentic meat-and-threes around town, but in the Music Valley neighborhood, this is the best choice. The decor is Opry-themed, and servers often jump up on stage to perform a quick number.

STEAK HOUSES

OLD HICKORY STEAKHOUSE $$$

2800 Opryland Dr., 866/972-6779

HOURS: Sun.-Thurs. 5pm-10pm, Fri.-Sat. 5pm-11pm

Steak houses are not traditionally bargain dining experiences, nor are resort restaurants. So knowing that this is a one-two punch on your wallet is good preparation. Once you're committed to spending cash on your tab, you'll be pleasantly surprised. This is Opryland's highest-end restaurant, and the food and service live up to that billing. The restaurant serves all the steak house staples, many made with herbs grown on site. Other menu items that earn acclaim include the cheese plates, Maine diver scallops, and foie gras. The restaurant's herb garden surrounds it in the hotel atrium, and there's patio seating so that you can enjoy the atrium's views. Validated hotel parking is available.

THAI
🅲 SUKHO THAI RESTAURANT ❺
2450 Music Valley Dr., 615/883-6050, www.sukhothainashville.com
HOURS: Mon.-Fri. 11am-2pm and 4:30pm-9pm, Sat. 4pm-10pm

When's the last time you dined at a restaurant encircled by a go-kart track? Welcome to Music Valley, where such contradictions are par for the course. This Thai restaurant has a nice ambience that is a complete departure from the go-kart track that surrounds it. It isn't the most authentic Thai kitchen in the city, but in Music Valley, it is one of the only solid international cuisine options. The pepper steak is excellent, and the native spice red and green curry is very good and scorching hot (though you can ask for it to be served mild). Takeout is available if you want to head back to the hotel after a long day of sightseeing.

South Nashville   Map 5

The highlight of the South Nashville dining scene is Nolensville Pike, where almost any type of ethnic cuisine you crave can be found. The restaurants in South Nashville tend to be casual and affordable.

CONTEMPORARY
THE YELLOW PORCH ❺❺
734 Thompson Ln., 615/386-0260, www.theyellowporch.com
HOURS: Mon.-Sat. 11am-3pm and 5pm-10pm

People who like Berry Hill's Yellow Porch are incredibly loyal. Located in a cute, comfortable house, the Yellow Porch serves solid American cuisine, with good salads, appetizers, and entrées, not to mention a good wine list and killer desserts. There is a small porch that is nice for dining in the summer, but it looks out on a traffic-heavy street.

CUBAN
BACK TO CUBA ❺
4683 Trousdale Dr., 615/837-6711
HOURS: Tues.-Sat. 11am-9pm

Nolensville Pike is Nashville's ethnic food mecca, so it stands to reason that Back to Cuba opened its doors here. On the menu are traditional Cuban favorites: giant grilled sandwiches of pork, ham, cheese, empanadas, and arroz con rice. For dinner, try the roast pork or grilled shrimp, and don't skip the lacy fried plantains and spicy black beans. It ain't Miami, but this is the closest you'll get to authentic Cuban food in these parts.

DINERS AND COFFEE SHOPS
GABBY'S ❺
493 Humphreys St., 615/733-3119, http://gabbysburgersandfries.com
HOURS: Mon.-Thurs. 10:30am-2:30pm, Fri. 10:30am-7pm, Sat. 11am-2:30pm

Gabby's is a largely lunch spot near Greer Stadium, home to the Nashville Sounds (dinner service is only on Friday). Locals love this tiny place thanks to the burgers made from grass-fed beef, sweet potato fries, or the veggie handmade black bean burger. Expect a wait, as the place is small, and more likely than not you'll sit at the counter to eat. Police officers, active military, and firefighters receive 20 percent off their bills.

🅲 THE PFUNKY GRIDDLE ❺
2800 Bransford Ave., 615/298-2088, www.thepfunkygriddle.com
HOURS: Tues.-Thurs. 8am-2pm, Fri. 7am-2pm, Sat.-Sun. 7am-3pm

This Berry Hill restaurant has a gimmick. The tables are outfitted with hibachi-type grills. You order pancakes, eggs, or breakfast potatoes, and you're served the ingredients to cook on your own. The potatoes are particularly well-seasoned, and pancakes are all you can eat with your choice of toppings and two kinds of

© MARGARET LITTMAN

Berry Hill has vegetarian eats thanks to the Sunflower Café.

batter. There are sandwiches and other dishes prepared in the kitchen, should you not want to make your own food. The menu includes many gluten-free options. Waits for a table can be long on the weekend.

SUNFLOWER CAFÉ ❺
2834 Azalea Pl., 615/457-2568,
www.sunflowercafenashville.com
HOURS: Mon.-Sat. 11am-2:30pm

This Berry Hill house is home to a vegetarian cafeteria-style restaurant with a changing selection of entrées and sides served in meat-and-three style, albeit without the meat. Many of the offerings are vegan and gluten-free as well. Sunflower uses local and sustainable ingredients, and that comes at a price. Some of the dishes, like the red bean chili, are flavorful, but others have that "this is good for you" aftertaste. Nashville has just a few vegetarian restaurants, so this place is worth checking out if you eschew meat.

ITALIAN
MAMA MIA'S ❺❺
4501 Trousdale Dr., 615/331-7207
HOURS: Mon.-Fri. 11am-2pm and 5pm-10pm, Sat. 5pm-10pm

For homemade, old-school Italian fare, go to Mama Mia's, which offers lasagna, ravioli, chicken, veal, and seafood dishes. Portions are huge, and the restaurant offers both ample parking and ample seating. This is an old-school joint, where you'll feel like you've stepped back in time to 1970. While the decor isn't fancy (or modern), it is cozy, homey, and welcoming. There can be a wait for tables on weekend nights. Mama Mia's doesn't have a liquor license, so bring your own wine along with your appetite.

KURDISH
DUNYA KEBOB ❺
2521 Nolensville Pike, 615/242-6664
HOURS: Mon.-Thurs. 11am-9:30pm, Fri.-Sat. 11am-10:30pm, Sun. noon-9:30pm

Nashville has a large Kurdish immigrant

population. If you haven't before, this is the place to try the cuisine. Kurdish specialties of chicken, lamb, beef, and seafood kebobs and gyro sandwiches fill the menu. The surroundings are strictly no frills, but for less than $10 you can leave feeling full, thanks to the use of fresh ingredients and sides of rice and grilled vegetables.

MEXICAN
LA HACIENDA TAQUERIA ⑤⑤

2615 Nolensville Pike, 615/256-6142, www.lahaciendainc.com
HOURS: Mon.-Thurs. 10am-9pm, Fri. 10am-10pm, Sat. 9am-10pm, Sun. 9am-9pm

Often chosen by Nashvillians as the best Mexican restaurant in a very crowded field, La Hacienda Taqueria is located within a colorful storefront on Nolensville Pike. The menu offers a dizzying array of choices—tacos, enchiladas, tamales, burritos, quesadillas, and *tortas*, just to name a few. Most come with your choice of chicken, chorizo, tripe, pork, or steak filling, and many have an authenticity often missing from Mexican restaurant fare. Combination platters, which offer three items plus rice and beans, are a good way to sample the options if you aren't sure what to order.

Greater Nashville
Map 6

BAKERIES
LA HISPANA PANADERIA ⑤

6208 Charlotte Pike, 615/352-3798
HOURS: Daily 6am-9pm

In a bright pink building in West Nashville stands La Hispana Panaderia, one of the city's great bakery bargains. People flock here from across town for inexpensive bread and pastries that are as good as the finest European bakery. Favorites include the crunchy white bread and their dense cookies and sweet tres leche cakes, craved by the most ardent sweet tooth.

BARBECUE
BAR-B-CUTIE ⑤

5221 Nolensville Pike, 615/834-6556, www.bar-b-cutie.com
HOURS: Daily 7am-9pm

Nashville isn't known for barbecue the way Memphis is, but there still are plenty of places from which to choose to try some smoked meats. It provides a clean, reliable sampling of barbecue, with plenty of non-pork options (not always the case in these parts). Some of the sides are pre-made, but all complement the meat well. Bar-B-Cutie is a chain with locations near the zoo (326 Harding Pl., 615/332-7585) and the airport (501 Donelson Pike, 615/872-0207).

JIM 'N' NICK'S BAR-B-Q ⑤

7004 Charlotte Pike, 615/352-5777, www.jimnnicks.com
HOURS: Sun.-Thurs. 11am-9pm, Fri.-Sat. 11am-10pm

Another barbecue chain, Jim 'n' Nick's is popular with Vanderbilt students and other west-siders who like the standards, such as pulled pork, ribs, and brisket, as well as the unusual, such as barbecue nachos. Unlike a lot of other barbecue places, Jim 'n' Nick's is not a hole in the wall. There's seating and a drive-through and a wine and cocktail menu. Try the cheese biscuits.

MARTIN'S BAR-B-QUE JOINT ⑤

7238 Nolensville Rd., 615/776-1856, http://martinsbbqjoint.com
HOURS: Sun.-Thurs. 11am-8pm, Fri.-Sat. 11am-9pm

One of a number of Nashville eateries that have been highlighted on the TV show *Diners, Drive-Ins and Dives,* Martin's is a favorite barbecue spot. On weekends this small shop is overflowing with folks wanting to fill up on pulled pork, spare ribs, and brisket. Meats are smoked for almost a full day, making them (and the surrounding area) flavorful. The sides are worth trying, too.

CONTEMPORARY

F. SCOTT'S ❶❷❸

2210 Crestmoor Rd., 615/269-5861

HOURS: Mon.-Thurs. 5:30pm-10pm, Fri.-Sat. 5:30pm-11pm

F. Scott's is an upscale restaurant and jazz bar with one of the best wine lists in Nashville. Diners are ushered into a black-and-white-tiled dining room, where the sounds of live jazz from the adjacent listening room follow them. Enjoy a relaxed meal with wine pairings and great conversation. Appetizers include rabbit tart, or pancetta and scallops with caviar, and entrées might be pan-seared seafood, dressed-up shepherd's pie, and grilled beef tenderloin. Save room for dessert: homemade ice cream, coconut cake, or a cheese plate paired with the perfect dessert wine.

THE WILD HARE ❶❷

316 White Bridge Pike, 615/818-0219, http://thewildharenashville.com

HOURS: Tues.-Sun. 11am-10pm

A nondescript eatery on the west side of town, The Wild Hare serves dishes made with local ingredients and interesting takes on classics. Favorites include the lobster pizza, the deviled eggs, and almost anything with bacon, plus lots of fried vegetables. There's a decent wine list and a friendly, laid-back vibe. The menu is sufficiently vegetarian-friendly to satisfy those who don't eat meat. Service is friendly, and parking isn't an issue.

DINERS AND COFFEE SHOPS

BOBBIE'S DAIRY DIP ❶

5301 Charlotte Ave., 615/463-8088

HOURS: Mon.-Sat. 11am-8pm, Sun. noon-8pm, closed winter

Go back in time to this old-fashioned burger and ice cream shop. You park and walk up to the window. Order and then sit at one of the few picnic tables until your shake or sundae is ready. On summer nights the place is packed with families, couples on date night, and more enjoying the simplest of pleasures. Hours vary based on the weather. A hot spell may encourage them to open their doors (er, windows) in early March. There's a second location downtown (223 4th Ave. N. 615/770-2770), but this is the classic.

◆ FOX'S DONUT DEN ❶

3900 Hillsboro Pike, 615/385-1021, www.foxsdonutden.com

HOURS: Mon.-Fri. 5am-midnight, Sat.-Sun. 6am-midnight

In general, eating at a joint that is as known for its signage as it is for its food is a bad idea. But at Fox's Donut Den, you get to take in the old-time neon sign that graces Hillsboro Pike (and was part of a rezoning debate in Green Hills) and eat a tasty doughnut at the same time. The sweet breakfast treat of your choice is a matter of personal preference, but the apple fritters are a local favorite.

FRENCH

TABLE 3 ❶❷

3821 Green Hills Village Dr., 615/739-6900, www.table3nashville.com

HOURS: Mon. 11am-9pm, Tues.-Thurs. 11am-10pm, Fri.-Sat. 11am-11pm, Sun. 10:30am-9pm

Amid the chains that surround the Mall at Green Hills is a surprising French food gem. The European-style bistro has solid steak frites, soups, salads, and omelets, the likes of which you'd find across the pond. Service is polite and accurate, if not speedy, and there's a small grocery that offers to-go items if that works better for your schedule. The mall has ample parking, but can be a zoo on weekend nights.

INDIAN

SHALIMAR ❶❷

3711 Hillsboro Pike, 615/269-8577, www.shalimarfinedining.com

HOURS: Mon.-Sat. 11am-2:30pm and 5pm-10pm

One of Nashville's oldest Indian restaurants, Shalimar offers fine food and efficient service. The Saturday lunch buffet brings in mall shoppers and ladies who lunch. At dinner, Shalimar takes on a slightly more elegant cast with vegetarian, chicken, lamb, and seafood entrées in popular preparations including masala, *biryani* (rice-based dish), tikka, *saag* (spinach-based

RESTAURANTS

dish), or korma. Shalimar is just a few blocks from the Mall at Green Hills.

ITALIAN

CAFÉ FONTANELLA ⬤⬤

4225 Whites Creek Pike, 615/724-1601, www.fontanelmansion.com/cafe-fontanella.php
HOURS: Mon.-Thurs. 11am-9pm, Fri. 11am-10pm, Sat. 10am-10pm, Sun. 10am-9pm

Café Fontanella is an Italian eatery that would not be a destination in and of itself, if it were not for its location. As the restaurant for the Fontanel Mansion complex, it is the best place to eat before a concert at the Woods at Fontanel or before or after touring the mansion. The barn-like space that houses the restaurant is pleasant and welcoming, parking is easy, and the porch has rocking chairs when you have to wait for a table. There's often live music, and the service is pleasant. The food is average traditional (think red sauce) Italian.

◨ CAFFE NONNA ⬤⬤⬤

4427 Murphy Rd., 615/463-0133, www.caffenonna.com
HOURS: Mon. 5pm-9pm, Tues.-Thurs. 11am-2pm and 5pm-9pm, Fri. 11am-2pm and 5pm-10pm, Sat. 5pm-10pm

For some of the best Italian food in Nashville, head west to the neighborhood of Sylvan Park, where you'll find Caffe Nonna. Inspired by Chef Daniel Maggipinto's own *nonna* (grandmother), the café serves rustic Italian fare. Appetizers include salads and bruschetta, and entrées include the divine Lasagne Nonna, made with butternut squash, ricotta cheese, spinach, and sage. The service at Caffe Nonna is friendly and attentive, and the atmosphere is cozy, but the space is small. Call ahead for a table.

MEXICAN

LOCAL TACO ⬤

4501 Murphy Rd., 615/891-3271, www.thelocaltaco.com
HOURS: Mon.-Sat. 11am-10pm, Sun. 11am-8pm

Sylvan Park's Local Taco is a small taco shop with a big patio. The taco varieties change often, and are as likely to be Korean or California-inspired as much as Mexican or Tex-Mex, as well as plain offbeat choices like a taco filled with fried mac and cheese. Prices are low, the margaritas are plentiful, and the joint is often jumping. Parking can be a challenge.

SOUTHERN

LOVELESS CAFE ⬤⬤

8400 Hwy. 100, 615/646-9700, www.lovelesscafe.com
HOURS: Daily 7am-9pm

The Loveless Cafe is an institution, and some may argue it's a state of mind. But this little café-that-could is increasingly a destination, too, for visitors not just to Nashville but the entire heartland of Tennessee. The Loveless got its start in 1951 when Lon and Annie Loveless started to serve good country cooking to travelers on Highway 100. Over the years the restaurant changed hands, but Annie's biscuit recipe remained the same, and it was the biscuits that kept Nashvillians, including many famous ones, coming back for more. In 1982, then owner George McCabe started the Hams & Jams mail-order business, and in 2003 the Loveless underwent a major renovation that expanded the kitchen and dining rooms, and added additional shops in the rear. The food at the Loveless is good, no doubt about it. The biscuits are fluffy and buttery, the ham salty, and the eggs, bacon, and sausage will hit the spot. The supper and lunch menu has expanded to include Southern standards like fried catfish and chicken, pit-cooked pork barbecue, pork chops, and meat loaf, as well as a few salads. Loveless is located about 20 miles from downtown Nashville; plan on a 30-minute drive out Highway 100. Once you get out of the congestion of the West End, it's a pretty trip.

If you are headed to adjacent **Loveless Barn** for the Wednesday night Music City Roots show, don't eat first. You can order from a limited Loveless menu and eat while you listen to the show.

PARK CAFE ⬤⬤⬤

4403 Murphy Rd., 615/383-4409, http://parkcafenashville.com
HOURS: Mon.-Fri. 4:30pm-10pm, Fri.-Sat. 4:30pm-11pm

Park Café is Sylvan Park's reliable upscale

HOT CHICKEN

Nashville's most sublime food experience is not to be found in a fine restaurant or even at a standard meat-and-three cafeteria. It is served on a plate with a slice of Wonder bread and a pickle chip. It is hot chicken, a very spicy pan-fried delicacy, made with bone-in breast and secret spices.

There are four shops that specialize in this regional treat: **400 Degrees** (319 Peabody St., 615/244-4467, www.400degreeshotchicken.com, Tues.-Fri. 11am-7pm, Sat. noon-5pm); **Pepperfire** (2821 Gallatin Pike, 615/582-4824, www.pepperfirechicken.com, Mon.-Sat. 11am-9pm), which allows you to call in your order so it's ready for pickup by the time you arrive; **Prince's Hot Chicken Shack** (123 Ewing Dr., 615/226-9442, Tues.-Thurs. 11:30am-10pm, Fri. 11:30am-4am, Sat. 2pm-4am), the most famous hot chicken shack, which has the longest lines; and **Bolton's Spicy Chicken & Fish** (624 Main St., 615/254-8015 and 2309A Franklin Pike, 615/383-1421, Mon.-Sat. 11am-9pm). Each has their special spices, but the basic idea is the same. Order it as spicy as you can take it, but not so hot that you can't enjoy the flavor. Panfrying takes time, so you're likely to wait wherever you go.

If you like perks like indoor seating, air-conditioning, or other menu choices with your hot chicken, you have some options. Several high-end restaurants including **The Southern Steak and Oyster** (150 3rd Ave. S., 615/724-1762, www.thesouthernnashville.com, Mon.-Thurs. 7:30am-10pm, Fri. 7:30am-midnight, Sat. 10am-midnight, Sun. 10am-10pm), **The**

Hot chicken—served on white bread with a pickle—is a Nashville specialty.

Catbird Seat (1711 Division St., 615/248-8458, www.thecatbirdseatrestaurant.com, Wed.-Sat. 5:45pm-9:45pm), and **Silo** (1121 5th Ave. N., 615/750-2912, www.silotn.com, Tues.-Sat. 4pm-11pm, Sun. 10:30am-2pm and 4pm-11pm) offer modern takes on this old favorite.

dinner-out spot, with a small but solid menu of meats and poultry. There's typically at least one vegetarian-friendly item on the menu. Like its sister restaurants **Eastland Cafe** (97 Chapel Ave., 615/627-1088, www.eastland-cafe.com, Mon.-Thurs. 5pm-10pm, Fri.-Sat. 5pm-11pm) and **Pomodoro East** (701 Porter Rd., 615/873-4978, www.pomodoroeast.com, Mon.-Sat. 4:30pm-10pm, Sun. 4:30pm-9pm), Park Cafe offers an impressive happy hour (Mon.-Thurs. 4:30pm-6:30pm, Fri.-Sat.

4:30pm-6pm), with specials on both food and drinks, that draws in the locals. The space is dark in a cozy way, great for a date or an intimate chat. Parking can be challenging on Murphy Road on the weekends.

PRINCE'S HOT CHICKEN SHACK ●
123 Ewing Dr., 615/226-9442
HOURS: Tues.-Thurs. noon-10pm, Fri. noon-4am, Sat. 2pm-4am
Out of all the food that you eat in Music City,

you'll likely still be dreaming about Prince's Hot Chicken when you get home. Hot chicken is panfried chicken that is also spicy, and is special to Music City. Prince's serves three varieties: mild, hot, and extra-hot. Most uninitiated will find the mild variety plenty spicy, so beware. It is served with slices of white bread—perfect for soaking up that spicy chicken juice—and a pickle slice. You can add a cup of creamy potato salad, coleslaw, or baked beans if you like. When you walk into Prince's, head to the back, where you'll place your order at the window, pay, and be given a number. Then take a seat—if you can find one—while you wait for your food. You can order to go or eat in. Your food is made to order, and Prince's is very popular, so the wait often exceeds 30 minutes. Take heart, though—Prince's chicken is worth the wait.

WENDELL SMITH $

407 53rd Ave. N., 615/383-7114
HOURS: Mon.-Sat. 6am-7:30pm

The 1950s vibe of this meat-and-three is hard to escape. It is a crowded spot with tiny booths and a liquor store (with the same name) next door. For decades locals have come here for friendly service and affordable food, and portions are large. This is the kind of place where mac and cheese counts as a vegetable, so don't expect to stick to a diet.

VIETNAMESE
KIEN GIANG $

5845 Charlotte Pike, 615/353-1250
HOURS: Daily 11am-9pm

Located just west of the Kroger grocery store, in a strip mall near the K&S World Market on a hill above Charlotte Avenue, Kien Giang is one of Nashville's favorite Vietnamese restaurants. The ambience is not fancy, and the service can be slow, but the spring rolls, pho, and other dishes are flavorful and authentic. Bring cash: Kien Giang does not accept plastic.

MISS SAIGON $

5849 Charlotte Pike, 615/354-1351
HOURS: Daily 7am-8:30pm

A renovation made Miss Saigon seem swanky in comparison to its neighbors, all of whom are authentic Vietnamese eateries in this area of town. Miss Saigon is in a strip mall on a hill off Charlotte Avenue; it can be easy to miss the driveway. But when you arrive you'll find more than ample parking, friendly staff, and a fresh menu with tasty spring rolls, *bahn mi* sandwiches, and many types of pho. Miss Saigon is usually buzzing, but there's rarely a wait for a table.

NIGHTLIFE

This is *Music City*. You're here for the nightlife. From concerts to theater, Nashville offers visitors plenty of entertaining diversions. No trip to Nashville is complete without listening to some live music. Music City overflows with musicians and songwriters and opportunities to hear them. So whether you love to two-step or you prefer something with a different kind of beat, be sure to make time for music during your visit.

Even before you arrive in the city, you can plan out your nights thanks to the Nashville Convention and Visitors Bureau (www.nashvillecvb.com). Through a handy feature on the bureau's website, you can check out upcoming concerts a month or more in advance. Many venues will let you buy tickets in advance over the phone or online. Now Playing

Nashville (www.nowplayingnashville.com), an initiative with the Community Foundation of Middle Tennessee, is a great resource for both entertainment listings and discounted tickets. Now Playing Nashville has a kiosk in the Nashville airport.

But don't panic if you can't plan ahead. One of the benefits of being in Music City is that there is always a show worth seeing somewhere. And because there are so many shows, there is always something that hasn't sold out.

Clubs listed in this chapter are categorized by their predominant music type, but keep in mind that variety is the name of the game. Most bars and clubs (except for honky-tonks) charge a cover when there is a band or performer, while songwriter nights and open mics are usually free.

HIGHLIGHTS

LOOK FOR  TO FIND RECOMMENDED NIGHTLIFE.

© MICHAEL JONES

The Bluebird Cafe

Best Cocktail: There are lots of mixologists who make a mean drink in Music City, but there's something about the entire experience that makes them taste better at **Holland House Bar and Refuge** (page 79).

Best Karaoke Joint: Wanna pretend that you can sing like a local? Head to **Lonnie's Western Room** to belt 'em out (page 79).

Songwriter Mecca: Go to **The Bluebird Cafe** if you want to hear the people who write the songs, not just sing them (page 87).

Best Place to See and Be Seen: The "it" places always change, but **The Stone Fox** is hip because of the creative minds that gather there (page 89).

Most Authentic Nashville Sound: Whether you come for Midnite Jamboree, Cowboy Church, or something else, the **Texas Troubadour Theatre** is where you're most likely to have a real Music City experience (page 89).

Best Outdoor Music Venue: The **Woods Amphitheater** provides that miles-away experience in the wilderness, even though it's just minutes away from the city (page 89).

Most Inventive Brewery: With coffee, hops, and oats, East Nashville's **Fat Bottom Brewing** has a new take on classic brews (page 90).

Bars

3 CROW

1020 Woodland St., 615/262-3345, www.3crowbar.com
HOURS: Daily 11am-3am
COST: $10
`Map 3`

3 Crow Bar is the epitome of East Nashville—friendly and eclectic, with local eccentrics and possibly rock stars. It is a particularly nice place to be on a sunny day when the garage door goes up and East Nashville in all its quirkiness walks by. This is also a great time to get the bushwhacker, a Southern concoction of rum, cream de cacao, and other secret ingredients, fed through a slushie machine. Need a place to lubricate work with a little lunch beer (open at 11am) and wireless Internet? You won't be alone.

CABANA

1910 Belcourt Ave., 615/577-2262,
www.cabananashville.com
HOURS: Mon.-Sat. 4pm-midnight
COST: No cover
`Map 2`

In Hillsboro Village, Cabana is a popular, if trendy, place to people-watch and unwind. It is a bar/restaurant/late-night hangout that attracts a youthful and well-dressed crowd. Lounge at the bar or in the expansive backyard. Choose from dozens of beers, wines, and excellent, albeit pricey, martinis.

CORSAIR ARTISAN DISTILLERY

1200 Clinton St., 615/200-0321,
www.corsairartisan.com
HOURS: Wed.-Fri. 4pm-8pm, Sat. 2pm-8pm
COST: $8 tour and tasting, $2 tour only
`Map 2`

This local distillery makes high-end spirits, including rum, whiskey, moonshine, and vodka. The team has won industry awards across the globe for its offbeat and limited-edition beverages. You can take a tour of the distillery to see how the whole thing works and then sample up to five of these creations. Weekend tours sell out, so book in advance.

EDGEFIELD SPORTS BAR AND GRILLE

921 Woodland St., 615/228-6422
HOURS: Mon.-Tues. 11am-midnight, Wed. 11am-1am, Thurs.-Sat. 11am-2am
COST: No cover
`Map 3`

Edgefield Sports Bar and Grille is a no-frills watering hole that caters to East Nashville residents. This small neighborhood joint has the classic amenities: pool, darts, foosball, skeeball, and backgammon. Locals love the burgers, but it is the no-pressure vibe that keeps them coming back.

FIDDLE AND STEEL

210 Printers Alley, 615/251-9002,
www.fiddleandsteel.com
HOURS: Daily 8pm-2:30am
COST: No cover
`Map 1`

When the hustle of Broadway gets overwhelming, duck into Printer's Alley and allow Fiddle and Steel to take the edge off. This bar puts a lot of energy into being friendly, and the regulars are in on it. It is a straight-up music saloon with country stars past, present, and future. It's also spacious with tables and an expansive sunken dance floor.

THE GREENHOUSE

2211 Bandywood Dr., 615/385-4311,
www.thefoodcompanynashville.com
HOURS: Daily 5pm-3am
COST: No cover
`Map 6`

Near the Mall at Green Hills, The Greenhouse offers specialty drinks, beers, and lots of hanging plants. To find it, look for the Green Hills Kroger and take a left. Its location means you'll find more locals than tourists. The two-story restaurant and bar has a nice patio in warm weather and plenty of TVs for the big game. The back parking lot is tiny.

NIGHTLIFE

TENNESSEE WHISKEY (AND WHERE TO DRINK IT)

© PETE RODMAN

Take a tour of Corsair Artisan Distillery.

When in Rome, do as the Romans do. When in Tennessee, drink Tennessee whiskey. Bourbon whiskey made in the Volunteer State is considered Tennessee whiskey, and there is no shortage of different whiskeys to sip. If you are up for a road trip, look at the different distilleries across the state (www.tennesseewhiskey.com) and go.

You won't even need to find a designated driver to accompany you to **The Jack Daniel's Distillery** (280 Lynchburg Hwy./ Hwy. 55, 931/759-4221, www.jackdaniels. com), which is located in a dry county. Tours and tastings are available at Marathon Village's **Corsair Artisan Distillery** (1200 Clinton St., 615/200-0321, www.corsairartisan.com), one of the area's newer small-batch distilleries.

For a whiskey cocktail at a bar, belly up to one of the following: **Holland House Bar and Refuge** (935 W. Eastland Ave., 615/262-4190, www.hollandhousebarandrefuge.com, Mon.-Thurs. 5pm-midnight, Fri.-Sat. 5pm-2am), **No. 308** (407 Gallatin Ave., 615/650-7344, daily 5pm-3am), and **Patterson House** (1711 Division St., 615/636-7724, www.thepattersonnashville.com, daily 5pm-3am).

◖ HOLLAND HOUSE BAR AND REFUGE

935 W. Eastland Ave., 615/262-4190,
www.hollandhousebarandrefuge.com
HOURS: Mon.-Thurs. 5pm-midnight, Fri.-Sat. 5pm-2am
COST: No cover
`Map 3`

Another Nashville mixology house that has received national attention, Holland House Bar and Refuge specializes in handmade, old-fashioned cocktails. The bar stocks an impressive selection of whiskey and bourbon, and hires bartenders who know how to use them. The happy hour is inventive and affordable (usually $5 per drink), and the cocktail menu changes seasonally.

◖ LONNIE'S WESTERN ROOM

208 Printers Alley, 615/828-7971,
www.lonnieswesternroom.com
HOURS: Daily 6pm-3am
COST: Two-drink minimum, donations to band encouraged
`Map 1`

If you think your karaoke skills can keep up with all the Music City pros, head to Lonnie's Western Room. This is the city's No. 1 spot for singing your heart out to pre-recorded tracks. Don't believe how serious it is? Seating is tiered and faces the stage. This is not a bar where you have your back to the singers. It is standing-room-only on the weekends; weeknights you can slip in and get a seat. Despite the name, folks play things other than Western music here.

NO. 308

407 Gallatin Ave., 615/650-7344
HOURS: Daily 5pm-3am
COST: No cover
`Map 3`

No. 308 is a sleek, mod hangout with hand-crafted drinks. Come during happy hour, when these custom cocktails are more budget friendly. This spot is the definition of a hipster hangout, with its unassuming entrace nestled next to a paint store. But for all the retro furniture, the funky themed nights, and the skinny jeans, No. 308 is a friendly neighborhood bar that happens to be better-looking and serves better drinks.

OAK BAR

231 6th Ave. N., 615/345-7116,
www.capitolgrillenashville.com
HOURS: Mon.-Sat. 11:30am-close, Sun. noon-close
`Map 1`

The basement of the historic Hermitage Hotel is home to the swanky Oak Bar, a practically perfect place to have a drink before going out on the town, to the theater at TPAC, or just for something to do downtown. The cocktails are well-crafted but not overly complicated (think: the classic Old Fashioned) and the service attentive. It can be hard to get a seat when the legislature is in session, but pre-theater on weekends you might have the place to yourself.

© RON MANVILLE

Patterson House is an option for a refined drink before a night on the town.

PARADISE PARK TRAILER RESORT
411 Broadway, 615/251-1515,
www.paradiseparkonline.com
HOURS: 11am-3am
COST: No cover
`Map 1`

Paradise Park Trailer Resort is divided into two spaces: The restaurant is on the right as you enter, the bar to your left. As the name suggests, it is decorated to look like a trailer park. Belly up to the bar to grab your drink, and stroll back to the dance floor, all the while feeling like you are outside. There are a few standard bar booths, but on Friday and Saturday nights, everyone is on the dance floor. The music is loud and generally includes bands playing covers of popular country songs. Paradise Park is a quintessential part of a downtown pub crawl. At some point, you're going to get hungry after (or while) drinking all that beer. This place can keep the beer parade going, but also claims to have the best burger in town, and you can still order it at 3am. The rest of the menu reflects the trailer resort theme with kitschy dishes like corn dogs, tater tots, and Frito pie, with the added benefit that the ingredients are sourced by real chefs.

PATTERSON HOUSE
1711 Division St., 615/636-7724,
www.thepattersonnashville.com
HOURS: Daily 5pm-3am
COST: No cover
`Map 2`

There's no sign on the exterior, but that hasn't kept people across the country from discovering Patterson House. Cocktails here are mixed with care, and there's no standing room. You must have a seat in order to be served. This contributes to a civilized cocktail hour, but also means long waits. This is not a pickup scene, but a place to savor your cocktail, from its creation to its last drop. Above Patterson House is acclaimed restaurant **The Catbird Seat** (1711 Division St., www.thecatbirdseatrestaurant.com, Wed.-Sat. 5:45pm-9:45pm).

Comedy

JAZZ 'N' JOKES
174 3rd Ave. N., 615/242-5653, http://jazzandjokes.com
HOURS: Show times vary; box office Tues.-Thurs. 10am-4pm, Fri. 10am-6pm, Sat. 4pm-6pm
COST: Generally $10-45, plus a two-item minimum
`Map 1`

Jazz and Jokes is a relatively new venue that showcases the talents of African American artists. They have a range of entertainment from R&B nights, karaoke, jazz, and comedy. This is a place for mature audiences, and it typically has a line out the door on weekend nights. Regulars think the food is better than most clubs, which is important when there is a two-item minimum.

ZANIES
2025 8th Ave. S., 615/269-0221,
www.nashville.zanies.com
HOURS: Show times Wed.-Thurs. and Sun. 7:30pm, Fri. 7:30pm and 9:45pm, Sat. 9pm and 11:15pm; may vary
COST: $20-25, plus a two-item minimum
`Map 2`

Zanies books big stand-up comedy acts. Think national names, like TV stars and stand-up comedians. Go wanting to laugh, and you will likely get what you paid for. There's a two-item minimum (drinks or food), neither of which is particularly remarkable. But you're there for the act, not the menu. Parking for the later weekend show can be tricky.

Gay and Lesbian

LIPSTICK LOUNGE
1400 Woodland St., 615/226-6343,
www.thelipsticklounge.com
HOURS: Tues.-Sat. 6:30pm-3am, Sun. 11am-7:30pm
COST: $5-10 for events like karaoke and trivia night
`Map 3`

Women outnumber men at the Lipstick Lounge, one of two lesbian bars on the same East Nashville intersection. This is a laid-back club with a better-than-average sound system and karaoke selection. Live music, pool, and great food attract a crowd nearly every night. The crowds are more mixed during the week than on the weekends, when it is mostly gay and lesbian.

MAD DONNA'S
1313 Woodland St., 615/226-1617,
http://maddonnas.com
HOURS: Tues.-Thurs. 11am-10pm, Fri. 11am-11pm, Sat. 10am-11pm, Sun. 10am-10pm
COST: No cover
`Map 3`

One of two East Nashville bars on the same intersection that cater to a lesbian clientele, Mad Donna's is a restaurant that becomes the place to hang on Tuesday nights. That's when drag queen bingo meets two-for-one drink specials. Do we really need to explain what happens next? In addition to drag queen bingo, the 2nd floor hosts karaoke and other festivities.

PLAY
1519 Church St., 615/322-9627, www.playdancebar.com
HOURS: Wed.-Sun. 9pm-3am
COST: $8 on drag show nights
`Map 2`

Right next door to club Tribe is Play, the city's highest-energy gay club, with drag shows and performances by adult-film stars. Though it is a gay bar, everyone is welcome as long as they're happy to be here. The drag shows are quality, but it is the dance floor (right next to the stage) that draws people in. On weekends that dance floor is packed. If you want more room to get your groove on, come on weeknights without drag shows.

TRAX
1501 Ensley Blvd., 615/742-8856
HOURS: Daily noon-3am
COST: No cover
`Map 5`

For a low-key evening of shooting pool or a happy-hour stop before dinner, TRAX is the place to go. The patio is a nice place to sit in warm weather. There is wireless Internet and big-screen televisions, but little in the way of ambience. The back parking lot is well lit, a perk when leaving in the wee hours.

TRIBE
1517 Church St., 615/329-2912, www.tribenashville.com
HOURS: Mon. and Fri.-Sat. 4pm-2am, Tues.-Thurs. and Sun. 4pm-midnight
COST: No cover
`Map 2`

You don't have to be gay to enjoy Tribe, but it helps to be beautiful, or at least well dressed. The dance floor here is one of the best in the city, and the atmosphere is hip. Martinis and other specialty drinks are the poison of choice at this Midtown club, which stays open until the wee hours. It has changed names and owners over the years, but has basically been the go-to gay dance spot for decades. It is next door to Play.

NIGHTLIFE

Live Music

COUNTRY AND BLUEGRASS

LAYLA'S BLUEGRASS INN

418 Broadway, 615/726-2799,
http://laylasbluegrassinn.com
HOURS: Mon. 8pm-midnight, Tues.-Thurs.
4pm-midnight, Sat. noon-2am, Sun. noon-midnight
COST: No cover, donations to band encouraged
Map 1

"Americana Inn" might be a more accurate name than "Bluegrass Inn," as this bar throws pretty much anything American at you. And their bookers have good taste. A cozy, dark dance hall, Layla's offers that honky-tonk trifecta: cheap beer, hot dogs, and no cover. It is often standing room only on Friday and Saturday nights, but that's not the only time to hear good music. Almost any time the lights are on, it's worth stepping inside. Head to the back entrance or the upper floor for more space.

LEGENDS CORNER

428 Broadway, 615/248-6334,
http://legendscorner.com
HOURS: Daily 11am-3am, 21 and up after 6pm
COST: No cover, donations to band encouraged
Map 1

Memorabilia of Nashville's past adorns the walls at Legends Corner, as you might expect from its name. This corner spot is smaller than some of the other honky-tonks, but it has the same all-day live music, without some of the crowds that the others attract.

NASHVILLE PALACE

2611 McGavock Pike, 615/889-1540,
www.nashvillepalace.net
HOURS: Sun.-Thurs. 4pm-11pm, Fri.-Sat. 11am-11pm
COST: No cover, donations to band encouraged
Map 4

The Nashville Palace is a restaurant, nightclub, and dance floor across from the Gaylord Opryland Hotel. If your image of Nashville is line dancing and whatever you've seen in movies, this place is more likely to meet your mental image than anywhere on Lower Broad. Live music is on tap daily starting at 5pm, and talent nights on Tuesday and Wednesday always draw a crowd.

ROBERT'S WESTERN WORLD

416 Broadway, 615/244-9552,
http://robertswesternworld.com
HOURS: Daily 11am-3am; ages 21 and older after 10pm
COST: No cover, donations to band encouraged
Map 1

Robert's Western World is often voted the city's best honky-tonk by locals. Originally a store selling boots, cowboy hats, and other country music regalia, Robert's morphed into a bar and nightclub with a good gift shop and even a Sunday morning church service. Many of the honky-tonks have similar acts playing similar music, but there's something about the energy of Robert's that makes it feel different from the rest.

THE STAGE ON BROADWAY

412 Broadway, 615/726-0504,
http://thestageonbroadway.com
HOURS: Mon.-Wed. 2pm-3am, Thurs.-Sun. 11am-3am
COST: No cover, donations to band encouraged
Map 1

The Stage is a honky-tonk that often plays second fiddle to the holy trinity—Robert's, Tootsie's, and Layla's—but gets its fair share of movie and TV cameo appearances. It has a large dance floor and music seven nights a week. Those under 21 are welcome before 6pm.

THE STATION INN

402 12th Ave. S., 615/255-3307, www.stationinn.com
HOURS: Doors open daily 7pm, show times vary
COST: $10-20, donations to band encouraged
Map 1

It doesn't look like much (or anything) from the outside, but inside this cinder block box is the city's most popular venue for bluegrass and roots music. The Station Inn is perhaps the country's best bluegrass club, and it showcases fine artists every night of the week. This homey and casual

COURTESY OF WILDHORSE SALOON

Learn to line dance and more at the Wildhorse Saloon.

club opens nightly at 7pm, with music starting about 9pm. This is a 21-and-over club, unless you come with a parent or guardian. There is no cover for the Sunday-night bluegrass jam, at which almost everyone who is anyone picks up an instrument and plays.

TOOTSIE'S ORCHID LOUNGE
422 Broadway, 615/726-0463, www.tootsies.net
HOURS: Daily 10am-2:30am
COST: No cover, donations to band encouraged
Map 1

Tootsie's Orchid Lounge's bright purple exterior makes it hard to miss, and has been for more than 50 years. This Lower Broad mainstay exudes classic country every day of the week beginning as early as 10am. On weekend nights there are typically bands playing both upstairs and downstairs, and folks clamoring to get in and out. Tootsie's has a back door that opens onto the alley next to the Ryman. This is how Opry stars could make it from the bar to the stage in time for their curtain call.

THE WHEEL
421 Broadway, 615/742-1676
HOURS: Sun.-Fri. 2pm-3am, Sat. 10am-3am
COST: No cover, donations to band encouraged
Map 1

The other honky-tonks along Lower Broad are better known. That makes them more crowded, but not necessarily better. Like most of the downtown honky-tonks, The Wheel is a long, narrow space where live bands play Western swing, bluegrass, rockabilly, and country all night long. The drinks are decently priced, the music loud, and the staff and regulars friendly. What else could you possibly want?

WILDHORSE SALOON
120 2nd Ave. N., 615/902-8200,
www.wildhorsesaloon.com
HOURS: Mon. 4pm-11pm, Tues.-Thurs. and Sun. 11am-11pm, Fri.-Sat. 11am-2am
COST: Cover varies based on show
Map 1

The Wildhorse Saloon is a boot-scootin', beer-drinkin' place to see and be seen, although almost exclusively by tourists. When the Wildhorse opened in 1994, promoters drove a herd of cattle through the streets of downtown Nashville. The huge dance floor is often packed with cowboys and cowgirls line dancing to the greatest country hits. Free dance lessons are offered every day (Mon.-Thurs. 6:30pm-8:30pm, Fri. 6pm-9:30pm, Sat. noon-9:30pm, Sun. 2pm-7:30pm). The Wildhorse books big-name acts many nights of the week, including country music, roots rock, and classic rock stars. The establishment is owned by Gaylord, the same folks who own the Ryman, Opryland, and the Opry, and often offers deals for hotel guests. There is a shuttle (with a charge) back to the Opryland Hotel for folks staying there.

JAZZ AND BLUES
B. B. KING BLUES CLUB
152 2nd Ave. N., 615/256-2727, www.bbkingclubs.com
HOURS: Sun. 11am-midnight, Mon.-Thurs. 11am-1am, Fri.-Sat. 11am-3am
COST: Cover varies based on show, typically under $10
Map 1

NIGHTLIFE

If you need to get that country twang out of your head, a good dose of the Memphis blues will do it. B. B. King Blues Club is a good place to start for a night of the blues. The club is a satellite of King's original Beale Street club, and it books live blues every night. The cover charge is usually under $10, unless B. B. King himself is making one of his rare appearances.

BOURBON STREET BLUES AND BOOGIE BAR

220 Printers Alley, 615/242-5837, www.bourbonstreetblues.com
HOURS: Daily 4pm-3am
COST: No cover, donations to band encouraged
Map 1

Located in the nightlife active strip of Printer's Alley, the Bourbon Street Blues and Boogie Bar is a club that is nothing fancy, but is where to go if you fancy New Orleans-style jazz and blues. This is a small live music venue, so you get to be up close with the act on stage. Drink prices are reasonable, and the shrimp burger is a favorite of many.

F. SCOTT'S

2210 Crestmoor Rd., 615/269-5861, www.fscotts.com
HOURS: Mon.-Thurs. 5:30pm-10pm, Fri.-Sat. 5:30pm-11pm
COST: No cover, two-drink minimum
Map 6

A fine-dining restaurant next door to the Mall at Green Hills, F. Scott's is also one of the city's premier venues for live jazz. The music goes well with the restaurant's art deco appeal. Come for dinner or for a few drinks at the bar while you listen in. Although there's no cover at the door, there is a two-drink minimum to listen if you are not dining.

NASHVILLE JAZZ WORKSHOP

1319 Adams St., 615/242-5299, www.nashvillejazz.org
HOURS: Vary based on show
COST: Cover varies based on show
Map 1

The Nashville Jazz Workshop is more than a venue: It is the musical heartbeat of the city's jazz scene. Locals come here for classes, lessons,

YES, MUSIC CITY HAS MORE THAN COUNTRY

It's true: Nashville is known for its country music. But Jack White relocated here. The Kings of Leon live here. The Black Keys are here. Robert Plant is often seen in 12 South. There is plenty of music being played, made, and heard in Music City that doesn't have a single note of twang (not that there is anything wrong with that).

If you're looking for jazz, blues, and rock music, you have plenty of options. For the best and most innovative in the rock music scene, start at **Third Man Records** (623 7th Ave. S., 615/891-4393, www.third-manrecords.com), the music store/music venue owned by Jack White. Many of the employees are in bands themselves and can tell you what's going on around town.

Other good non-country venues include **The Stone Fox** (712 51st Ave. N., 615/953-1811, www.thestonefoxnashville.com), **The Family Wash** (2038 Greenwood Ave., 615/226-6070, www.family-wash.com), and **The 5 Spot** (1006 Forrest Ave., 615/650-9333, www.the5spotlive.com).

and lectures. But if you just want to listen, no worries. This is a great venue for jazz in all its definitions: from New Orleans sound to contemporary, performed by big names and serious students.

ECLECTIC

THE BASEMENT

1604 8th Ave. S., 615/254-8006, www.thebasementnashville.com
HOURS: Show times vary; doors open one hour before show time
COST: Cover varies
Map 2

The Basement calls itself a cellar full of noise, but it's a good kind of noise. Indie rock is the most common art form here, but they book other types of acts, too. The Basement's New Faces Night on Tuesday is a popular place to hear singer-songwriters. Admission is 21 and over, unless accompanied by a parent or guardian. The brick walls and subterranean feel give the Basement its cool atmosphere. It is nestled under **Grimey's New and Preloved Music** (1604 8th Ave. S., 615/254-4801, www.grimeys.com, Mon.-Sat. 11am-8pm, Sun. 1pm-6pm), one of the city's best record stores. Park behind the club and on side streets.

CAFÉ COCO

210 Louise Ave., 615/321-2626, www.cafecoco.com
HOURS: 24 hours a day, seven days a week
COST: $5
`Map 2`

Coffee shop by day, bar and live music venue by night. That describes Elliston Place's Café Coco, and, frankly, Nashville as a whole. The space is small, but it offers a wide cross section of live music. Monday is songwriter's night, Tuesday is open-mic poetry, and Thursday is open-mic music. Jazz and rock bands play other nights, when the cover is $2-5.

CANNERY BALLROOM

1 Cannery Row, 615/251-3020, www.mercylounge.com
HOURS: Vary based on show
COST: Cover varies
`Map 1`

Located in an old warehouse that has housed a flour mill, jam factory, and country music concert hall, Cannery Ballroom and its sister **Mercy Lounge** are two cool venues for live music. Cannery Ballroom is a large, somewhat cavernous space with lots of nice cherry-red touches, hardwood floors, and a shiny red bar. It can hold up to 1,000 people. The Mercy Lounge upstairs is a bit more intimate, with a capacity of up to 500 people. The Mercy Lounge hosts 8 off 8th on Monday nights, an open mic where eight different bands get to perform three songs. Both venues book rock, country, soul, and all sorts of other acts.

DOUGLAS CORNER CAFÉ

2106 8th Ave S., 615/292-2530, www.douglascorner.com
HOURS: Mon.-Sat. 6pm-midnight
COST: Cover varies
`Map 2`

The Douglas Corner Café offers a Tuesday-night open mic and country and other acts the rest of the week. It is known as a place where singer-songwriters show off their wares, and it is laid-back in both attitude and ambience. An intimate setting, full menu, and decent acoustics make this a popular choice for music listening. Several live albums have been recorded here.

THE EAST ROOM

2412 Gallatin Ave., 615/335-3137
HOURS: Vary by event
COST: Cover varies
`Map 3`

One of the city's newer music venues, the East Room is best known for hosting **East Nashville Underground** (www.eastnashvilleunderground.com), a quarterly festival of indie and other non-country sounds. The space has high ceilings, comfy couches, and plenty of room to see the eclectic artists who perform here. Other events include midnight shows and even movie screenings.

EXIT/IN

2208 Elliston Pl., 615/321-3340, www.exitin.com
HOURS: Vary based on show
COST: Cover varies
`Map 2`

For decades the Exit/In has been a favorite rock music venue, booking alternative country, blues, and reggae as well. Located on Elliston Place, the club is convenient to the Vanderbilt campus and therefore Vanderbilt students. While Exit/In wows in terms of rock acts booked and rock history made, the venue itself is a little worn around the edges. Don't expect luxury facilities. Drink prices are slightly higher than you might think the venue warrants.

NIGHTLIFE

TENNESSEE WALTZING

In Nashville you hardly need to find a dance club to boogie. There is (quite literally) music in the streets; people will start moving whenever the mood strikes. The carillon bells play "The Tennessee Waltz" every hour on the hour at Bicentennial Mall, and it can be hard to resist the urge to start waltzing right there in public.

But if you want a more structured dance environ, no worries. There are dance floors, lessons, and places to cut the rug all over town. For dancing downtown, try **Seen** (114 2nd Ave. S., 615/251-0064, www.seennashville.com, Tues. and Thurs.-Sat. 10pm-3am).

Downtown's **Wildhorse Saloon** (120 2nd Ave. N., 615/902-8200, www.wildhorsesaloon.com, Mon. 4pm-11pm, Tues.-Thurs. and Sun. 11am-11pm, Fri.-Sat. 11am-2am) offers dance lessons every single day of the week. This stop isn't considered particularly authentic by locals, but the lessons are free, the music is loud, and there's usually a good crowd.

Monday nights transform East Nashville's **The 5 Spot** (1006 Forrest Ave., 615/650-9333, www.the5spotlive.com, daily 8pm-3am) into a sock hop to '50s and '60s music. Despite taking place on a school night, it is regularly packed and lasts into the wee hours.

THE 5 SPOT

1006 Forrest Ave., 615/650-9333, www.the5spotlive.com
HOURS: Daily 8pm-3am
COST: $2-10
Map 3

Fans of ABC's *Nashville* know The 5 Spot as the grungy (in terms of both decor and sound) home to indie rock wannabes. With its heavy red curtains and eclectic mix, The 5 Spot has earned the title as the go-to spot on Monday with its Dance Party, playing old-school rap, traditional, and rock. Every third Sunday of the month, Dr. Sketchy shows up, giving patrons an opportunity to draw models dressed in burlesque attire, with drink specials and contests. The crowd is equally eclectic and changes depending on the night's theme.

THE LISTENING ROOM CAFÉ

217 2nd Ave. S., 803/466-0830,
http://listeningroomcafe.com
HOURS: Mon.-Thurs. 11am-11pm, Fri.-Sat. 11am-midnight
COST: No cover
Map 1

This venue aims to be the best sound in town, a tall order in a city filled with sound. Some would say that they've come pretty close to living up to those claims. Musical offerings include up-and-coming singer-songwriters. This is a listening room, so the volume inhibits conversation, but there are no rules against it. The Listening Room Café serves better-than-bar food to eat while you listen.

THE RUTLEDGE

410 4th Ave. S., 615/782-6658,
www.therutledgelmv.com
HOURS: Mon. 6am-2am, Tues.-Sun. 5pm-2am
COST: Cover varies
Map 1

A music venue designed by performers, The Rutledge has some of the most ear-pleasing acoustics in the city. An intimate brick venue, it seats only 250, and there's not a bad one among them. Even standing at the bar puts you in good listening radius of the stage. The Rutledge books a wide variety of acts, hosts industry events, and even puts on tribute shows now and then.

SPRINGWATER

115 27th Ave. N., 615/320-0345,
www.springwatersupperclub.com
HOURS: Daily 11am-3am
COST: Cover varies
Map 2

There are basically three things you need to know about Springwater: It's a dive bar. The beer is cheap. It's cash only. All of the rest of the details derive from these three. It's an actual dive bar, not a hip bar trying to be a dive. Although, somehow it has become hip, either because of this or in spite of it. The acts here are the very definition of eclectic. People-watching is especially entertaining, and more so after a few cheap beers.

THAT'S COOL

2309 Franklin Pike, 615/712-6466,
www.thatscoolnashville.com
HOURS: Mon.-Sat. 5:30pm-2am
COST: Cover varies, typically less than $10
Map 2

An unassuming bar with a large live music space, That's Cool specializes in letting lesser-known acts have their time in the spotlight. You'll sit on comfy couches and armchairs, be waited on by a friendly bar staff, and admire the visual art of local artists while listening to bands play. The music here runs the gamut from the experimental to the ordinary. You're unlikely to see any named stars here, but you're also unlikely to pay more than $10 to get in the door. Parking is rarely an issue here.

3RD AND LINDSLEY

816 3rd Ave. S., 615/259-9891,
www.3rdandlindsley.com
HOURS: Vary based on show
COST: Cover varies
Map 1

3rd and Lindsley is a neighborhood bar and grill that showcases rock, alternative, progressive, Americana, soul, and R&B music. Over the years they have developed a reputation for solid bookings, though if you were just driving down the street you wouldn't think a place that rocks could reside inside. Monday nights feature The Time Jumpers, a world-class Western swing jam band. 3rd and Lindsley serves a full lunch and dinner menu, the bar is well stocked, and the club offers good sound quality and an adequate dance floor and seating. The atmosphere isn't particularly quirky or welcoming, but you came here for music, not decor.

12TH AND PORTER

114 12th Ave. N., 615/320-3754,
www.12thandporterlive.com
HOURS: Vary based on show
COST: Cover varies, typically starts at $5
Map 1

For decades 12th and Porter has been a favorite venue for live music in the city. Ownership has changed over the years, and with it, the venue's atmosphere (and cleanliness). No longer a restaurant, too, 12th and Porter still reliably books all kinds of acts. It remains a popular choice for music-label showcases, and legendary performers have been known to stage impromptu shows here. The space is big, if not fancy, and the crowd varies depending on the act. The online calendar is kept updated. 12th and Porter is often a venue for festivals including Americana Music Fest and Tin Pan South.

NIGHTLIFE

Live Music Venues

C THE BLUEBIRD CAFE

4104 Hillsboro Pike, 615/383-1461,
www.bluebirdcafe.com
HOURS: Daily 5:30pm-close
COST: $7-12
Map 6

The Bluebird Cafe is where Nashville's real music magic happens. It's an unassuming room, small and, depending on the night, a bit cramped, but when people talk about how they heard so-and-so play in Nashville, odds are pretty good that it was here. The Bluebird is famous for its songwriters' nights, open mics, and performances in the round. Musicians aren't up on a stage, they are right there, with you. Since it is a small room, reservations are required, and this is not the place to plan to talk to your neighbor while the music plays. You will be shushed. Not every performer on the calendar is someone recognizable, but odds are, they've written something that is. It's worth the risk to find out.

COUNTRY MUSIC HALL OF FAME

222 5th Ave. S., 615/416-2001,
www.countrymusichalloffame.org
HOURS: Jan.-Feb. Wed.-Mon. 9am-5pm, Mar.-Dec.
daily 9am-5pm
COST: Free with museum admission or museum
membership
Map 1

The Country Music Hall of Fame hosts concerts, readings, and musical discussions regularly in an auditorium located inside the hall. These daytime events are often aimed at highlighting one type of country music or another, often in conjunction with a themed exhibit. The Hall of Fame is well respected, and often you'll find big names playing. Admission is free with your paid admission to the hall, so it is a good idea to plan your trip to the hall on a day when there's a concert scheduled (separate admission to concerts is not available). Check the website for a listing of upcoming events. Museum members get access to small concerts as well.

THE GRAND OLE OPRY

2804 Opryland Dr., 615/871-6779, www.opry.com
HOURS: Shows Tue., Fri., and Sat.; Opry Classics
Shows Thurs.
COST: Prices vary based on show, typically $39-54
Map 4

If there's any one thing you really must do while in Nashville, it's go to see the Grand Ole Opry. Really. Even if you think you don't like country music. For more than 80 years this weekly radio showcase of country music has drawn crowds to Nashville. Every show at the Opry is still broadcast live on WSM, a Nashville AM radio station. Shows are also streamed online, and some are televised on cable. But nothing beats the experience of being there. Often there is an additional Tuesday evening show. Since this is a radio broadcast, shows start and end right on time. Every Opry show is divided into 30-minute segments, each of which is hosted by a different member of the Opry. This elite country music fraternity includes dozens of stars that you've

heard of and others you haven't. The host performs two songs; one at the beginning of their half-hour segment and one at the end. In between they will introduce two or three other performers, each of whom will sing about two songs. In between segments, the announcers read radio commercials and stagehands change around the stage set.

MARATHON MUSIC WORKS

1402 Clinton St., 615/891-1781,
www.marathonmusicworks.com
HOURS: Show times vary; box office Mon.-Fri.
noon-1pm
COST: Prices vary based on event
Map 2

Housed in the revitalized Marathon Village, the home of the former Marathon Motor Works, this venue brings a modern take to an old space. This brick-lined warehouse has two bars, a fun loft-like VIP space, and plenty of room to cut a rug when the acts warrant it. An eclectic cross section of acts are booked here; this is definitely not a country music only club. There's a parking lot in the back, and sometimes there is available free parking on the street.

THE RYMAN AUDITORIUM

116 5th Ave. N., 615/889-3060, www.ryman.com
HOURS: Show times vary; box office and tours daily
9am-4pm
COST: Self-guided tour $13 adults, $6.50 children
ages 4-11; backstage tour $17 adults, $10.50 children
ages 4-11
Map 1

The most famous music venue in Nashville, the Ryman Auditorium continues to book some of the best acts in town, of just about every genre you can imagine. On the good side, the hall still boasts some of the best acoustics around. On the bad, the pew-style bench seats aren't all that comfortable. But seeing the reverence performers have for this venue makes it hard to notice anything else. Musicians love to show off the acoustics here, often playing a song or two without a mic.

☾ THE STONE FOX

712 51st Ave. N., 615/953-1811,
www.thestonefoxnashville.com
HOURS: Mon.-Fri. 5pm-3am, Sat.-Sun. 11am-3am
COST: Cover varies, typically starts at $5
Map 6

Music City It Boy William Tyler and his mul-titalented family opened this music venue/res-taurant in Sylvan Park in 2012, and almost immediately it became the über-hip place to see a show in Nashville. Thanks to the Tylers' con-nections they've been able to book acts across genres, including Lambchop, Paul Burch, and Rosanne Cash. The bar serves both local beers and cheap PBR-type brews. Locals like the brunch and food menu, but unlike most other venues, it is hard to see (and hear) the bands in the club from the tables.

☾ TEXAS TROUBADOUR THEATRE

2416 Music Valley Dr., 615/859-1001,
http://etrecordshop.com/tttlogo.htm
HOURS: Vary by performance
COST: Prices vary based on event
Map 4

Adjacent to the **Ernest Tubb Record Shop** (2416 Music Valley Dr., Ste. 110, 615/889-2474, http://etrecordshop.com) the Texas Troubadour Theatre is home to a number of classic events, including the weekly **Midnite Jamboree** and **Cowboy Church,** as well as other events. The theatre is nicer than you might expect, being in a strip mall, with roomy pew seating, good views of the stage, and a fun concessions stand. The record shop is open late after Midnite Jamboree, so you can buy the works of the stars you've just heard. Every Sunday morning at 10am, locals and tourists dressed in anything from shorts to Stetsons gather here for a lively praise-and-worship country gospel church.

☾ WOODS AMPHITHEATER

4225 Whites Creek Pike, 615/724-1600,
http://woodsamphitheater.com
HOURS: Vary based on show
COST: Prices vary based on event
Map 6

Opened in 2010, this 4,500-seat outdoor con-cert venue is nestled, as its name suggests, in the woods at Fontanel, a spot that used to be the home of country star Barbara Mandrell. The Woods Amphitheater has space for pic-nicking on the lawn during a concert and VIP boxes, as well as folding chairs for a more traditional concert experience. This is an idyllic place to see a show, with the sunset over the city's horizon. Fontanel often oper-ates free shuttles to and from downtown, for those who don't want to make the short drive to Whites Creek for a concert. This can be a bonus, as the driveway to the parking lot can get congested.

Pubs

12 SOUTH TAPROOM AND GRILL

2318 12th Ave S., 615/463-7552,
http://12southtaproom.com
HOURS: Mon.-Sat. 11am-midnight
COST: No cover
Map 2

The extensive list of brews on tap has earned 12 South Taproom and Grill a loyal local fol-lowing. The above-average bar food includes several vegetarian-friendly options, but peo-ple come here because of the beer. Expect a crowd—in all likelihood it will be standing room only on weekends. The staff knows their stuff and can help direct you to the right brew for your tastes.

THE BEER SELLAR

107 Church St., 615/254-9464, www.beersellar.net
HOURS: Mon.-Sat. 2pm-3am, Sun. noon-3am
COST: No cover
Map 1

Duck into The Beer Sellar to experience its "50 taps, 100 bottles, and 1 bitching jukebox." Located right downtown, this is a cozy bar that feels more like a neighborhood joint than something you'd find in the heart of a major

NIGHTLIFE

metropolitan business district. Its beer focus distinguishes it from the tourist-heavy kitsch or the honky-tonk vibes of its neighbors.

BLACKSTONE RESTAURANT AND BREWERY

1918 West End Ave., 615/327-9969, www.blackstonebrewery.com
HOURS: Mon.-Thurs. 11am-midnight, Fri.-Sat. 11am-1am, Sun. 11am-10pm
COST: No cover
`Map 2`

Blackstone Restaurant and Brewery is a local favorite, with its own brand of craft beers, a cozy fireplace, and a laid-back vibe. The space is huge, with lots of tables, fireplace-adjacent seating, and bar stools. Given its size and proximity to the Vanderbilt campus, you'd think it'd be a loud party house, but it is actually a welcoming place to have a beer with friends.

BOSCOS

1805 21st Ave. S., 615/385-0050, http://boscosbeer.com
HOURS: Mon.-Sat. 11am-1:30am, Sun. 10:30am-12:30am
COST: No cover
`Map 2`

Boscos calls itself a beer-lover's restaurant. While food is important here, it is Boscos' reputation for good beer that keeps patrons coming back. Boscos serves more than 50 different handcrafted beers every year. It was the winner of the Great American Beer Festival 2011 with its Hefeweizen. Stake out a front window seat to people-watch in always-hopping Hillsboro Village while you drink your beer. Despite being a big space with high ceilings, it is remarkably easy to have an intimate conversation here.

◖ FAT BOTTOM BREWING

900 Main St., 615/678-5895, www.fatbottombrewing.com
HOURS: Tues.-Fri. 4pm-10pm, Sat. 2pm-10pm
`Map 3`

This is a brewery, so it is about the beer. But the new pub, located in an old mattress factory in East Nashville, is also about the food. Seasonal salads, a number of good burgers, a

© MARGARET LITTMAN

East Nashville's Fat Bottom Brewing serves up sass as well as ales.

cheese plate, and other better-than-bar-fare make up the menu here and make it a good destination for a meal with your beer. There's a lovely outdoor beer garden in warm-weather months, but the brick-lined indoor space is cozy, too. Each of the beers has a Vargus-girl-style icon to distinguish it.

FLYING SAUCER

111 10th Ave. S., 615/259-3039, www.beerknurd.com
HOURS: Mon.-Wed. 11am-1am, Thurs.-Sat. 11am-2am, Sun. noon-midnight
COST: No cover
`Map 1`

A few blocks from downtown, behind the Frist Center for the Visual Arts and Union Station, you'll find one of the city's most popular beer bars. The selection is huge, with imports, local brews, and everything in between. Monday is pint night, when you can get $2.50 pints of just about any of the beers on the wall. Weekday volume is manageable, but this place is packed on weekends.

THE GOLD RUSH

2205 Elliston Pl., 615/321-1160,
www.goldrushnashville.com
HOURS: Daily 11am-3am
COST: No cover
Map 2

Since 1974 The Gold Rush has been the place to go for a beer on Elliston Place. It still is. Although the stools are a little time-worn, this remains a beloved late-night mellow hangout. The barbecue is better than you might expect, and the beer is cheap. Billiards, darts, and football on the TV round out the classic bar amenities.

JACKALOPE BREWING CO.

701 8th Ave. S., 615/873-4313, www.jackalopebrew.com
HOURS: Thurs.-Sat. 4pm-8pm, Sun. noon-4pm
COST: No cover; $7 tour and tasting
Map 1

Jackalope offers tastings of its craft brews, and tours of its taproom. The beer selection changes monthly, so there's always an excuse to go back and try another. Jackalope's beers include Rompo Red Rye Ale, Thunder Ann American Pale Ale, and Bearwalker Maple Brown. Growlers are available for purchase as well.

ROCK BOTTOM RESTAURANT & BREWERY

111 Broadway, 615/251-4677, www.rockbottom.com
HOURS: Sun.-Thurs. 11am-11pm, Fri.-Sat. 11am-midnight
COST: No cover
Map 1

A popular downtown brewpub, Rock Bottom Restaurant & Brewery is an imposing place right near Riverfront Park. A national chain, Rock Bottom serves food as well as its brewed-in-house craft beers. The staff is friendly and competent, prices are reasonable, and they accommodate large parties without blinking an eye.

YAZOO TAP ROOM

910 Division St., 615/891-4649, www.yazoobrew.com
HOURS: Thurs.-Fri. 4pm-8pm, Sat. 2:30pm-6:30pm
COST: No cover; $6 tours
Map 1

Yazoo is the local craft beer of choice, and it can be found in most bars around town. Other bars, however, do not have the selection of the taproom. Beer connoisseurs are very happy here. Hours change with the season, so check the website for updates. The taproom also fills growlers in case you want to take something to a party. The local food trucks like to park outside.

NIGHTLIFE

ARTS AND LEISURE

Before Nashville was Music City, it was the Athens of the South, a city renowned for its cultural, academic, and artistic life. Universities, museums, and public arts facilities created an environment for artistic expression unparalleled in any other Southern city. It has an opera company of its own, not to mention an award-winning symphony (and symphony center), an innovative and growing visual arts scene, and ample opportunities to sample contemporary and classic music, film, and theater.

But the arts are not the only way to get out and experience Nashville's native pursuits. Folks who come to Music City from elsewhere remark on how green and lush Nashville is. It is true: Nashville has good parks, numerous sports teams, accessible waterways, and nice weather to enjoy them all. In 2013 5th Avenue

(also known as 5th Avenue of the Arts) was renovated with an art-themed streetscape.

Most of the city's arts attractions are concentrated downtown, with blocks of galleries clustered together. This area is always interesting, but really comes alive during the **First Saturday Art Crawl** (www.nashville-downtown.com), which takes place on the first Saturday of each month. There are free shuttles to take art lovers from gallery to gallery. Downtown is also dotted with interesting public art projects, including the iconic red *Ghost Dancer* sculpture on the banks of the Cumberland River.

Speaking of the river, the Cumberland is a great place to start looking for recreational opportunities in Nashville. It winds its way through the city (and state), offering up pretty

HIGHLIGHTS

LOOK FOR  TO FIND
RECOMMENDED ARTS AND ACTIVITIES.

© MARGARET LITTMAN

The mist rises at Cumberland Park, one of the city's most photographed spots.

Best Live Radio Show for $10: The Wednesday-night **Music City Roots** show at the Loveless Barn is the best opportunity to see many up-and-coming acts for less than the cost of dinner (page 102).

Most Lycopene-Laden Festival: Tomato art, tomato costumes, tomato music: anything tomato-themed goes at the **East Nashville Tomato Art Festival** (page 105).

Green Space Most Oft Seen on TV: The proximity to the river downtown and the Tennessee Titans' stadium, means **Cumberland Park** is in beauty shots in many TV panoramas of Music City (page 108).

Best Place to Get on Your High Horse: Want to ride your horse in a public park without dragging that trailer all over the suburbs? Head to the **Equestrian Center** in Warner Parks (page 109).

Easiest Way to Rent a Bike: Just walk up to one of more than 20 **Nashville B-Cycle** stations across the city, don your helmet, and start pedaling. It is almost that simple (page 112).

Only Sport in Town that Shows the Score on a Guitar: Greer Stadium is home to the minor-league **Nashville Sounds** and a guitar-shaped scoreboard (page 116).

Most Tongue-in-Cheek Tour: There's a lot to love about Nashville, but there's a lot to mock, too. **Nash Trash Tours** does both best (page 118).

vistas, ample paddling and boating access, and more. Walking, hiking, and even horseback-riding are available on well-tended trails in the city's 108 parks. The Greenways, of which there are 19, connect large portions of the city with outdoor space. Bike rentals, yoga studios, paddleboard rentals, and other options are available for those who want to be active while in town.

The Arts

GALLERIES

AARON DOUGLAS GALLERY

Fisk University, 1000 17th Ave. N., 615/329-8685, www.fisk.edu

HOURS: Tues.-Fri. 11am-4pm, Sat. 1-4pm, Sun. 2pm-4pm

COST: Free

Map 2

Unassumingly nestled on the Fisk University campus is the Aaron Douglas Gallery, which houses the school's collection of African, African American, and folk art works. It also hosts visiting exhibits and others by Fisk students and faculty. The gallery is named after painter and illustrator Aaron Douglas, who also established Fisk's first formal art department, and is located on the top floor of the Fisk library. Nearby **Cravath Hall** is home to several Aaron Douglas murals that are worth seeing.

THE ARCADE

244 5th Ave. N.

HOURS: Vary by gallery; first Sat. of the month 6pm-9pm

COST: Free

Map 1

If the second floor of the Arcade looks locked up, it's because a number of small galleries and artists have spaces here, and their public hours are erratic at best. During the monthly **First Saturday Art Crawl** (www.nashvilledown-town.com), however, all the doors are open and the lights are on. This is the best place and time to see innovative and affordable art in the city, when the energy is high and the wine flows. Galleries feature artwork in mediums like sculpture, photography, paintings, and print-making. If you see something you like, buy it. Many of these galleries are essentially pop-up shops, and it may be hard to find the works again next month.

ART + INVENTION GALLERY

1106 Woodland St., 615/226-2070, www.artandinvention.com

HOURS: Fri.-Sat. 11am-6pm, Sun. noon-5pm, or by appointment

COST: Free

Map 3

The Art + Invention Gallery is an East Nashville institution. Proprietors Meg and Bret MacFayden put on 5-6 shows each year, including the signature Tomato Art Show, part of the annual Tomato Art Festival in August (www.tomatoartfest.com), and are well loved for their support of other Music City creative types. The shop stocks handmade decorative art, jewelry, pottery, knit goods, and more. Art + Invention was the go-to East Nashville creative boutique before the streets were lined with them.

THE ARTS COMPANY

215 5th Ave. N., 615/254-2040, www.theartscompany.com

HOURS: Tues.-Sat. 11am-5pm

COST: Free

Map 1

One of downtown's most accessible and eclectic galleries, The Arts Company offers exhibits of the works of local and national artists, with contemporary works ranging from the avant-garde to the everyday. The works are shown in a gallery space in an inviting historic building. Unlike some other galleries, The Arts Company, one of the area's first galleries, typically has worked with a wide range of prices.

FISK'S STIEGLITZ COLLECTION

When photographer Alfred Stieglitz died in 1946, his wife, Georgia O'Keeffe, herself one of the most important artists of her generation, was left with the responsibility of giving away his massive art collection. Stieglitz had collected more than 1,000 works by artists including Arthur Dove, Marsden Hartley, O'Keeffe, Charles Demuth, and John Marin. He also owned several African sculptures.

Stieglitz's instructions regarding this art collection were vague. In his will he asked O'Keeffe to select the recipients "under such arrangements as will assure to the public, under reasonable regulations, access thereto to promote the study of art."

O'Keeffe selected several obvious recipients for parts of the collection: the Library of Congress, the National Gallery of Art in Washington, the Metropolitan Museum of Art, the Art Institute of Chicago, and the Philadelphia Museum of Art. Nashville's Fisk University was a surprise, and Carl Van Vechten, a writer, photographer, and friend of Stieglitz and O'Keeffe, is credited with making the suggestion. Van Vechten was keenly interested in African American art and was close friends with Fisk president Charles Johnson.

O'Keeffe and Fisk were not an easy partnership. According to an account by C. Michael Norton, when she first visited the university, a few days before the Carl Van Vechten Gallery would open on campus, O'Keeffe ordered major changes to the gallery space, eventually flying in a lighting designer from New York on the day before the opening. At the opening ceremony on November 4, 1949, held at the Memorial Chapel at Fisk, O'Keeffe declined President Johnson's invitation to the lectern and spoke from her chair, saying curtly: "Dr. Johnson wrote and asked me to speak and I did not answer. I had and have no intention of speaking. These paintings and sculptures are a gift from Stieglitz. They are for the students. I hope you go back and look at them more than once."

The Stieglitz Collection at Fisk consists of 101 remarkable works of art, including two by O'Keeffe, 19 Stieglitz photographs, prints by Cezanne and Renoir, and five pieces of African tribal art.

For years, cash-strapped Fisk has sought to sell parts of the collection to raise funds. In 2012, Walmart heiress Alice Walton's Crystal Bridges Museum in Bentonville, Arkansas, acquired a 50 percent share in the collection for $30 million. Now the 101-piece collection will rotate between Crystal Bridges and Fisk's Carl Van Vechten Gallery every two years. While some decry the deal as not following the stipulations in O'Keeffe's will, others see it as the only option to keep the collection in the public eye and Fisk solvent. The influx of cash should help maintain the collection and provide for new resources, such as a printed catalog of the impressive works.

CARL VAN VECHTEN GALLERY

Fisk University, 1000 17th Ave. N., 615/329-8720
HOURS: Tues.-Sat. 10am-5pm
COST: $10 adults, $6 seniors, free for children
Map 2

The Carl Van Vechten Gallery is named for the art collector who convinced artist Georgia O'Keeffe to donate to Fisk University a large portion of the work and personal collection of her late husband, Alfred Stieglitz. The college still retains 50 percent of the collection, although they have sold the other half to Crystal Bridges Museum of American Art, in Arkansas, to raise funds for the cash-strapped private school. The legal battle waged in courts for more than seven years. Beginning in fall 2013, the collection will rotate between Crystal Bridges and the Van Vechten every two years. Other exhibits will be on display when the Stieglitz collection is in Arkansas. The collection includes works by Stieglitz and O'Keeffe, as well as acclaimed European and American artists including Pablo Picasso, Paul Cezanne, Pierre-Auguste Renoir, Diego Rivera, Arthur Dove, Gino Severini, and Charles Demuth. It is truly a remarkable collection and one worth seeing, but call ahead to confirm hours,

THE SCULPTURE OF WILLIAM EDMONDSON

The first African American artist to have a one-man show at the Museum of Modern Art in New York was Nashville-born sculptor William Edmondson (1874-1951).

Edmondson was born in the Hillsboro area of Nashville. He worked for decades as a laborer on the railroads, a janitor at Women's Hospital, and in other similar jobs before discovering his talent for sculpture in 1929. Edmondson told the Nashville *Tennessean* that his talent and passion were God-given: "God appeared at the head of my bed and talked to me, like a natural man, concerning the talent of cutting stone He was about to bestow. He talked so loud He woke me up. He told me He had something for me."

A prolific sculptor, Edmondson worked exclusively with limestone, and he created angels, women, doves, turtles, rabbits, and other "varmints." He also made tombstones. Edmondson never learned to read or write, and he called many of his works "mirkels" because they were inspired by God.

In the 1930s, Louise Dahl-Wolfe, a photographer for *Harper's Bazaar* magazine, brought Edmondson and his work to the attention of Alfred Barr, the director of the Museum of Modern Art. Barr and other trustees of the museum admired what they termed as Edmondson's "modern primitive" work, and they invited him to display a one-man show at the museum in 1938. In 1941, the Nashville Art Museum put on an exhibit of Edmondson's work.

Edmondson continued to work until the late 1940s, when he became ill with cancer. After his death in 1951 he was buried in an unmarked grave at Mount Ararat Cemetery in Nashville. The city park at 17th Avenue North and Charlotte Avenue is named in honor of Edmondson.

Some of Edmondson's work is on display at the Cheekwood Museum.

---

particularly when school is not in session. Ring the bell to the right of the door to be let in.

LEQUIRE GALLERY

4304 Charlotte Ave., 615/298-4611,
www.lequiregallery.com
HOURS: Tues.-Sat. 10am-3pm
COST: Free
Map 6

Sculptor Alan LeQuire is known for two iconic Nashville works: *Musica*, the Music Row sculpture controversial for its unclad figures, and *Athena*, the massive golden goddess at the Parthenon. His Sylvan Park gallery is more diverse, exhibiting both his own work and that of other sculptors. In addition to having works on display, LeQuire Gallery also teaches classes and workshops for those who want to get in touch with their artistic side.

OVVIO ARTE

425 Chestnut St., 615/838-5699, www.ovvioarte.com
HOURS: By appointment
COST: Free

Map 5

Transplanted New Yorkers Theo Antoniadis and Veta Cicolello opened Ovvio Arte in 2008. This art gallery and performance space is a venue for the unexpected. It offers regular theater, dramatic readings, and art shows. An evening here is sure to highlight Nashville's offbeat, creative side. This is not a static gallery: It is a performance space where art, music, and theater collide. The space is 2,500 square feet large, built in a 1937 garage.

THE RYMER GALLERY

233 5th Ave. N., 615/752-6030,
www.therymergallery.com
HOURS: Tues.-Sat. 11am-5pm
COST: Free
Map 1

Perhaps the most cosmopolitan of all Nashville's galleries, The Rymer Gallery installs thought-provoking exhibits with works from artists of national renown. The Rymer is also home to Nashville's Herb Williams (www.herbwilliamsart.com), a gifted artist who creates sculpture from crayons.

Williams's work has been on display in the White House and other prestigious addresses.

SARRATT GALLERY

Vanderbilt University, 2301 Vanderbilt Pl., 615/322-2471, www.vanderbilt.edu/sarrattgallery
HOURS: Sept.-mid-May Mon.-Fri. 9am-9pm, Sat.-Sun. 10am-10pm, mid-May-Aug. Mon.-Fri 9am-4:30pm
COST: Free
Map 2

The Sarratt Gallery is housed in the main student center on the Vanderbilt campus, which has a more contemporary bent than the other on-campus gallery, the **Vanderbilt Fine Arts Gallery** (1220 21st Ave. S., 615/343-1702). The Sarratt frequently exhibits the work of alumni and students and kicks off the shows with popular opening receptions. The annual holiday sale is one of the best places to shop for artisan crafts in the city. The tall space is in a well-trafficked lobby of the student center, alongside a small courtyard with a fountain.

TWIST ART GALLERY

73 Arcade, 888/535-5286, www.twistartgallery.com
HOURS: Thurs.-Sat. 11am-3pm, first Sat. of the month 6pm-9pm
COST: Free
Map 1

The upper level of **The Arcade** (244 5th Ave. N.), houses several artist studios that open as galleries during downtown's monthly First Saturday Art Crawl. One favorite is the innovative, multi-room Twist Art Gallery, which exhibits different artists and works each month.

VANDERBILT UNIVERSITY FINE ARTS GALLERY

Vanderbilt University, 1220 21st Ave. S., 615/343-1702, www.vanderbilt.edu/gallery
HOURS: Sept.-early May Mon.-Wed. and Fri. noon-4pm, Thurs. noon-8pm, Sat.-Sun. 1pm-5pm; early May-mid-June Tues.-Fri. noon-4pm, Sat. 1pm-5pm
COST: Free
Map 2

In 2009 this university gallery moved into the historic 1928 McKim, Mead and White building on Vanderbilt's pretty Peabody campus.

The moved prompted a shift of the gallery's mission as well. Today the gallery is home to a permanent collection of more than 6,000 objects of art that are exhibited throughout the years. Exhibitions can be up for several months at a time and are often tied in with special lectures and other events on campus.

ZEITGEIST ARTS

516 Hagan St., 615/256-4805, www.zeitgeist-art.com
HOURS: Tues.-Sat. 11am-5pm
COST: Free
Map 5

For years Zeitgeist was the cornerstone—literally and figuratively—of Hillsboro Village. Its small, bright space attracted high-quality artists and well-heeled collectors. In 2013 the gallery moved to a bigger, reclaimed historic space with Manuel Zeitlin Architects. The exhibited art changes monthly, depending on which artists the gallery is featuring.

THEATER

ACTORS BRIDGE ENSEMBLE

Neuhoff Studio, 1312 Adams St., 615/498-4077, www.actorsbridge.org
HOURS: Show and class times vary
COST: General admission $18, students and seniors $12
Map 1

New theatrical works are given the spotlight by the Actors Bridge Ensemble, a theater company for both new and seasoned actors. The ensemble brings provocative and new plays to theaters across Nashville, and offers classes at their Neuhoff Studio, a space that once was a slaughterhouse. Actors Bridge is also the professional theatre company in full-time residence at Belmont University's Troutt Theater Complex. The ensemble approach means everyone gets to try everything, from acting to lighting to manning the box office.

ARTISTS' COOPERATIVE THEATRE

Darkhorse Theater, 4610 Charlotte Ave., 615/726-2281, www.act1online.com
HOURS: Show times vary
COST: $12
Map 6

COURTESY OF NASHVILLE SHAKESPEARE

Nashville Shakespeare's summer productions welcome anyone who loves the Bard.

Artists' Cooperative Theatre is an organization dedicated to bringing theatrical gems, both classic and modern, to Nashville audiences. Founded in 1989, ACT 1, as it is called, has presented productions of more than 90 of the world's greatest plays, using both classical and modern plays to describe and comment on the human condition. Each year the theater puts on four or five productions. Past productions include *Dr. Horrible's Sing-Along Blog*, *The Night of the Iguana*, *The Imaginary Invalid*, and *Pirates of Penzance*.

CIRCLE PLAYERS

Shamblin Theatre, 3901 Granny White Pike,
615/332-7529, www.circleplayers.net
HOURS: Show times vary
COST: $18 adults, $15 students and seniors
Map 5

Circle Players is the oldest nonprofit, all-volunteer arts association in Nashville. As a community theater, all actors, stagehands, directors, and other helpers are volunteers. The company stages four or five performances every year at a variety of theater locations around the city. Performances include classic theater, plus stage adaptations of popular cinema and literature. They often perform at Shamblin Theatre on the Lipscomb University campus.

NASHVILLE SHAKESPEARE

161 Rains Ave., 615/255-2273, www.nashvilleshakes.org
Map 5

The city's Shakespeare troupe brings the Bard to Music City audiences all year long. The winter performances take place at the Belmont University's **Troutt Theater** (2100 Belmont Blvd.). But it is the summer show, held outside at **Centennial Park** (2500 West End Ave.), which really grabs headlines. Nashville Shakespeare was founded in 1988. Since then is has worked to get the Bard's words to audiences who might not otherwise be exposed to these classics. Many of its performances are designed to be inexpensive or free, and are often mounted in parks and schools. Also fun are the monthly Shakespeare Allowed readings at the main public library.

Everyday folks, not actors, gather to read the works as they were meant to be heard: aloud.

TENNESSEE REPERTORY THEATRE

Andrew Johnson Theater, 505 Deaderick St., 615/782-4000, www.tennesseerep.org

HOURS: Box office Mon.-Fri. 10am-5pm, performances Tues.-Thurs 6:30pm, Fri. 7:30pm, Sat. 2:30pm and 7:30pm

COST: $25-43

Map 1

The Tennessee Repertory Theatre is Tennessee's largest professional theater company. It stages a number of big-name shows and off-Broadway productions annually. The Rep performs in the Tennessee Performing Arts Center, located in the James K. Polk Cultural Center in downtown Nashville. This is the same building that houses the Tennessee State Museum, plus some Nashville Opera performances, and the Nashville Ballet. Some of their productions have included *The Crucible, I Hate Hamlet,* and *Doubt.* The season runs October-May.

BALLET

NASHVILLE BALLET

Andrew Jackson Hall, 505 Deaderick St., 615/782-4040, www.nashvilleballet.com

HOURS: Box office Mon.-Fri. 10am-5pm, show times vary

COST: $35-72

Map 1

Founded in 1981 as a civic dance company, the Nashville Ballet became a professional dance company in 1986. Entertaining more than 40,000 patrons each year, the ballet performs both classical and contemporary pieces. The 22-person ballet often performs at the Tennessee Performing Arts Center in the James K. Polk Cultural Center downtown. Productions have included *Romeo and Juliet, The Nutcracker,* and *Sleeping Beauty.*

OPERA

NASHVILLE OPERA ASSOCIATION

Andrew Jackson Hall, 505 Deaderick St., 615/832-5242, www.nashvilleopera.org

HOURS: Box office June-July Mon.-Thurs. 9am-5pm, Aug.-May Mon.-Fri. 9am-5pm; show times vary

COST: Varies by show

Map 1

Middle Tennessee's only opera association, the Nashville Opera Association puts on an average of four mainstage performances per season (Oct.-Apr.) and does a six-week tour to area schools. The opera performances typically take place at the Tennessee Performing Arts Center in the James K. Polk Cultural Center downtown. The opera's headquarters, the **Noah Liff Opera Center** (3622 Redmon St., 615/832-5242) hosts private events and some smaller performances.

DINNER THEATER

CHAFFIN'S BARN DINNER THEATRE

8204 Hwy. 100, 615/646-9977, www.dinnertheatre.com

HOURS: Thurs. noon and 6pm, Fri.-Sat. 6pm, Sun. noon

COST: Varies based on show, military discounts are available

Map 6

Chaffin's Barn Dinner Theatre was Nashville's first professional theater and continues to put on Broadway-style plays for dinner patrons. As the name suggests, these performances take place in a theater that looks like a barn from the outside. There's nothing cutting-edge about the shows or the meal, but they are family-friendly fun.

MISS JEANNE'S MYSTERY DINNER THEATRE

600 9th Ave. S., 615/902-9566, www.missjeannes.com

HOURS: Thurs.-Sun. 7pm

COST: $50

Map 1

If mystery is what you're into, have dinner at Miss Jeanne's Mystery Dinner Theatre, where you and your friends try to guess who done it while eating a Southern feast. This dinner-and-a-show theater offers plenty of discounts, includes those for seniors, members of the military, and groups larger than 10, making a night of whodunit more affordable.

ARTS AND LEISURE

CHILDREN'S THEATER
NASHVILLE CHILDREN'S THEATRE

724 2nd Ave. S., 615/254-9103,
www.nashvillechildrenstheatre.org
HOURS: Box office Mon.-Fri. 8:30am-4pm, show
times Tues.-Fri. 10am and 11:45am, Sat. 11am, Sun. 2pm
COST: $19 adults, $12 seniors and students, $12
children ages 2-17
`Map 1`

Nashville Children's Theatre is the oldest children's theater company in the United States. During the school year, the company puts on plays for children from preschool to elementary-school age in its colorful theater, a space that was renovated in 2005. In the summer there are drama classes for youngsters, plus lots of activities that include Mom and Dad. Recent years have included original NCT productions as well as nationally recognized plays.

REAL LIFE PLAYERS

Darkhorse Theater, 4610 Charlotte Ave.,
615/300-3592, www.darkhorsetheater.com
HOURS: Thurs.-Sat. 6:30pm
COST: $10
`Map 6`

Teenagers own and operate the Real Life Players, a stalwart theater company that produces original plays written by Nashville teens. The subject matter of the plays produced is relevant to teenagers, but don't expect fluff. Topics covered have ranged from religion to family to gender roles. Profits are donated to teen-related community organizations.

WISHING CHAIR PRODUCTIONS

615 Church St., 615/862-5800,
http://nashvillepubliclibrary.org/wishingchair
HOURS: Show times typically Tues.-Wed. 9:30am,
10:30am, and 11:30am, but may vary
COST: Free
`Map 1`

Neither adults nor kids should miss the marionette shows at the Nashville Public Library. Using marionettes from the collection of former library puppeteer Tom Tichenor (dating back to the 1940s), plus others acquired from Chicago's Peekaboo Puppet Productions, the library's children's room staff put on excellent one-of-a-kind family entertainment. The group also partners with the Nashville Symphony and the Nashville Jazz Workshop, among other local institutions. Schoolchildren sometimes get to see the Wishing Chair Puppet Truck in their school parking lots.

CLASSICAL MUSIC
NASHVILLE SYMPHONY ORCHESTRA

Schermerhorn Symphony Center, One Symphony Pl.,
615/687-6400, www.nashvillesymphony.org
HOURS: Show times vary
COST: $35-85
`Map 1`

The Nashville Symphony Orchestra is housed in the remarkable Schermerhorn Symphony Center next to the Country Music Hall of Fame, one of the downtown buildings that was renovated as a result of 2010 flood damage. Nominated for four Grammies and selling more recordings than any other American orchestra, the symphony is a source of pride for Music City. Costa Rican conductor Giancarlo Guerrero is the symphony's seventh music director. The symphony puts on more than 200 performances each year, including classical, pops, and children's concerts. Its season spans September-May. Buying tickets online is a breeze, especially since you can easily choose where you want to sit. There is discounted parking for symphony-goers in the Pinnacle at Symphony Place, across the street from the Schermerhorn. During the summer, the symphony plays its Community Concerts series at locations across the city.

CINEMA
BELCOURT THEATRE

2102 Belcourt Ave., 615/383-9140, www.belcourt.org
COST: Evenings $8.75 adults, $6.25 seniors, $7.25
students/military/children under 12; matinees $7.25
adults, $6.25 seniors, $6.75 student/military, $7.25
children under 12
`Map 2`

Once the home of the Grand Ole Opry (as is true of so many buildings in Nashville), the Belcourt Theatre is the city's best venue for independent films. Built in 1925 as a silent movie house, the Belcourt now screens a refreshing variety of independent and unusual films, plus hosts live music concerts and other quirky performances and film fests. In the summer the Belcourt screens some films outdoors. Parking in the theater's Hillsboro Village lot is free for moviegoers. Ask for a code when you buy your ticket.

REGAL CINEMAS GREEN HILLS
3815 Green Hills Village Dr., 615/269-5910, www.regmovies.com
COST: $11.25 adults, $10 students, $8 seniors and children
Map 6

The Regal Cinemas Green Hills is a large shopping mall movie theater, but one that shows more mainstream arty flicks than some of the others in town. The theaters are in a separate building than the main mall, connected to a parking garage. Park in that garage and use the walkway to access the theater, to avoid the mess that the mall lot can become on weekend nights. This is also the site of the annual Nashville Film Festival each April.

PERFORMANCE VENUES
BLAIR SCHOOL OF MUSIC
2400 Blakemore Ave., 615/322-7651, http://blair.vanderbilt.edu
COST: Varies by event
Map 2

The Blair School of Music presents student, faculty, and visiting artist recitals frequently during the school year. Blair's ensembles include woodwind, string, brass, and big band. Vanderbilt University's music school, Blair addresses music through academic, pedagogical, and performing activities.

DYER OBSERVATORY
1000 Oman Dr., 615/373-4897, www.dyer.vanderbilt.edu
COST: Varies by event
Map 6

A working space observatory operated by Vanderbilt University, Dyer Observatory has

emerged as a popular venue for music, thanks to two ongoing concert series. **Music on the Mountain,** with Blair School of Music, and **Bluebird on the Mountain** ($105 per carload) with the Bluebird Cafe, bring live music to this dramatic and one-of-a-kind spot. Imagine a night of fine music enjoyed under the stars, with the fresh air and the atmosphere of the forest all around you.

WAR MEMORIAL AUDITORIUM
301 6th Ave. N., 615/782-4040, www.wmarocks.com
COST: Varies by show
Map 1

Built in 1925 to honor Tennesseans who died in World War I, the War Memorial Auditorium is one of several live music venues that once was the home of the Grand Ole Opry (in this case 1939-1943). After the floods of 2010, it again hosted the Opry while the Opry House was under renovation. The space has a crescent-shaped stage and is known for having good acoustics, which attracts a wide variety of acts. Today the venue welcomes live musical acts, comedians, and others, including The Avett Brothers, Mavis Staples, and Ira Glass.

CONCERT SERIES
BLUEGRASS NIGHTS AT THE RYMAN
116 5th Ave. N., 615/889-3060, www.ryman.com/bluegrass
HOURS: late June-late July Thurs. 7:30pm
COST: $27.50, or $147 for a season pass
Map 1

In 1945 Earl Scruggs brought his banjo to the stage of the Ryman Auditorium, and with that bluegrass became a vital part of the Grand Ole Opry. This summer series, which takes place on Thursday nights, honors that legacy. Bluegrass features some of the best pickers in the country. Starting in June and ending in July, this Ryman Auditorium series is always popular. Season passes are available, and many locals take advantage of that because they don't want to miss one of these shows.

ARTS AND LEISURE

JAZZ ON THE CUMBERLAND

Cumberland Park, 592 S. 1st St., 615/731-9001, http://jazzblues.org

HOURS: May-Oct. third Sun. 5:30pm

COST: Free

`Map 1`

For a laid-back evening in a one-of-a-kind setting, check out the Tennessee Jazz and Blues Society's concert series Jazz on the Lawn. On the third Sunday of the month from May through October, jazz and blues artists take the stage on the lawns of some of Nashville's most historic homes, including **Belle Meade Plantation** (5025 Harding Pike) and **Cheekwood** (1200 Forrest Park Dr.). Bring your own picnic and blanket.

LIVE ON THE GREEN

10 Public Square, Public Square Park, 615/242-5600, www.liveonthegreen.net

HOURS: Aug.-early Sept. Thurs. 5pm

COST: Free

`Map 1`

During Thursday nights in late summer, Public Square Park transforms for Live on the Green.

The outdoor concert series tends to attract a lot of indie rock acts, and in recent years the names have gotten bigger, with performances from Alabama Shakes, Los Lonely Boys, and Brett Dennen, among others. Live on the Green's audience is young, cool, and socially aware. Food and arts and crafts vendors line the sidewalks under tents.

◖ MUSIC CITY ROOTS

Loveless Barn, 8400 Hwy. 100, 615/646-9700, http://musiccityroots.com

HOURS:

COST: $10 adults, $5 children ages 6-18

`Map 6`

As great as the Opry is (and it is *great*), sometimes the music seems a little dated. On Wednesday nights you can experience an Opry-style live radio show, but with more cutting-edge country, Americana, and bluegrass acts. This hip, high-energy, multiple-hour, multiple-act show includes live interview segments with the artists, on-the-air commercials, and an audience that often gets up and dances. Stay until the very end, for the Loveless Jam, when all the night's performers cram onstage for one last song.

Festivals and Events

WINTER
ANTIQUES AND GARDEN SHOW OF NASHVILLE

1200 Forrest Park Dr., 615/352-1282, www.antiquesandgardenshow.com

COST: $20

`Map 6`

More than 150 dealers set up in the Nashville Convention Center for this upscale home and garden show in February. One of the largest such shows that combines both indoor furniture and outdoor, garden antiques, the event includes workshops, demonstrations, and vintage finds to meet most budgets and tastes. Proceeds from the show benefit the Cheekwood Botanical Garden and Museum of Art.

BATTLE OF NEW ORLEANS COMMEMORATION

4580 Rachel's Ln., 615/889-2941, www.thehermitage.com

COST: Free

`Map 6`

At the Battle of New Orleans Commemoration, The Hermitage, Andrew Jackson's home, is free to the public. The free day is typically on a weekend closest to January 8, which is when the event took place in 1815. The Battle of New Orleans was one of the final battles in the War of 1812 and is considered one of President Jackson's biggest legacies. The event includes a traditional wreath-laying on the general's grave.

MUSIC CITY BOWL

LP Field, 1 Titans Way, www.musiccitybowl.com
COST: Varies based on lineup
`Map 1`

The Music City Bowl pits a Southeastern Conference team against a Big Ten rival. This nationally televised football game is held at LP Field. The festivities typically include a night-before free concert downtown and a parade of the collegiate athletes. Hometown team the Vanderbilt Commodores have played in the bowl several times in recent years. When that happens there is a big black and gold cheering section.

NEW YEAR'S EVE/BASH ON BROADWAY

1st Ave. and Broadway,
www.visitmusiccity.com/newyearseve
COST: Free
`Map 1`

Sure, every city has some celebration to ring in the year. But Music City goes all out. In recent years Nashville has been one of the nationally televised locations for celebs to be filmed welcoming Baby New Year in all his glory. This Bash on Broadway event, held right downtown, always includes several bands, at least one of which tends to be fairly high profile. New Year's Eve in downtown Nashville also includes—what else?—a giant musical note drop.

SPRING
COUNTRY MUSIC MARATHON

Centennial Park, 2500 West End Ave.,
http://runrocknroll.competitor.com/nashville
COST: $150, with discounts for early registration; free for spectators
`Map 2`

Part of the Rock 'n' Roll Marathon circuit, this race is good fun for both participants and spectators. In addition to the course's hardcore 26.2 miles, there's a half marathon, wheelchair marathons and half marathons, and a kids' event. There's plenty of live music (more than 28 stages) along the course, which winds its way through the city. High school cheerleading squads root for the runners.

ROCK YOUR RUN

Every marathon is part spectacle. But the **Country Music Marathon,** which includes a half-marathon distance, too, is as known for the performances as it is for the racing. After all, it is called the Country *Music* Marathon. Spectators and runners alike cite the event's music vibe for keeping them motivated. In 2013 more than 28 stages were set up along the route, to keep arms pumping and legs moving for the course of the race. After the 26.2 miles, everyone is invited to a post-race concert. All runners get into the concert for free with their race number; spectators and townsfolk can buy tickets for about $35.

While some folks enter this event to win, it not unusual to see runners hula-hooping or dancing to the music as they go by. It is all part of the Nashville beat.

NASHVILLE FASHION WEEK

Citywide, http://nashvillefashionweek.com
COST: $25-350

Nashville's creative class isn't just musically inclined. There's a rich fashion design community. And the first week of April is the time to see it in all its runway glory. Events take place across the city all week, ranging from runways to workshops to parties with the city's best-dressed folks.

NASHVILLE FILM FESTIVAL

Regal Cinemas Green Hills, 3815 Green Hills Village Dr.,
www.nashvillefilmfestival.org
COST: $12 individual tickets
`Map 6`

Film lovers throughout the country look forward to the Nashville Film Festival, held every April at the Regal Cinemas Green Hills. The film festival was founded in 1969 as the Sinking Creek Film Celebration. These days more than 20,000 people attend the week-long event, which includes film screenings, industry panels, and lots of parties. Lots of locals volunteer to help put on the event,

ARTS AND LEISURE

which screens many regional films not shown at other festivals.

RUNNING OF THE IROQUOIS STEEPLECHASE

7311 Highway 100, 800/619-4802, www.iroquoissteeplechase.org

COST: $15 general admission, children under 12 free

Map 6

For something a little different, plan to attend Steeplechase at Percy Warner Park. Taking place on the second Saturday of May, the race is the nation's oldest continuously run weight-for-age steeplechase in the country. Fans in sundresses or suspenders and hats enjoy watching some of the top horses in the country navigate the racecourse. A general admission ticket gets you a seat on the hillside overlooking the stadium. Pack a blanket, food, and drinks (and mud boots if it has rained recently, which is not uncommon), and you'll have an excellent day. Various tailgating tickets are available and are priced according to how good the view is from the parking spot. If you want to tailgate, you'll need to buy tickets well in advance.

TENNESSEE CRAFTS FAIR

Centennial Park, 2500 West End Ave., 615/736-7600, www.tennesseecrafts.org/craft-fairs.html

COST: Free

Map 2

Known as TACA, this crafts fair isn't a beaded friendship bracelet kind of thing. More than 200 artists are juried and selected for their quality works. You'll find jewelry, painting, ceramics, and many other media on display here, as well as food and activities to keep the kids busy. Held in Centennial Park, this is not a place to expect a bargain, but you may find a work of art you'll keep for years. The fair repeats in September.

TIN PAN SOUTH SONGWRITERS FESTIVAL

Citywide, www.tinpansouth.com

COST: $90 festival pass, free-$12 individual tickets

Many Nashville music events celebrate the performers. But the Tin Pan South Songwriters Festival honors the people who come up with the lyrics for all those great tunes. So while you may not recognize most of the names on the lineup, you're sure to get a good introduction to the people behind the famous words. Typically held the last week of March or first week in April, Tin Pan South, organized by the Nashville Songwriters Association International, schedules performances at venues across the city.

SUMMER

CMA FEST

Various locations downtown, 800/745-3000, www.cmafest.com

COST: $145 four-day pass

Map 1

What was once called Fan Fair, and is now known as CMA Fest, is a four-day mega-music show in downtown Nashville. The stage at Riverfront Park along the Cumberland River is occupied by day with some of the top names in country music, with as many as 400 performers. At night the hordes move to LP Field across the river to hear a different show every night. Four-day passes, which cost between $145 and $350 per person, also give you access to the exhibit hall, where you can get autographs and meet up-and-coming country music artists. This is one of Nashville's biggest events of the year, and you are wise to buy your tickets and book your hotel early. Get a room downtown so you don't need a car; parking and traffic can be a nightmare during the festival. Locals tend to steer clear of downtown during CMA Fest.

CMT MUSIC AWARDS

Location varies annually, www.cmt.com

COST: $50-120

Country music fans vote on their favorite performers' videos and TV performances through CMT's website. The first weekend in June, the winners of those awards are feted in award-show style from a Music City venue like Bridgestone Arena. There's a red carpet, but in true Nashville fashion, you might see some boots with those black-tie outfits. Attendees

CMA Fest is one of Nashville's biggest tourist attractions.

will enjoy the many performances that occur between award presentations.

EAST NASHVILLE TOMATO ART FESTIVAL

Woodland St. and 11th Ave., www.tomatoartfest.com
COST: Free
Map 3

The East Nashville Tomato Art Festival is a tongue-in-cheek celebration of tomatoes and the hip, artsy vibe of East Nashville. Events include a parade of tomatoes, the "Most Beautiful Tomato Pageant," biggest and smallest tomato contests, tomato toss, and Bloody Mary taste-off. The festival usually takes place on the second Saturday of August. Feel free to come dressed as a tomato, or at least all in red.

INDEPENDENCE DAY

1st Ave. and Broadway, www.visitmusiccity.com
COST: Free
Map 1

Independence Day is celebrated in a big way in Music City with fireworks and a riverfront concert that's broadcast live on television. The event attracts more than 100,000 people every year. Like any Nashville event, the stage (often on a barge in Riverfront Park) is filled with lots of live music, and the fireworks display offers some serious pyrotechnics. Arrive downtown early to enjoy these festivities: You'll need extra time to park, and you'll want to stroll and listen before the fireworks begin.

MUSIC CITY BREWER'S FESTIVAL

Music City Walk of Fame, Demonbreun St.,
www.musiccitybrewersfest.com
COST: $49 general admission
Map 1

The Music City Brewer's Festival is a one-day event held in July at the Music City Walk of Fame downtown. Come to taste local brews, learn about making your own beer, and enjoy good food and live music. There are typically about 50 different brewers and 100 different beers, plus live music and other entertainment. Tickets are required; the event benefits local charities and almost always sells out.

ARTS AND LEISURE

COURTESY NASHVILLE CONVENTION & VISITORS CORP.

MUSIC CITY HOT CHICKEN FESTIVAL

700 Woodland St., 615/219-9590

www.hotchickenfestival.com

COST: Free

`Map 3`

The temperature is almost always hot at the Music City Hot Chicken Festival in July, but so is the chicken. This east-side event is a feast of Nashville's signature spicy pan-fried dish. Because hot chicken is made individually, the lines are long. But music, cooking contests, and other activities help pass the time. This is a great way to sample one of the classic Music City culinary delights.

NASHVILLE PRIDE FESTIVAL

Riverfront Park, 100 1st Ave. S., 615/844-4159, www.nashvillepride.org

COST: $5 general admission

`Map 1`

Early June sees Nashville's gay, lesbian, bisexual, and transgender community show its rainbow colors at the Nashville Pride Festival, a three-day event at downtown's Riverfront Park. This is not just the average Pride parade. There's an artists' village, where local artisans show off their wares, plus live music, a drag stage, and much more.

FALL

BBQ, BEER, AND BOURBON

Nashville Municipal Auditorium, 417 4th Ave. N., www.beerandbourbon.com/nashville/show-info

COST: $45

`Map 1`

The name really says it all. This is a daylong event where you can taste a selection of beverages, including 40 different bourbons and 60 different beers. What goes well with all those drinks? Pulled pork, brisket, and other delicious barbecue. This is an event that tours nationally, but it is such a good fit for Tennessee that it takes on its own Music City flavor.

CELEBRATE NASHVILLE CULTURAL FESTIVAL

Centennial Park, 2500 West End Ave., 615/955-0881, http://celebratenashville.org

COST: Free

`Map 2`

The Metro Parks department took over this multicultural celebration from the Scarritt-Bennett Center. International organizations set up in Centennial Park and offer food, dance, music, crafts, and other pieces of different cultures from around the world. There are separate activity areas for teens and younger children.

CUMBERLAND RIVER DRAGON BOAT FESTIVAL

Riverfront Park, 100 1st Ave. S., www.nashvilledragonboat.com

COST: $65 for individual paddlers; free for spectators

`Map 1`

The Cumberland River Dragon Boat Festival is a one-day race in September that takes place at Riverfront Park, and is part of a 2,300-year-old tradition. More than 40 boats with big dragon heads and 20 costumed paddlers each race each other on the water near LP Field. There are plenty of river-themed activities for spectators, too, including a DragonLand themed area for kids. Proceeds from the event benefit watershed conservation projects.

FALL FEST

Belle Meade Plantation, 5025 Harding Pike, 615/356-0501, www.bellemeadeplantation.com

COST: $10

`Map 6`

The Belle Meade Plantation hosts its biggest fundraising event of the year, Fall Fest, every September. The two-day festival features antiques, arts and crafts, live music, and children's activities. Browse for antiques or just take in the sights and sounds of the plantation. The leaves are typically changing in the landscape during this event, and the home is open for tours.

GOSPEL MUSIC ASSOCIATION DOVE AWARDS

Allen Arena, Lipscomb University, 1 University Park Dr., www.gospelmusic.org

COST: Ticket prices vary

`Map 6`

Gospel music used to host its annual awards

night in April. In 2013 the Gospel Music Association Dove Awards were moved to October. Still billed as gospel music's biggest night, the event is now held at Lipscomb University Allen Arena. The live performances are also broadcast on television.

GREEK FESTIVAL

Holy Trinity Greek Orthodox Church, 4905 Franklin Pike, 615/333-1047, http://nashvillegreekfestival.com
COST: $2 adults, free children 12 and under
Map 5

Nashville's annual Greek Festival is hosted by the Holy Trinity Greek Orthodox Church and held in September. For more than 25 years Nashville residents have flocked here for homemade Greek food and entertainment, which includes dancing and tours of the historic cathedral. Oopa!

JOHN MERRITT CLASSIC

LP Field, 1 Titans Way, 615/963-5841, www.merrittclassic.com
COST: $10-45
Map 1

The John Merritt Classic, held over Labor Day, starts with fashion shows and live music concerts, and culminates with a football contest between the Tennessee State University Tigers and another historically black collegiate football team. The annual showdown is named for legendary former TSU football coach John Ayers Merritt.

NDFESTIVAL

Belcourt Theatre, 2102 Belcourt Ave., 615/846-3150, www.belcourt.org
COST: Admission varies by event
Map 2

Nashvillians love the Belcourt Theatre, the indie movie theater/concert venue in Hillsboro Village. And they love the nDFestival because it is the Belcourt's largest fundraiser and keeps the doors open the rest of the year. The multi-day events in this fest are filled with fashion shows, music, film, and other cultural activities. You never know what you'll see at nD.

OKTOBERFEST

7th Ave. and Monroe St., 615/818-3959, www.nashvilleoktoberfest.com
COST: Free
Map 1

Oktoberfest is a Nashville tradition. Held in historic Germantown north of the Bicentennial Mall, this weekend festival is enhanced by its setting in what was once Nashville's German enclave. The events include a walk-run, church services, and a street fair with German music, food, and other entertainment. Oktoberfest usually takes place in mid-October.

SOUTHERN FESTIVAL OF BOOKS

Legislative Plaza, Union St. and 6th Ave. N., 615/770-0006, www.humanitiestennessee.org
COST: Free
Map 1

The Southern Festival of Books is held during the second full weekend of October on Legislative Plaza in downtown Nashville. Featuring book readings, autograph sessions with well-known and regional authors, and discussions, the festival, organized by Humanities Tennessee, is a must for book lovers. It has activities for children, too.

ARTS AND LEISURE

Recreation

Nashvillians work hard, as is evidenced by the numbers of businesses headquartered here, the number of venture capitalists who fund those companies, and the numbers of new music careers launched. But Nashvillians play hard, too. That makes Music City a good place to get out and play, whether you are an athlete yourself or you prefer spectator sports.

Football, baseball, and hockey are the trifecta of professional sports in Nashville, but people feel as strongly about college teams as they do about the professional ones. Even Vanderbilt University, which historically has not been an SEC football powerhouse, has enjoyed good seasons in recent years.

Nashville's location on the Cumberland River means it is a lush, green city, with lots of places to enjoy water sports, as well as parks for biking, horseback riding, and other outdoors activities. Nashville's mild winters mean there are only a few days of the year where it might be too cold to exercise outdoors.

PARKS

Nashville's Metro Parks department oversees 12,000 acres of open space, including 108 parks and 19 greenways that help connect all those green spaces to one another. The parks system includes almost everything your recreational heart might desire, including dog parks, swimming pools, tennis courts, walking trails, horseback riding, golf, disc golf, and spray parks, which are appreciated during the hot Tennessee summers.

An interactive map on the Metro website (www.nashville.gov) allows you to search for parks by geographic location or activity.

CENTENNIAL PARK
2500 West End Ave., 615/862-8424, www.nashville.gov
HOURS: Daily sunrise-11pm
COST: Free
Map 2
Nashville's best city park, Centennial is best

known as home of the Parthenon, and that edifice is the center of activity in this 132-acre gem. In addition to the museum and historical site, the park is also a pleasant place to relax. A small lake provides a habitat for ducks and other water creatures; paved walking trails are popular for walking during nice weather. The park hosts many events during the year, including Shakespeare in the Park each August and September. There's almost always something going on here, particularly in the summer, when live music frequently fills the trees. Centennial Park is home to one of Nashville's three official dog parks, as well as marked running trails, bicycle rental stations, children's play areas, and almost anything else you can expect from a park.

◖ CUMBERLAND PARK
592 S. 1st St., 615/862-8508, www.nashville.gov/parks
HOURS: Daily sunrise-sunset
COST: Free
Map 1

This 6.5-acre park is one of Nashville's newest, and if you count by the number of times it has been featured on ABC's TV show *Nashville*, the most popular. TV drama aside, this is a remarkable space, nestled on the banks of the Cumberland River, next to LP Field. It includes a kid-friendly rock-climbing wall, trails with native plants, misting stations, and educational information about how the Cumberland River is essential to the area's ecosystem. There are nice public restrooms and a concession stand here. The regular free parking is not available when there is an event at LP Field.

EDWIN AND PERCY WARNER PARKS
7311 Highway 100, 615/352-6299, www.nashville.gov/parks
HOURS: Daily sunrise-sunset
COST: Free
Map 6

The largest city parks in Tennessee, Edwin and Percy Warner Parks are a 2,600-acre oasis

GREEN IN THE CITY

Nashville has a remarkable network of connected green spaces thanks to its **Greenways** (615/862-8400, www.nashville.gov/greenways). The master plan is for this system to eventually connect the entire city. Today there are more than 190 miles of paved pathways and primitive trails used by bicyclists, runners, and dog walkers, all of which connect different parts of the city to each other. The Greenways run through the city's prettiest natural areas and, in places, along the Cumberland River. Some Greenways include nature centers and other educational facilities. For the most part, the routes are clean and safe. The long-term plan is for every Nashville resident to live within one mile of a Greenway. Good maps are available for download from Greenways for Nashville (www.greenwaysfornashville.org) as well as from the official website.

of forest, fields, and quiet pathways located just nine miles southwest from downtown Nashville. Nashvillians come here to walk, jog, ride bikes and horses, and much more. The parks have scenic drives, picnic facilities, playgrounds, cross-country running trails, an equestrian center, bridle trails, a model-airplane field, and athletic fields. Percy Warner Park is also home to the Harpeth Hills Golf Course, and Edwin Warner Park has a nature center that provides year-round environmental education. The nature center also hands out maps and other information about the park.

HAMILTON CREEK PARK

2901 Bell Rd., 615/862-8472,
www.nashville.gov/parks/water/marina.asp
HOURS: Daily sunrise-sunset
COST: Free
`Map 6`

Most of the access areas on Percy Priest Lake are managed by the Corps of Engineers, but

Metro Nashville operates Hamilton Creek Park, on its western shore. There's a sailboat marina here, where locals dock their boats, and this is a pretty spot from which to watch regattas and other sailing events. Storage for boats and paddleboards is available at a nominal fee for locals.

HORSEBACK RIDING
🄲 EQUESTRIAN CENTER

2500 Old Hickory Blvd., 615/370-8051
HOURS: Daily sunrise-sunset
COST: Free for 1-9 horses, $44 permit for 10-25 horses
`Map 6`

Those who love horses are fans of the Equestrian Center in Warner Parks, best known for the annual Iroquois Steeplechase Horse Race it hosts each May. But a 10-mile bridle path is open to horseback riding year-round. Because these trails are the only public horse trails in the county, they are crowded, and your horses need to share the trails with dogs, runners, and walkers.

TWIN FORKS HORSE TRAIL

J. Percy Priest Lake, 3737 Bell Rd., Nashville,
615/889-1975, www.lrn.usace.army.mil
HOURS: Daily 24 hours
COST: Free
`Map 6`

Hikers and horseback riders alike appreciate this 18-mile trail located in the East Fork Recreation Area on the southwestern shore of Percy Priest Lake and into the Stones River. The trail is wooded and well maintained and perfect for horseback riding, but the emphasis here is on the trail, not the vistas. If what you really want is views of the water, select a different vantage point. Come prepared: This trail can be muddy after a rainstorm.

HIKING AND BIKING
ANDERSON ROAD FITNESS TRAIL

Anderson Rd. and Couchville Pike, 615/889-1975,
www.lrn.usace.army.mil
HOURS: Daily sunrise-sunset
COST: Free
`Map 6`

The 14,200-acre J. Percy Priest Lake is big, and

ARTS AND LEISURE

© MARGARET LITTMAN

Rent a bike from a Nashville B-Cycle station and explore Music City on two wheels.

as a result is the heart of Nashvillians' water-based recreation. But the big lake and its banks are divided into smaller pieces, and this trail is a good one to consider if you want to get out and stretch your muscles. It is called a "fitness trail," but all the fitness is on your own accord: There are no hurdles or obstacles or any man-made equipment. It does have great views of the water and plenty of shade, which is welcome during Nashville's summers.

LONG HUNTER STATE PARK

2910 Hobson Pike, Hermitage, 615/885-2422,
http://tn.gov/environment/parks/LongHunter
HOURS: Daily 7am-sunset
COST: Free
Map 6

The State of Tennessee operates this park on the eastern shore of Percy Priest Lake. It offers mountain biking trails, both a two-mile loop and a four-mile loop. In addition there are several hiking trails around the lake, with a number of good vantage points and views of

the water. Boats are available for rentals during the summer season. Both group and backcountry camping is available.

NATCHEZ TRACE PARKWAY

Southwest of Nashville, 800/305-7417,
www.nps.gov/natr
HOURS: Daily 24 hours
COST: Free
Map 6

The first destination for bikers around Nashville is the Natchez Trace Parkway, a historic two-lane, 444-mile blacktop scenic drive that originates in Nashville and journeys south through the Tennessee and Mississippi countryside, eventually terminating in Natchez, Mississippi. The parkway is closed to commercial traffic, and the speed limit is strictly enforced, making it popular for biking. Biking the Trace can be an afternoon outing or a weeklong adventure. The National Park Service maintains three campgrounds along the Trace, plus five bicyclist-only campsites with more modest amenities. The northernmost bike campsite is located at the intersection of the Trace and Highway 50, about 36 miles south of Nashville. When biking on the Trace, ride in a single-file line and always wear reflective clothing and a helmet.

RADNOR LAKE STATE NATURAL AREA

1160 Otter Creek Rd., 615/373-3467,
http://tennessee.gov/environment/parks/RadnorLake
HOURS: Daily 6am-sunset
COST: Free
Map 6

Just seven miles southwest of downtown Nashville, Radnor Lake State Natural Area provides a natural escape for visitors and residents of the city. Eighty-five-acre Radnor Lake was created in 1914 by the Louisville and Nashville Railroad Company, which impounded Otter Creek to do so. The lake was built to provide water for the railroad's steam engines. By the 1940s, the railroad's use of the lake ended, and 20 years later the area was threatened by development. Local residents, including the Tennessee Ornithological Society,

THE NATCHEZ TRACE PARKWAY

The first people to travel what is now considered the Natchez Trace were probably the Choctow and Chickasaw Indians, who made the first footpaths through the region. French and Spanish traders used the 500 miles of intertwining Indian trails that linked the Mississippi port of Natchez to the Cumberland River.

Early white settlers quickly identified the importance of a land route from Natchez to Nashville. In 1801, the Natchez Trace opened as an official post road between the two cities. Boatmen who piloted flatboats from Nashville and other northern cities to Natchez and New Orleans returned along the Trace by foot or horse, often carrying large sums of money. One historian characterized the diverse array of people who used the Trace as "robbers, rugged pioneers, fashionable ladies, shysters, politicians, soldiers, scientists, and men of destiny, such as Aaron Burr, Andrew Jackson, and Meriwether Lewis."

The Trace developed a reputation for robberies, and few people traveled its miles alone. Many thieves disguised themselves as Indians, fanning the flames of racial distrust that existed during this period of history. By 1820, more than 20 inns, referred to as "stands," were open. Many were modest—providing food and shelter only.

In 1812, the first steamship arrived at Natchez, Mississippi, marking the beginning of the end of the Trace's prominence. As steamboat travel became more widespread and affordable, more and more people turned away from the long, laborious, and dangerous overland route along the Trace.

The road's historical importance is evident in the fact that it was not easily forgotten. While it faded from use, the Natchez Trace was remembered. In 1909, the Daughters of the American Revolution in Mississippi started a project to mark the route of the Trace in each county through which it passed. The marker project continued for the next 24 years and eventually caught the attention of Mississippi Rep. Thomas J. Busby, who introduced the first bills in Congress to survey and construct a paved road along the route of the old Natchez Trace.

During the Great Depression, work on the Natchez Trace Parkway began under the Public Works Administration, the Works Project Administration, and the Civilian Conservation Corps. Following the New Deal, construction slowed dramatically, and it was not until 1996 that the final leg of the parkway was completed.

The 445-mile parkway follows the general path of the old Natchez Trace; in a few places, they fall in step with each other. More than 100 miles of the parkway lie within Tennessee. It runs along the Western Highland Rim through Davidson, Williamson, Hickman, Maury, Lewis, and Wayne Counties. The **National Park Service** (800/305-7417, www.nps.gov/natr) publishes a fold-out map and guide to the parkway.

The parkway passes scenic overlooks, historic sites, and quiet pastures. In many places along the route, you have the opportunity to walk along the original Trace.

successfully rallied against development, and Radnor Lake State Natural Area was established in 1973.

There are six miles of hiking trails around the lake, and Otter Creek Road, which is closed to vehicular traffic, is open to bicycles and walkers. A nature museum at the visitors center (Sun.-Thurs. 9am-4pm, Fri.-Sat. 8am-4pm) describes some of the 240 species of birds and hundreds of species of plants and animals that live at Radnor.

THREE HICKORIES NATURE TRAIL

2910 Hobson Pike, Hermitage, 615/885-2422, www.lrn.usace.army.mil

HOURS: Daily sunrise-sunset
COST: $4
Map 6

The Three Hickories Nature Trail is an easy, 1.6-mile trail found in the Cook Recreational Area. It is the kind of walk you can do with a stroller, small children, and/or groups of varying fitness levels. There are pretty views of the

ARTS AND LEISURE

BIKING MUSIC CITY

Nashville is no Portland; you won't see a bicycle rack at every storefront. But the city has a growing bike culture, and it is easy to pedal your way across the city to see its highlights.

The first step is to bring your own bike, rent one from one of the shops listed in this chapter, or borrow one. City residents (with a local ID) can check out a bike from **Nashville GreenBikes** (http://nashvillegreenbikes.org). Once you have your two wheels it is easy to connect to more than 90 miles of greenways and 133 miles of on-road bike lanes and shared-use bike routes.

The **Music City Bikeway** (map downloadable from www.nashville.gov/bikeways) offers a 26-mile route that covers the city from east to west and includes city streets, Greenway paths, and more. It goes by the Nashville Farmers' Market, which has the most creative bike racks in the city, in the shape of bright vegetables. Eight miles of the bikeway include streets with designated bike lanes. Another good set of downloadable maps is available from Walk/Bike Nashville (www.walkbikenashville.org).

lake, and you'll feel like you are miles away from the city even though it takes fewer than 30 minutes to get here from downtown.

BIKE SHOPS AND RENTALS
CUMBERLAND TRANSIT
2807 West End Ave., 615/321-4069,
www.cumberlandtransit.com
HOURS: Mon.-Fri. 9am-7pm, Sat. 9am-6pm, Sun. noon-5pm
Map 2

One of the city's most beloved independent outdoors shops, Cumberland Transit stocks and services bikes (as well as plenty of other gear). Brands carried include Trek, Gary Fisher, and Yakima (you need a rack after you buy all the good sports equipment). The store also hosts a number of how-to workshops.

EAST SIDE CYCLES
103 S. 11th St., 615/469-1079, www.eastside-cycles.com
HOURS: Mon.-Fri. 11am-7pm, Sat. 10am-6pm
COST: $20-60/day
Map 3

This neighborhood bike show has everything anyone with two wheels could want. There are high-end bikes for sale, rentals for just getting around town, and repair and service if you don't know what to do to get your own bicycle back on the road. There are bike seats and other gear to make biking with your kids easy

(and even toys to keep them occupied while you shop). The store has bike tools around back if you need DIY repair during off hours.

◖ NASHVILLE B-CYCLE
Citywide, 615/625-2153, www.nashville.bcycle.com
HOURS: Daily 24 hours
COST: Up to $45 for 24 hours

Nearly 200 bikes are available for rental at 20 different stations across Music City, with new locations being added regularly. A 24-hour pass is $5, plus hourly rental. The first hour is free, and each additional half hour is $1.50. You must sign up for a membership in advance and bring your own helmet.

TRACE BIKES
8080 Highway 100, 615/646-2485,
www.tracebikes.com
HOURS: Mon-Fri. 10am-6pm, Sat. 10am-5pm
COST: $50/day
Map 6

Formerly located next to the Loveless Cafe near the Natchez Trace Parkway, Trace Bikes is now in The Shoppes on the Harpeth. This is still a picture-perfect location for getting out and riding a bike on this lovely route. Bikes and gear are also available for sale, and the shop leads biking events.

FITNESS
CENTENNIAL SPORTSPLEX

222 25th Ave. N., 615/862-8480, www.nashville.gov
HOURS: Mon.-Thurs. 5:30am-8pm, Fri. 5:30am-6pm,
Sat. 9am-5pm
COST: Fitness center daily rate $7 adults, $6 students,
seniors, and children ages 5-12
Map 2

The Centennial Sportsplex has 15 lighted outdoor tennis courts and four indoor courts, as well as a ball machine, pro shop, and concession stand, but is best known for its indoor ice skating rink. Indoor courts may be booked up to three days in advance. Outdoor courts can be reserved up to six days in advance. The Sportsplex organizes numerous tennis tournaments, leagues, and classes during the year.

YOGA STUDIOS
HOT YOGA PLUS

2214 Elliston Pl., 615/321-8828, www.hotyogaplus.com
COST: $15-20 single class
Map 2

Hot Yoga Plus is a local chain, with this location near the Vanderbilt campus, as well as suburban locations. It is one of the most popular in the area, and you'll see cars with their stickers across town. The emphasis, as its name suggests, is on hot yoga. The thermostats are turned up and practitioners sweat it out while doing their poses. Class size can be large here; this isn't the studio for one-on-one work.

KALI YOGA

1011 Fatherland St., 615/260-5361,
www.kaliyugayoga.com
COST: $13 single class, $45 for 1 week unlimited
Map 3

Locals like the classes at this East Nashville yoga studio because there's something for everyone, be it hot yoga or restorative candlelight yoga. The space is small, and the class sizes are limited to accommodate that, so yogis get attention from their instructors and have room to stretch their arms in warrior pose. Packages are available for those who want to attend more than one class.

STEADFAST AND TRUE

1207-A Villa Pl., 615/320-9642,
www.steadfastandtrueyoga.com
COST: $10-15 single class
Map 2

Steadfast and True is for people who feel, well, steadfast in their commitment to yoga. With a focus on ashtanga, this isn't a studio for newcomers to the practice, although the instructors are welcoming to everyone. Basically, this is a studio that takes yoga seriously, but doesn't take itself too seriously. It is located in Edgehill Village, near the Belmont campus.

12 SOUTH YOGA

2814 12th Ave. S., 615/385-3600,
www.12southyoga.com
COST: Free beginners' classes; other classes require
10-week registration $135
Map 2

One of the city's most popular yoga studios, 12 South is known for its well-trained and knowledgeable instructors. This isn't the least expensive studio in town, but its devoted following suggests that the cost is worth it. Mats and other accessories are available for those who do not own their own.

GOLF
GAYLORD SPRINGS GOLF LINKS

18 Springhouse Ln., 615/458-1730,
www.gaylordsprings.com
HOURS: Mon.-Fri. 7am-sunset, Sat.-Sun.
6:30am-sunset
COST: Apr.-Nov. 15 Mon.-Thurs. $65/18 holes, Fri.-Sun.
$75/18 holes, Nov. 16-Mar. Mon.-Thurs. $55/18 holes,
Fri.-Sun. $65/18 holes
Map 4

Golfers like this 6,842-yard Larry Nelson-designed course, saying it delivers one of the state's best golf experiences. Don't miss the comforts of the 43,000-square-foot clubhouse or the scenery of the links-like layout bordered by limestone cliffs and the Cumberland River. It is located near the Gaylord Opryland Resort in Music Valley.

ARTS AND LEISURE

HARPETH HILLS GOLF COURSE

2424 Old Hickory Rd., 615/862-8493, www.nashville.gov
HOURS: Vary based on season
COST: Mon.-Fri. $28/18 holes, Sat.-Sun. $30/18 holes
Map 6

Nestled in Percy Warner Park, Harpeth Hills is a public course with a solid reputation. It was designed in 1965 and renovated in 1991. Golfers can appreciate the natural beauty of the surrounding parks while they hit the links. Affordable lessons are available at many of Metro Nashville's public courses, including this one.

MCCABE GOLF COURSE

100 46th Ave. N., 615/862-8491, www.nashville.gov
HOURS: Vary based on season
COST: Mon.-Fri. $24/18 holes, Sat.-Sun. $26/18 holes
Map 6

The city's Sylvan Park area is home to the public McCabe Golf Course, a large 27-hole course. Built in 1942 and renovated in 2007, the course is challenging enough for regular golfers but accessible for those who are new to the sport. A new driving range with target greens opened in 2012. Tee times can be reserved up to seven days in advance.

NASHBORO GOLF CLUB

1101 Nashboro Blvd., 615/367-2311,
http://nashborogolf.com
HOURS: Vary based on season
COST: Mon.-Thurs $36/18 holes, Fri.-Sun. $45/18 holes
Map 6

Larger bunkers and water hazards dot the 6,887 yards in this private golf course, which is open to the public. The course was designed by Benjamin J. Wihry. There's a clubhouse and pro shop for all your associated golfing needs.

SHELBY GOLF COURSE

2021 Fatherland St., 615/862-8474, www.nashville.gov
HOURS: Vary based on season
COST: $16/18 holes
Map 3

The first public golf course in Music City is still one of Nashville's favorites. Located in the popular East Nashville Shelby Park, the 18-hole

course is particularly friendly to new golfers. It also hosts a respected junior golf program. The par 72 course has the same rates on weekends as weekdays. Tee times can be reserved up to seven days in advance.

TED RHODES GOLF COURSE

1901 Ed Temple Blvd., 615/862-8463, www.nashville.gov
HOURS: Vary based on season
COST: Mon.-Fri. $24/18 holes, Sat.-Sun. $26/18 holes
Map 6

In 1992 this North Nashville golf course was renovated, thanks to a design by Gary Roger Baird. The greens run along the banks of the Cumberland River, which means there are pretty views and lots of wildlife alongside the putting greens and fairways. The 18-hole course is an easy one to walk, making it a good choice for a little extra exercise. Tee times can be reserved up to seven days in advance.

TWO RIVERS GOLF COURSE

2235 Two Rivers Pkwy., 615/889-2675,
www.nashville.gov
HOURS: Vary based on season
COST: Mon.-Fri. $24/18 holes, Sat.-Sun. $26/18 holes
Map 4

Near both the airport and the Music Valley Opryland complex is this public 18-hole course. It has great views of the downtown skyline and a design that is challenging for even the most experienced golfer. Two Rivers' golf pros offer affordable lessons ($99 for five weeks) lessons for beginners at the beginning of the season.

WATER SPORTS
ELM HILL MARINA

3361 Bell Rd., Nashville, 615/889-5363,
www.elmhillmarina.com
HOURS: Office and boat house Mon.-Sun. 8am-7pm
COST: Boat rental $65-315
Map 6

Boating, fishing, and water sports are among the most popular activities on J. Percy Priest Lake. Elm Hill Marina is the marina closest to downtown Nashville, and as a result, it is one of the busiest. Lots of locals rent slips and have their boats docked here. But even if you don't have a boat of your own, you can rent one. The Pontoon boats ($220 for a half day) are popular with the party crowd. Elm Hill also has an out-doors store with essentials like sunscreen and key rings that float, and a restaurant with typi-cal seaside fair.

J. PERCY PRIEST LAKE

3737 Bell Rd., Nashville, 615/889-1975,
www.lrn.usace.army.mil
HOURS: Daily 24 hours
COST: Free
Map 6

J. Percy Priest Lake was created in the mid-1960s when the Army Corps of Engineers dammed the Stones River east of Nashville. The lake is a favorite destination for fishing, boating, swimming, paddling, and picnicking. The lake sprawls over 14,200 acres. Access is provided through more than a dozen different parks and access areas on all sides of the lake. Many of these areas bear the names of communities that were inundated when the lake was created.

The lake's visitors center, operated by the Army Corps of Engineers, is located at the site of the dam that created the lake. The visitors center is located on Bell Road at exit 219 off I-40 heading east from downtown Nashville. There you will find a lake overlook and one of four marinas on the lake.

NASHVILLE PADDLE CO.

www.nashvillepaddle.com
COST: $25 for two-hour rental, $40 for four-hour rental, $80 private lessons

Middle Tennessee's flatwater lakes and riv-ers are perfect for paddling. Nashville Paddle Co. offers stand-up paddleboard (SUP) in-struction and lessons for both adults and kids. Lessons take place at one of several launches on Percy Priest or Old Hickory Lakes or on the Cumberland River. Rentals are also available for those who want to take boards and go for a weekend. All reservations are made online. With a local yoga teacher, Nashville Paddle Co. offers SUP yoga as well as PaddleFit classes, which are workouts that use both land and water to get your core in tip-top shape.

NASHVILLE SHORES

4001 Bell Rd., Nashville, 615/889-7050,
www.nashvilleshores.com
HOURS: Vary by season
COST: $32 adults, $27 seniors and children under 48 inches
Map 6

Nashville Shores is a great destination for a hot summer day. This water and amuse-ment park features miles of sandy beaches along the shore of J. Percy Priest Lake, pools, waterslides, and water sports. Admission to the park includes the opportunity to take a 45-minute lake cruise on *The Shoreliner,* which looks like an old steamboat and has a paddlewheel in the back.

OLD HICKORY LAKE

876 Burnett Rd., Old Hickory, 615/822-4846,
www.lrn.usace.army.mil
HOURS: Daily 24 hours
COST: Free
Map 6

One of two lakes formed by the damming of the Cumberland River (the other is Percy Priest), Old Hickory is named after President Andrew Jackson, whose plantation was nearby. The lake includes eight marinas, an arboretum, and more than 40 places to launch a boat (or paddleboard) and get out on the water. There are beaches, picnic areas, and sailboat marinas, as well as two campgrounds.

SUP MUSIC CITY

J. Percy Priest Lake, 3737 Bell Rd., Nashville,
808/255-8002, http://supmusiccity.com
HOURS: By appointment only
COST: $35 for two hours, $80 for half day
Map 6

Hawaii transplant Chip Cathey teaches stand-up paddleboarding (SUP) on J. Percy Priest Lake, both in private lessons and group set-tings. Cathey is a knowledgeable waterman who can get new paddlers up and moving. Racing training, corporate training, and other packages are also available for those who want to take their paddling to the next level.

COURTESY OF NASHVILLE SHORES

Nashville Shores is a great place to cool off in the hot summer.

TIP-A-CANOE
1279 Hwy 70, Kingston Springs, 800/550-5810,
www.tip-a-canoe.com
HOURS: Vary by season
COST: $50 (approx.) for two hours for two people
`Map 6`

Tip-a-Canoe has been offering canoe and kayak rentals on the Harpeth River on the west side of town since before the Narrows of the Harpeth was a state park. All that experience has paid off. Boat rentals include shuttle service from where you get off the river back to the beginning where your car is parked. Shuttles are also available (for a fee) for those who have their own boats. The Harpeth is typically a Class I river, but some times of the year is a Class II. If you have concerns about your paddling ability, call ahead for river conditions.

WAVE COUNTRY
2320 Two Rivers Pkwy., 615/885-1052,
www.nashville.gov/parks
HOURS: Mon.-Thurs. 11am-5pm, Fri.-Sat. 10am-6pm,
Sun. 11am-6pm
COST: $12 adults, $10 children ages 3-12
`Map 4`

When the summer gets hot, as it does in Tennessee, locals line up to take their kids to Wave Country. Located near Music Valley, this water park has exciting slides, a wave pool, and sand volleyball courts, as well as a play area for smaller kids. Wave Country is managed by the city parks commission.

SPECTATOR SPORTS
Baseball
◖ NASHVILLE SOUNDS
534 Chestnut St., 615/690-4487,
www.nashvillesounds.com
HOURS: Box office Mon.-Fri. 9am-6pm
COST: Reserved game day $14, advance $12; general admission game day $10, advance $8; military discounts available
`Map 5`

What an appropriate name for a minor-league baseball team in Music City. The Sounds are a AAA affiliate of the Milwaukee Brewers, and they play about 30 home games a year

June-October. Before the 2008 season opener, the team invested $1 million in stopgap improvements to the aging Greer Stadium, their home in South Nashville. Finding a new home for the Sounds is an ongoing topic of conversation around town. Wherever they go, the guitar-shaped scoreboard better go with them. There's an alcohol-free section of the stadium, which often appeals to families with small kids.

Football
NASHVILLE KANGAROOS
3500 West End Ave., 615/403-7377, http://nashvillekangaroos.org
HOURS: Varies by game
COST: Free
`Map 6`

The most distinctive brand of football played in Nashville is Australian rules. The Nashville Kangaroos were founded in 1997 and were one of the first Australian football teams in the United States. The "Roos" play at Elmington Park and sometimes practice with Vanderbilt's own Aussie rules squad. One of the missions of the club is to promote cultural understanding and exchange, so the social calendar can be just as grueling as the sports one. The Roos also sponsor a women's netball team.

NASHVILLE STORM
1800 Stratford Ave., www.nashvillestormonline.com
HOURS: Apr.-Aug.
COST: $10 adults, free for children ages 14 and under
`Map 3`

For a different football experience than the NFL's Titans, head to East Nashville's Stratford High School and catch a home game of the minor-league Storm. The team is composed of amateur and former pro players and has won championship titles several years in a row.

TENNESSEE TITANS
LP Field, 1 Titans Way, 615/565-4000, www.titans-online.com
HOURS: Varies by game
COST: Varies by game
`Map 1`

You simply cannot miss 68,000-seat LP Field,

home of the Tennessee Titans. The stadium, which was finished in 1999 and renovated after the 2010 flood, towers on the east bank of the Cumberland River, directly opposite downtown. Since their move to the stadium in 1999, the Titans have sold out almost every home game. They play September-December. Tickets sell out early—often months in advance. If you want to see a game on short notice, your best bet is the online NFL ticket exchange, where season ticket holders can sell their seats to games they don't want to attend.

Ice Hockey
NASHVILLE PREDATORS
501 Broadway, 615/770-2344, http://predators.nhl.com
HOURS: Varies by game
COST: $20-350
`Map 1`

Nashville celebrated the 10th anniversary of its National Hockey League franchise, the Predators, in 2008. It was a sweet victory for fans, who fought to keep the team in the city in the face of lackluster support from the community with a "Save the Predators" campaign. The Predators play in the 20,000-seat Bridgestone Arena, located on Broadway in the heart of downtown. Home games include live country music performances and other activities for the fans. The regular season begins in October and ends in early April.

TOURS
GENERAL JACKSON SHOWBOAT
2812 Opryland Dr., 615/458-3900, www.generaljackson.com
HOURS: Show times generally daily noon and 7pm
COST: $57-91
`Map 4`

Gaylord Opryland's General Jackson Showboat offers campy, big-budget-style musical shows on the stage of a giant riverboat as it lumbers down the Cumberland River. Show dates and times vary by season, but typically there are midday lunch and evening dinner cruises. A smaller boat, the *Music City Queen,* offers tailgating cruises before Titans football games. Because of the meal and the live entertainment,

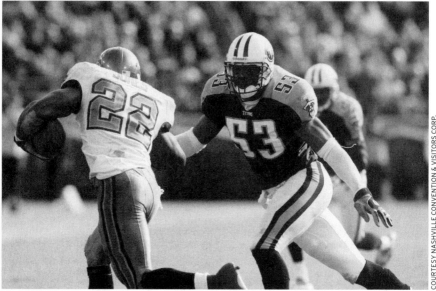

COURTESY NASHVILLE CONVENTION & VISITORS CORP.

The NFL's Tennessee Titans are part of Nashville's fabric.

these cruises aren't necessarily the best way to see the river, as you're focused on the stage, rather than the scenery.

GRAY LINE TOURS

2416 Music Valley Dr., 615/883-5555 or 800/251-1864
HOURS: Vary depending on tour
COST: $40-47 adults, $20-24 children
Map 4

Nashville's largest tour company, Gray Line, offers more than 12 different sightseeing tours of the city. The three-hour Discover Nashville tour includes entrance to the Ryman Auditorium, the Country Music Hall of Fame, and stops at other city landmarks. The three-hour Homes of the Stars tour takes you past the homes of stars including Alan Jackson, Vince Gill, Dolly Parton, and the late Tammy Wynette. There is also a one-hour downtown trolley tour and a downtown walking tour.

NASH TRASH TOURS

Meeting point: 900 Rosa Parks Blvd., 615/226-7300 or 800/342-2123, www.nashtrash.com
HOURS: Generally daily 11am and 2:30pm
COST: $32
Map 1

Nashville's most notorious tour guides are Sheri Lynn and Brenda Kay Jugg, sisters who ferry good-humored tourists around town in a big pink school bus. The Nash Trash Tour is a raunchy, rollicking, rib-tickling tour of city attractions, some of which you won't even find in this guidebook. Be prepared to be the butt of some of the jokes yourself—their "I Got Trashed" T-shirts have a double meaning. You'll snack on canned cheese, and there's even a pit stop to buy beer. These tours are not appropriate for children or adults who aren't comfortable laughing at themselves and others. As Sheri Lynn says: "If we haven't offended you, just give us some time." Nash Trash Tours sell out early and often. If you think you want this perspective on the city, make your reservation now. Tours depart from the **Nashville Farmers' Market** (900 Rosa Parks Blvd).

NASHVILLE PEDAL TAVERN

1516 Demonbreun St., 615/390-5038,
www.nashvillepedaltavern.com
Hours: Daily 11:30am-11pm
COST: Mon.-Thurs. $325, Fri.-Sat. $400
Map 2

Have 15 friends and a taste for beer? Then the Nashville Pedal Tavern is for you. You board what is basically a giant group bicycle and pedal together to move forward through downtown or Midtown, stopping at various pubs on the route. Members of your party pass out food and drink while you pedal. Each tour includes between two and five pub stops; at each spot there's a special for Pedal Tavern customers. Expect to be photographed by people on the street as you ride by.

SEGWAY TOURS

119 3rd Ave. S., 615/244-0555,
www.segwayofnashville.com
HOURS: Daily 9am, 10am, 1pm, and 3pm
COST: $75 per person
Map 1

Explore Music City atop a different two-wheeled vehicle on a 2.5-hour sanctioned Segway tour. You'll cover about 10 miles of ground, navigating past pedestrians and tourists stuck in car traffic, passing by many of the big tourist sites, including the Country Music Hall of Fame, Fort Nashborough, and Bridgestone Arena. Riders must be older than 14. Helmets and other gear are provided, as is pre-tour Segway training.

TENNESSEE CENTRAL RAILWAY

220 Willow St., 615/244-9001, www.tcry.org
HOURS: Tour times vary; museum Tues., Thurs., and Sat. 9am-3pm
COST: Around $32
Map 5

The Tennessee Central Railway Museum offers an annual calendar of sightseeing and themed railway rides in central Tennessee, including kids' trips, Old West shoot-outs, and murder mysteries. Excursions include fall foliage tours, Christmas shopping expeditions, and trips to scenic small towns. All trips run on the Nashville and Eastern Railroad, which runs east, stopping in Lebanon, Watertown, Cookville, or Monterrey. These tours are not just train rides, but well-organized volunteer-led events. You might get "robbed" by a Wild West bandit (the cash goes to charity) or taken to a scenic winery. The volunteers know their railroad trivia, so feel free to ask questions. The cars vary depending on what is available, but there is a car that doubles as a gift shop and another that is a concession stand, although you are welcome to bring your own food on the train. Trips sell out early, so book your tickets well in advance.

ARTS AND LEISURE

SHOPS

Nashville's new reputation as an "it" city has shown off the city's restaurants, music venues, and outdoor rec opportunities. But its shopping has gotten short shrift. It is true that Nashville is not a world-class shopping city. Fairly or not, locals still stock up when they head to New York City or Atlanta.

But if you like the thrill of the hunt, you'll find more than enough stuff to fill an extra space in your suitcase. The area malls run the gamut from discount to high-end, and most of the big-name chain stores can be found in or near them (think Nordstrom, Lululemon, Urban Outfitters, Gap, Forever 21, and many, many others). If you're willing to venture out beyond the malls, there are endless opportunities for one-of-a-kind merchandise, from antiques and vintage goods to the handmade.

One of the best all-around shopping districts is Hillsboro Village, the commercial district that borders Vanderbilt University in Midtown. Upscale clothing stores, used books, and trendy housewares are just a few of the things you'll find in this neighborhood, best explored on foot. East Nashville is mecca for those who crave handmade goods. Fine boutiques cater to the well-heeled in tony West End and 12 South.

And don't pass up the opportunity to buy Western wear in Music City. Seriously, don't go home without a pair of boots.

COURTESY OF THIRD MAN RECORDS

HIGHLIGHTS

LOOK FOR **◖** TO FIND
RECOMMENDED SHOPS.

COURTESY OF KATY KATTELMAN

Shop at Katy K Designs Ranch Dressing for authentic western duds.

◖ Where to Find the Ultimate Pair of Jeans: 12 South's **Imogene + Willie** sells denim that is made just for your assets. They're pricey, but custom-cut and designed to last a lifetime (page 126).

◖ Where to Find a Piece of Italy in Nashville: Named for the Italian grandfather the owner never knew, **Peter Nappi** offers high-end boots custom-made in Italy. The shop also has a stage for live music (page 127).

◖ Most Iconic Nashville Images: Since 1879 **Hatch Show Print** has been churning out letterpress signage for concerts, shows, and businesses. Take home a piece of the Music City aesthetic (page 130).

◖ Best Place to Browse for Tunes: Grimey's New and Preloved Music goes above and beyond the typical music shop with live music, helpful staff, and enthusiastic customers who love to hang out and browse (page 133).

◖ Best Place to Buy Something Other than Country Music: Jacky White's **Third Man Records** is a rock-lovers heaven, with music selected to fit the icon's favorite styles (page 134).

◖ Best Retail Strips for the Etsy Set: East Nashville's **1108 Shops at Woodland** and **Shoppes on Fatherland** are chock-full of one-of-a-kind purses, neckties, jewelry, and all other things made by local artists (page 136).

◖ Where to Buy Iconic Western Wear: Yoked shirts and bolo ties are just costumes. If you want to take a piece of this signature style home with you, **Katy K Designs Ranch Dressing** is the place to start (page 137).

Antiques and Vintage Goods

ANTIQUE ARCHAEOLOGY
1300 Clinton St., 615/810-9906,
www.antiquearchaeology.com
HOURS: Mon.-Sat. 10am-6pm, Sun. noon-5pm
Map 2

The second retail location for American Picker Mike Wolfe, this store is almost a museum to American "things." All the pieces aren't necessarily for sale, but there are stories behind all of them. There are stories, too, about the building itself, which was the Marathon Motor Works car factory. Fans of the History Channel's *American Pickers* can find fun show T-shirts as well as rub elbows with some of the show's chief "pickers."

EIGHTH AVENUE ANTIQUES MALL
2015 8th Ave. S., 615/208-2414,
www.8thavenueantiquemall.com
HOURS: Tues.-Sat. 10am-5pm, Sun. noon-5pm
Map 2

Antiquers, pickers, and other lovers of vintage goods like to browse in this multi-dealer mecca of all things old. The folks with booths here specialize in dolls, jewelry, furniture, and other treasures of times gone by. There's ample parking, and individual dealers sometimes advertise sales on Facebook.

FLIP
1100 8th Ave. S., 615/256-3547, http://hip2flip.com
HOURS: Mon.-Sat. 10am-7pm
Map 2

Flip is a rare beast: a high-end consignment store that exclusively serves men. The selection is well curated, and the staff is helpful not only in finding something in your size, but also in helping you think about your style. The store stocks newer trends, but is focused on classic suits and other items that have stood the test of time. Flip refers clients to a tailor for the perfect fit.

GASLAMP ANTIQUE AND DECORATING MALL
100 Powell Place, Ste. 200, 615/297-2224,
www.gaslampantiques.com
HOURS: Mon.-Sat. 10am-6pm, Sun. noon-6pm
Map 5

Near the old 100 Oaks Mall in South Nashville, you'll find one of the city's largest and most popular antiques malls. It may be squeezed behind a Staples and next to a Home Depot, but its wares are anything but big-box style. It has more than 150 vendors and a great selection of all types of antiques.

HIP ZIPPER
1008 Forrest Ave., 615/228-1942, www.hipzipper.com
HOURS: Tues.-Thurs. noon-6pm, Fri.-Sat. 10am-5pm
Map 3

This East Nashville vintage stalwart is so packed with gems from days gone by that it can be hard to work your way around the racks. Working through the inventory is part of the fun, though. Come here to find men's and women's vintage clothing, handbags, and accessories. Goods are also available for rent, if you're in town for a music video, film, or other production.

LOGUE'S BLACK RAVEN EMPORIUM
2915 Gallatin Pike, 615/562-4710,
http://blackravenemporium.blogspot.com
HOURS: Tues.-Sat. 11am-6pm
Map 3

If your idea of vintage includes a little Goth-punk-horror, this is where you want to shop. The upstairs is a mix of books, DVDs, music, clothing, and horror memorabilia. The basement is where the serious fun happens. On weekends, Logue's Cult Fiction Underground Theatre plays select horror films and other cult performance arts.

OLD MADE GOOD
3701B Gallatin Pike, 615/516-8505,
www.oldmadegood.com
HOURS: Tues.-Sat. 11am-6pm, Sun. noon-5pm
Map 3

Locals call this indie craft shop "OMG." It's filled with everything vintage, reclaimed,

OLD SCHOOL

COURTESY NASHVILLE FLEA MARKET

You never know what you'll find at the monthly Tennessee State Fairgrounds Flea Market.

Folks rummaged their way through yard sales and flea markets long before there was a History Channel show that told them how. But even more people love the hunt for that long-forgotten gem thanks to *American Pickers*. The show's host, Mike Wolfe, has just two **Antique Archaeology** stores in the country, and one of them is in Nashville (1300 Clinton St., 615/810-9906, www.antiquearchaeology.com), in the early 1900s Marathon Village car factory. Head here to see some of the shows favorite "picks," plus new logoed merchandise and the occasional real find.

Other favorite retailers who know how to salvage goods include East Nashville's **Old Made Good** (3701B Gallatin Pike, 615/516-8505, www.oldmadegood.com) and **Hip Zipper** (1008 Forrest Ave., 615/228-1942, www.hipzipper.com).

If you'd rather sift through the dregs and dirt yourself, Nashville has no shortage of flea markets and thrift stores. The best bet for furniture, art, and other funky finds is the **Tennessee State Fairgrounds Flea Market** (625 Smith Ave., 615/862-5016, www.nashvilleexpocenter.org) held on the fourth weekend of every month at the Tennessee State Fairgrounds.

repurposed, and locally made, ranging from housewares to clothing and jewelry. The proprietors have an eye for the quirky and a decidedly politically incorrect sense of humor: Beware: You may see a four-letter word embroidered on

throw pillows. The shop is a hub of crafty community activities. Stop by for no other reason than to see the gold glitter floors.

SHOPS

WONDERS ON WOODLAND
1110 Woodland St., 615/226-5300
HOURS: Thurs.-Sat. 11am-6pm, Sun. noon-5pm
Map 3
Wonders on Woodland inhabits the front room of this East Nashville building. It is stocked with a well-curated selection of jewelry and other collectibles in a mix of mid-century and Victorian styles (yes, they can go together rather well). The jewelry comes in a great range of costs and styles. It is a great place to find a quirky gift for quirky people.

Books

BOOKMAN BOOKWOMAN USED BOOKS
1713 21st Ave. S., 615/383-6555,
www.bookmanbookwoman.com
HOURS: Mon.-Wed. 10am-6pm, Thurs.-Fri. 10am-8pm, Sat. 9am-8pm, Sun. 11am-5pm
Map 2
Even when Nashville was losing chain bookstores, its residents were never without somewhere to shop for something to read. This Hillsboro neighborhood mainstay is chock-a-block with used books, including cheap paperbacks and rare must-haves, as well as new books ordered specifically for local book clubs. The organizational system here can take some figuring out, but browsing is part of the charm.

EAST SIDE STORY
1108 Woodland St., Unit B, 615/915-1808,
www.eastsidestorytn.com
HOURS: Tues.-Fri. 1pm-6pm, Sat. 10am-6pm
Map 3
East Side Story prides itself on being Nashville's only all-local bookstore. That means owner Chuck Beard and his wife, Emily, stock the small shop specifically with works by local authors and about the area. The store may seem no bigger than your guest closet, but there's no shortage of activities, events, and passion about the local literary community here.

HOWLIN' BOOKS
1702 8th Ave. S., 615/942-9683, http://howlinbooks.com
HOURS: Mon.-Fri. 11am-8pm, Sat. 10am-8pm, Sun. 1pm-6pm
Map 2
One of the city's newest bookstores, Howlin' specializes in the literary offshoots of the wildly popular new and used music store: new and used, music, arts, pop culture, modern lit, poetry, magazines, and children's books. Like Grimey's, the music store that spawned it, Howlin' hosts many public events.

MCKAY
636 Old Hickory Blvd., 615/353-2595,
http://mckaybooks.com
HOURS: Mon.-Thurs. 9am-9pm, Fri.-Sat. 9am-10pm, Sun. 11am-7pm, extended hours in summer
Map 6
A Knoxville institution now with locations across the state, McKay encourages readers to return books, CDs, and DVDs for store credit after they've read or listened to or watched them. That means the giant Nashville location is always buzzing with sellers as well as buyers. McKay has a fun energy and is cleaner and better organized than most used bookstores.

PARNASSUS BOOKS
3900 Hillsboro Pike, Ste. 14, 615/953-2243,
www.parnassusbooks.net
HOURS: Mon.-Sat. 10am-8pm, Sun. noon-5pm
Map 6
A famous owner (novelist Ann Patchett) and the willingness to open a new independent bookstore in the "books-are-dead" year of 2011 allowed Parnassus Books to make national headlines. Located in a strip mall across from the Mall at Green Hills, Parnassus specializes in a well-edited selection, personal service, and literary events for both kids and adults.

The storytelling is just part of the fun at Parnassus Books.

COURTESY OF PARNASSUS BOOKS

Clothing and Accessories

BOUTIQUE BELLA

2817 West End Ave., 615/467-1471, www.boutiquebella.com
HOURS: Mon.-Sat. 10am-6pm
Map 2

Boutique Bella specializes in jeans. With a tremendous range of designers including J Brand, 7 for All Mankind, AG Adriano Goldschmeid, and Rock & Republic, and an equal selection of sizes, those looking for jeans that actually fit are bound to find their Holy Grail. The boutique is cute as a button, particularly the perfectly adorable dressing rooms. Sale racks are fantastic.

BULLETS AND MULLETS

1108 Division St., 615/678-7631, www.bulletsmullets.com
HOURS: Mon.-Thurs. 11am-7pm, Fri.-Sat. 11am-9pm, Sun. noon-6pm
Map 1

Can you think of a more fun store name? The inventory at Bullets and Mullets lives up to its name. Come here for funky dresses, trendy accessories, Hello Kitty goodies, and other kitschy must-haves. The inventory skews a little young, but the store is entertaining regardless of your age. There's a second location (168 Opry Mills Dr., 615/649-0858, Mon.-Sat.10am-9pm, Sun. 11am-7pm) in the Opry Mills mall.

DCXV

727 Porter Rd., www.dcxvclothing.com
HOURS: Tues.-Fri. 1pm-6pm, Sat. noon-6pm
Map 3

All around town you see "We believe in Nashville" murals painted on building walls with the elements of the state flag. This is the shop of the minds behind those signs. In a small space in the hip strip mall along Porter Road (this whole strip is a repurposed housing complex), you'll find creative clothing and accessories, lots of great energy, and, of course, the best T-shirts that show your Nashville love.

H. AUDREY
4027 Hillsboro Pike, 615/760-5701, http://haudrey.com
HOURS: Mon.-Sat. 10am-7pm, Sun. noon-6pm
Map 6

This boutique, owned by renowned singer/songwriter Holly Williams (Hank Jr.'s daughter) aims to fill a niche in Nashville for the well-heeled. Williams specifically aims at clients who would shop at Barney's, Saks, and Bergdorf's if those stores had local outposts. The shop is exquisitely edited with an eye for detail. Upstairs, there is a small loft space showcasing portraits of renowned musicians by equally renowned photographers.

HABIT
2209 Bandywood Dr., 615/292-9399,
http://habitboutiqueclothing.blogspot.com
HOURS: Mon.-Sat. 10am-5:30pm
Map 6

This little white cottage, with whitewashed floors and a bright country loft feel, satisfies casually sophisticated tastes. Habit's owners find the best of new and known designers, including Joie, Rebecca Taylor, and Ella Moss, to offer lovely selections to their discriminating customers.

HATWRKS
1027 8th Ave. S, 615/491-9009, www.hatwrks.com
HOURS: "Open Most Days," call ahead to confirm hours
Map 2

Owner/milliner Gigi Haskins creates fine custom hats for men and women, made on location with devices and machines that are as enchanting as the products themselves. Besides her own label of cloche, fascinators, boaters, porkpies, bowlers and fedoras, she carries an impressive array of some of the most trusted brands available, including the ubiquitous Stetson, historic Dobbs, and gorgeous Louise Green. She can also rehab your grandfather's favorite hat to make it new again.

◖ IMOGENE + WILLIE
2601 12th Ave. S., 615/292-5005,
www.imogeneandwillie.com

HOURS: Mon.-Fri. 11am-7pm, Sat. 11am-5pm, Sun. 1pm-5pm
Map 2

When this denim shop opened in an old gas station in 2009, it seemed like it was catering to a very niche market: a place to buy $200 jeans. But in the years since, the brand has thrived, getting into national retailers like Anthropologie, expanding into other product lines, and building a loyal local following, all by having products that are highly customizable and basically custom-sewn to fit. Come here to get your pair made; they're designed to last forever, and you're likely to see a Music City celeb while you shop.

JAMIE
4317 Memphis-Bristol Hwy, 615/292-4188,
www.jamie-nashville.com
HOURS: Mon.-Fri. 10am-5:30pm, Sat. 10am-5pm, summer Mon.-Fri. 10am-5pm, Sat. 10am-4:30pm
Map 6

Jamie has long been the height of couture for Nashville women who want something without rhinestones. Brands stocked include Prada, Missoni, Vera Wang, and Jason Wu, so come here for attentive service and killer shoes, but be prepared to pay for it. There's also a salon on-site for makeup and hair services.

MODA
2511 12th Ave. S., 615/298-2271,
http://modanashville.com
HOURS: Mon. noon-5pm, Tues.-Sat. 10:30am-6pm
Map 2

MODA's elegantly eclectic boutique features women's designer clothing, accessories, jewelry, gifts, and even a bit of locally made baby clothes. The atmosphere is bright yet minimalist, adding to the spacious feel, and the style is casual and the dressier side of casual. The staff is friendly and attentive without being intrusive.

OTIS JAMES
1300 Clinton St., 615/638-1469,
www.otisjamesnashville.com
HOURS: Call first; generally Mon.-Fri. 10am-6pm
Map 2

Housed in the old Marathon Motor Works

© SEAN HAGWELL

Find hand-crafted men's accessories at Otis James.

car factory, this men's shop hand makes linen, wool, and silk bow ties. You wouldn't think that'd be something in demand in our world of casual Fridays, but thanks to details like the hand-painted labels, these are some of the most coveted goods in town. Don't miss the made-to-order ball caps.

☾ PETER NAPPI

1308 Adams St., 615/248-3310,
http://peternappi.com/studio
HOURS: Mon.-Sat. 11am-6pm, and by appointment

Phillip Nappi, grandson of the shop's namesake, has made boot- and shoe-making an art (again). The shop's studio is in Italy, where artisans create footwear in the old-world style in limited runs with the highest quality vegetable-tanned leathers. But the retail location in Germantown is totally Music City. The reclaimed space is a workshop, store, and live music venue where customers may purchase tempting shoes, handbags, hats, and jewelry or place custom orders.

POSH

4027 Hillsboro Pike, 615/269-6250,
www.poshonline.com
HOURS: Mon.-Sat. 10am-7pm, Sun. noon-6pm
Map 6

One of the city's hippest clothing shops, Posh stocks a large selection of clothing for both men and women, as well as a drool-worthy shoe department, handbags, and other accessories. The back room's sales area is a bargain-hunter's wet dream. Regular prices can be on the higher end. Fashions are stylish and ran the gamut from casual to night-on-the-town. There is another Posh boutique in Green Hills (1801 21st Ave. S., 615/383-9840).

SCARLETT BEGONIA

2805 West End Ave., 615/329-1272,
http://scarlettbegonia.com
HOURS: Mon.-Sat. 10am-6pm, Sun. 1pm-5pm
Map 2

For decades Vanderbilt students have shopped in this boutique, which specializes in fair trade goods. You might think it is all

SHOP LIKE A ROCK (OR COUNTRY) STAR

By now you know that Music City's name is well-earned. Many bona fide stars call this fair city home. Not only that, but they buy clothes (and boots, don't forget the boots) for their stage and screen appearances in Nashville.

You can emulate their style without looking like you're dressing for a Halloween party by starting at these favorite shops:

If you have serious cash to spend, head to **Manuel Exclusive Clothier** (1922 Broadway, 615/321-5444, http://manuelamericandesigns. com), where you can have a bedazzled rhinestone suit made just for you.

If your stage career isn't quite justifying the custom expense yet, hightail it to **Katy K Designs Ranch Dressing** (2407 12th Ave. S., 615/297-4242, www.katyk.com), which boasts used and new Western wear, much of it designed by Katy herself.

Owned by a celeb herself (Hank Jr.'s daughter Holly) **H. Audrey** (4027 Hillsboro Pike, 615/760-5701, http://haudrey.com) is the choice for stars who want a more refined look, maybe for that talk show appearance.

How can you consider yourself a star until you have a custom-made signature hat? You can get that done at **Hatwrks** (1027 8th Ave. S., 615/491-9009, www.hatwrks.com).

Ecuadorian sweaters that smell like patchouli. There is some of that, but the merchandise is much more varied and sophisticated. Come here for pretty dresses, fun skirts, and jewelry in a variety of price ranges. Women's clothing is stocked in a wide cross section of sizes. Puppets, toys, and other gifts are also on the shelves.

THE PERFECT PAIR

2209 Bandywood Dr., Ste. I, 615/385-7247, http://theperfectpairnashville.com
HOURS: Mon.-Sat. 10:30am-5:30pm
Map 6

For women who love the pursuit of the perfect shoe, there's no better place than this well-edited shop. High-fashion pumps and flats meet the quintessential Music City boots on these shelves. The inventory is limited, so you leave feeling like what you've purchased won't be worn by every woman in town. The shop also stocks jewelry and handbags, but shoes are what makes The Perfect Pair worth stopping by.

TWO OLD HIPPIES

401 12th Ave. S., 615/254-7999, www.twooldhippies.com/nashville
HOURS: Mon.-Thurs. 11am-8pm, Fri.-Sat. 11am-9pm, Sun. noon-6pm

Map 1

The owners of Two Old Hippies lived the era of "Peace, Love, and Rock 'n' Roll" with gusto, and they do their best to bring those ideals to the present day, particularly the rock 'n' roll part. There's an actual '69 VW Microbus right in the middle of the store to set the mood. Shop here for vintage-looking band shirts and other Nashville-style gifts. Non-shoppers can noodle away on premium guitars or listen to live music.

UAL

2918 West End Ave., 615/340-9999, www.shopual.com
HOURS: Mon.-Sat. 10am-8pm, Sun. noon-6pm
Map 2

Bargain-hunting fashionistas cannot skip UAL. Designer samples of clothes, handbags, shoes, and jewelry are shoved onto crowded racks in this shop near the Vanderbilt campus. UAL stocks both men's and women's frocks, but the women's selection is significantly larger. Label-loving shoppers can find great prices on goods, but a little digging is involved. If you are typically a Target shopper, these prices might still seem high.

Crafts

HAUS OF YARN

265 White Bridge Pike, 615/354-1007,
www.hausofyarn.com

HOURS: Mon.-Wed. and Fri. 10am-5:30pm,
Thurs. 10am-7pm, Sat. 10am-4pm,
Sun. noon-5:30pm

Map 6

Both local knitters and those from out of town flock here. Haus of Yarn's large, well-stocked shop offers things stores in bigger cities don't. The shelves here are filled with some of the country's best selection of yarns. The staff and owner are avid knitters, so there are hundreds of shop models that help you visualize what the yarns will look like in a finished garment. Come in on Friday and meet Stanley, a sweet rat terrier rescued by one of the staff from in front of the store. He models many knit goods from the shop's stock.

RED DOG BEADS

1006 Fatherland St., Ste. 206, 615/530-1074,
www.reddogbeads.com

HOURS: Tues.-Fri. 10am-6pm, Sat. noon-6pm, Sun. noon-4pm

Map 3

Red Dog Beads has been a Nashville mainstay, although not necessarily in one location. The shop moved from Inglewood to an all-mobile setup to East Nashville, where the small space is jam-packed with beads, jewelry-making supplies, and finished goods. There are also class offerings such as stringing parties for all ages, wire wrapping, and finding construction.

Flea Markets

NASHVILLE FARMERS' MARKET FLEA MARKET

900 Rosa Parks Blvd., 615/880-2001,
www.nashvillefarmersmarket.org

HOURS: Fri.-Sun. 8am-6pm

Map 1

This flea market, located next to Bicentennial Mall State Park, and connected to the Nashville Farmers' Market, tends to be of the tube sock and T-shirt variety, not furniture and collectibles. Still, there are always a few diamonds in the rough, and the location can't be beat. It's not worth making a separate trip; instead, stop here on your way to the farmers market or Bicentennial Mall, and you may be pleasantly surprised.

TENNESSEE STATE FAIRGROUNDS FLEA MARKET

500 Wedgewood Ave., 615/862-5016,
www.nashvilleexpocenter.org

HOURS: Mar.-Nov. fourth weekend of the month Fri. 8am-5pm, Sat. 7am-6pm, Sun. 7am-4pm, Dec.-Feb. fourth weekend of the month Fri. noon-5pm, Sat. 7am-5pm, Sun. 7am-4pm

Map 5

Nashville's largest flea market takes place on the fourth weekend of every month at the Tennessee State Fairgrounds. It is a bargain-lover's dream, with thousands of sellers peddling clothes, crafts, and all sorts of vintage and used housewares, often at lower prices than you'd find in bigger cities. The fairgrounds are located on 4th Avenue, south of downtown. Admission is free; parking is $5.

Gifts

FABU

4606 Charlotte Pike, 615/383-0505, http://shopfabu.com
HOURS: Mon.-Sat. 10am-6pm, Sun. 1pm-5pm
Map 6

Fabu is located in a cute little converted house, and the owners have done a sweet job making that location work. Each room has its own theme or style: pop culture, masculine, kids, for the kitchen, and, of course, a room devoted to the holiday that's just around the corner. It is the kind of place to go to find something for the person that has everything, the folks holding down the fort at home, or a gift for yourself.

FIRE FINCH BOUTIQUE

1818 21st Ave. S., 615/385-5090, www.firefinch.net
HOURS: Mon.-Sat. 10am-6pm, Sun. noon-5pm
Map 2

Country music sweetheart Taylor Swift is one of the locals who loves to shop here. Fire Finch is the go-to shop for trendy jewelry, handbags, and accessories. Look here for candles, books, scarves, and more. The downtown location (305 Church St., 615/829-3533) also has a few home decor items as well.

◖ HATCH SHOW PRINT

316 Broadway, 615/256-2805,
www.countrymusichalloffame.org/our-work
HOURS: Mon.-Fri. 9am-5pm, Sat. 10am-5pm
Map 1

Part gallery/part storefront, Hatch Show Print is one of Nashville's best-known places to buy and see art. Hatch has been making colorful posters for more than a century, and their iconic letterpress style is now one of the trendiest looks in modern design. They continue to design and print handouts, posters, and T-shirts for local and national customers. Visitors to the shop can gaze at the cavernous warehouse operation and buy small or large samples of their work, including reproductions of classic country music concert posters. This is a great place to find a special souvenir of your trip to Nashville, or just to see another part of

COURTESY NASHVILLE CONVENTION & VISITORS CORP.

Hatch Show Print created the signature look of many classic country music posters.

Music City's history. Hatch posters are up all over town, including in the airport. At press time, the Hatch Show Print shop had plans to move from Broadway into new space at the Country Music Hall of Fame and Museum.

PANGAEA

1721 21st Ave. S., 615/269-9665, www.pangaeanashville.com
HOURS: Mon.-Thurs. 10am-6pm, Fri.-Sat. 10am-9pm, Sun. 1pm-5pm
Map 2

Pangaea carries clothing, silver jewelry, mirrors, lanterns, frames, and trinkets that are funky, kitschy, eclectic, and boho-chic. The wares come from the Southwest, Mexico, Asia, India, Nashville, and everywhere in between—and in almost every price range. The shop is chock-full of goods. If you're the kind of browser who likes to look at every little thing, plan to be here awhile.

PRETTY PRETTY POP POP

1006 Fatherland St., #201, 615/915-1172,
www.prettyprettypoppop.com
HOURS: Tues.-Sun. 11am-6pm
`Map 3`

Pretty Pretty Pop Pop may have a silly name, but the staff here is serious about its goods. They make all-natural, vegan bath, beauty, and hair products that smell and look as good in your bathroom as they feel in your bathtub. The fragrances are fresh, not overpoweringly perfumed. They are also made entirely in East Nashville and have that special East Nashville sense of humor. The bath bombs are a crowd favorite.

THRIVE

1006 Fatherland St., 615/944-1534,
www.thrivestores.com
HOURS: Tues.-Sat. 10:30am-6pm
`Map 3`

Thrive is a retail store with a cause. Owner Mark Wood decided to change his corporate life into one that had personal meaning and global impact. He began by making beeswax candles: a simple act that led him on a greater journey. Thrive, the store, continues to sell his locally made candles, but works hard at honoring the earth and its citizens with fair trade practices. Thrive stocks teas, organic chocolate, clothing, and other small things that can have a big impact.

Gourmet and Specialty Foods

BANG CANDY COMPANY

1300 Clinton St., 615/587-4819,
www.bangcandycompany.com
HOURS: Tues.-Sat. 10am-5pm
`Map 2`

Once a food cart hawking gourmet marshmallows around town, Bang Candy Company is now a candy store/coffee shop hybrid. It is *the* place to go for a sweet treat. The shop attracts a diverse clientele with Antique Archeology shoppers and local hipsters all lingering among the sweets. The marshmallows and caramels are handmade in-house, and include offbeat flavors such as absinthe and rose cardamom. Take home a flavored simple syrup for mixing your own cocktails.

THE BLOOMY RIND

501 Gallatin Ave., 615/429-9648,
http://thebloomyrind.com
HOURS: Mon.-Fri. 11am-7pm, Sat. 10am-6pm, Sun. noon-4pm
`Map 3`

The Bloomy Rind, located inside Porter Road Butcher's space, is the city's favorite cheese shop. Folks head to East Nashville from the other side of the river for handcrafted, all-natural American artisan cheeses. The stock includes a particular emphasis on Southern cheeses. Hours may be extended during the holiday season.

PEANUT SHOP

19 Arcade, 615/256-3394, www.nashvillenut.com
HOURS: Mon.-Fri. 9am-5pm, Sat. noon-3pm
`Map 1`

Walking into the Peanut Shop is a trip back in time. The floorboards creak; nuts are roasting, boiling, or getting candied; and everything is still measured on the original over/under scale. This was the first home of Planters Peanuts, and the original destination of generations of Nashvillians on coffee break (as it still is today). Though they specialize in nuts, there's also a generous assortment of candies and, in the summer, ice cream.

Home Decor

ASHBLUE

2170 Bandywood Dr., 615/383-4882, www.ashblue.com
HOURS: Mon.-Fri. 10am-6pm, Sat. 10am-5pm
`Map 6`

Imagine a shop that carries everything from fine jewelry to funky furniture to garden accessories, and that's AshBlue. People come here for everything from bridal registries to hostess gifts. If you're visiting Music City via airplane, you'll likely have to ship your finds home, because you're not going to want to limit yourself to what will fit in a carry-on.

DAVIS COOKWARE

1717 21st Ave. S., 615/298-4728
HOURS: Mon.-Fri. 10am-5:45pm, Sat. 10am-5:30pm
`Map 2`

Davis Cookware has been in business in this location so long that they still have a painted sign on the side of the building that advertises their business. Like that sign, it's a little old-fashioned. The shop stocks all the essentials of cooking and crams them into every nook and cranny. The layout isn't entirely organized, but that's probably because the owners do like to show customers around and love a conversation. This is the only store in town that stocks Lodge Cast Iron cookware, and they sharpen knives on-site, with skill. They also specialize in fine coffees and teas and have an encyclopedic knowledge on the subject.

GREEN WAGON

1100 Forrest Ave., 615/891-1878,
www.greenwagonnashville.com
HOURS: Tues.-Sat. 10am-6pm, Sun. noon-5pm
`Map 3`

The Green Wagon is East Nashville's source for all things green. Not just a place to shop for eco-friendly goods, although it is that, the store is a place where you can go to talk about what really will help the earth and what is just green washing. In addition to the education piece of it, the Green Wagon is a great place to buy handmade gifts and eco-friendly bath and body products, and attend local green events. It is located in a repurposed old house, which is apropos of the mission.

LOTUS LEAF HEALTHY MARKET

223 Donelson Pike, 615/884-9021,
www.lotusleafhealthymarket.com
HOURS: Mon.-Thurs. 11am-5:30pm, Fri.-Sat. 11am-2pm
`Map 6`

Lotus Leaf Healthy Market is a destination for their selection of loose tea and herbs alone. But there is more to the market. Find Green Pergola soaps and body products. Drink a cup of tea while perusing the shelves for supplies for healthy eating. This is the place to find ingredients for tasty vegetarian, vegan, raw, and gluten-free cuisine.

Kids

FAIRYTALES BOOKSTORE

114B S. 11th St., 615/915-1960,
www.fairytalesbookstore.com
HOURS: Tues.-Fri. noon-7pm, Sat.-Sun. 10am-6pm
`Map 3`

This is kid heaven. Housed in one-half of a cute little house, this bookstore has what children—and adults—need to express themselves in most every art form. The books are wonderful, but there are toys, games, and crafting supplies, too. Everything is touchable, and there's a secure play area for trying things out. There's a quiet room with a couch and a cup of tea for breaks for mom, and events, too: story time, art classes for kids and adults. Be forewarned: The other side of the house is home to the **Pied Piper Creamery** (114 S. 11th St., 615/227-4114, www.thepiedpipercreamery.com, Mon.-Thurs. noon-9pm, Fri.-Sat. noon-10pm, Sun. 1pm-9pm), an excellent ice cream shop.

PHILLIPS TOY MART

5207 Harding Pike, 615/352-5363,
www.phillipstoymart.com
HOURS: Mon.-Sat. 9am-5:30pm
Map 6

Phillips Toy Mart is the sort of toy store children and adults dream about. They not only have the nostalgia factor on their side with Lincoln Logs and Tinker Toys, but they also have the modern craves like Webkinz. Not to be missed is the model train setup in the back, which most likely will enchant grandpa and grandson into starting a train set together. Phillips is also old-school toy store enough to carry a full selection of kites, from beginner to stunt, and model-making supplies.

Music

ERNEST TUBB RECORD SHOP

417 Broadway, 615/255-7503, http://etrecordshop.com
HOURS: Daily 24 hours
Map 1

The Texas Troubadour, Ernest Tubb, founded his famous record store on Broadway in 1947. It remains an excellent source of classic and modern country music recordings, as well as DVDs, books, clothing, and souvenirs. At the back of the shop you can see the stage where Ernest Tubb's Midnite Jamboree was recorded and aired after the Grand Ole Opry on Saturday nights. (The Jamboree still airs, but it's recorded at the Texas Troubadour Theatre in Music Valley.) This location is great for late-night browsing after honky-tonking and eating on Lower Broad. The Music Valley shop (2416 Music Valley Dr., 615/889-2474) has more elbow room.

FANNY'S HOUSE OF MUSIC

1101 Holly St., 615/750-5746,
www.fannyshouseofmusic.com
HOURS: Mon.-Sat. 11am-6pm, Sun. 1pm-5pm
Map 3

In another city, Fanny's might be considered an unusual place. It's a woman-owned, guitar-centered music store with a vintage clothing shop mixed in. But in Nashville, it's par for the course. The staff can help you find a guitar that's comfortable for you to play, regardless of gender or size. There are new, used, and vintage guitars and gear, and the guitar-techs do a superb job of getting the road dings out of your axe. There are almost always folks sitting around jamming while you shop.

◖ GRIMEY'S NEW AND PRELOVED MUSIC

1604 8th Ave. S., 615/254-4801, www.grimeys.com
HOURS: Mon.-Sat. 11am-8pm, Sun. 1pm-6pm
Map 2

Grimey's is one of the best places in the city to go for new and used CDs, DVDs, and vinyl. You'll find a wide selection of not just country, but rock, folk, blues, R&B, and other genres as well. But Grimey's is more than a store: It's

© DOYLE DAVIS

Browse pre-loved tunes at Grimey's.

an institution. The staff are knowledgeable and friendly, and the clientele passionate and loyal. In-store live performances literally make the sound come alive. Music fans could spend hours here. Plan accordingly. **Grimey's Too** (1702 8th Ave. S., 615/942-9683), just down the block, is just as good as the original.

THE GROOVE

1103 Calvin Ave., 615/227-5760,
http://thegroovenashville.wordpress.com
HOURS: Mon.-Sat. noon-8pm, Sun. noon-6pm
Map 3

The Groove stocks some CDs, but mainly it's all about the vinyl. The shop stocks a good selection of new and used vinyl, and the folks behind the counter know what they're doing, so the records are in the right genre. In contrast with many stores for record diggers, this is a bright and airy place in a sunny house. Instead of smelling like dust and basement, it smells faintly of incense. They have a turntable listening station and host live bands.

GRUHN GUITARS

2120 8th Ave. S., 615/256-2033, www.gruhn.com
HOURS: Mon.-Fri. 9:30am-5:30pm, Sat.
9:30am-2:30pm
Map 2

If you want to make your own music, head to Gruhn Guitars, a guitar shop with one of the best reputations in the music world. Founded by guitar expert George Gruhn, the shop is considered by some the best vintage guitar shop in the world. For 50 years shiny guitars, banjos, mandolins, and fiddles hung on the walls of the Broadway storefront. In 2013 the shop moved, but the sign—and the quality—remains the same.

LAWRENCE RECORD SHOP

409 Broadway, 615/256-9240,
http://lawrencerecordshop.com
HOURS: Tues.-Sat. 10am-6pm
Map 1

Lawrence Record Shop has all new records, 45s, cassettes, and CDs, in descending order

of importance. "All new" is quite a trick for some of these media. The stock is almost exclusively leftover cutouts from dusty warehouses and rusty factories. This can mean some serious gems for collectors. It takes some digging—the store has four floors and is 180 feet deep. Opening hours are on the early side in comparison to most of the other Lower Broad businesses, so plan ahead and come early.

PHONOLUXE RECORDS

2609 Nolensville Pike, 615/259-3500
HOURS: Fri.-Sat. 10am-7pm, Sun. noon-6pm
Map 5

Phonoluxe Records owner Mike Smyth has always marched to the beat of his own drum. He never lost faith in vinyl, so in the 1990s, when everyone started buying CDs, he stocked up on LPs. Now that people remember why they loved vinyl in the first place, he has the stock to attract collectors and music lovers. The location is a bit out of the way, and the hours are eccentric, but this only increases the romance. Smyth pulls gems from his own vault every week, so it's worth checking back regularly. All genres are represented.

◖ THIRD MAN RECORDS

623 7th Ave. S., 615/891-4393,
www.thirdmanrecords.com
HOURS: Mon.-Sat. 10am-6pm, Sun. 1pm-4pm
Map 1

Third Man is a record label, recording studio, and record store all in one fairly small building. The idea behind the label is simple: All the music in the building has Jack White's stamp on it in some way. It's not a bad thing. Blue Series records are recorded by bands traveling through town, recording one or two songs, and available on 7-inch vinyl. Green Series are records of non-musical ideas: spoken word, poetry, or instructional discussions. There are the bands on the label, too, full-length LPs, and reissues of unusual and beautiful things.

COURTESY THIRD MAN RECORDS

Music fans can't resist a stop at Jack White's Third Man Records.

Pets

WAGS & WHISKERS

1008 Forrest Ave., back side of building, 615/228-9249, www.wagsandwhiskersnashville.com

HOURS: Mon.-Fri. 10am-8pm, Sat. 10am-6pm, Sun. noon-5pm

Map 3

Wags and Whiskers carries holistic dog and cat food, and offers self-serve dog washing stations. The washing stations are big metal tubs set at a height that won't break your back. They also stock a cornucopia of treats, including dog-safe bones in the freezer. Wags and Whiskers is a little tricky to find, on the back side of vintage purveyor Hip Zipper, in the basement, but it's worth the trip.

CAT SHOPPE/DOG STORE

2824 Branford Ave., 615/297-7877, www.thecatshoppedogstore.com

HOURS: Mon.-Sat. 10am-6pm, Sun. 1pm-4pm

Map 5

This store is an aminal lover's dream, worth the trip just to soothe the nerves and relax. The atmosphere is peaceful, and kittens and cats, available for adoption, roam everywhere. The staff is knowledgeable about pet issues and is extremely helpful. The dog half of the store features discounted high-end dog food, Thundershirts, and a seemingly endless array of dog paraphernalia sorted by breed.

SHOPS

Shopping Districts and Centers

1108 SHOPS AT WOODLAND
1108 Woodland St., 615/226-6670
HOURS: Vary by store
`Map 3`

A collection of quirk shops nestled near East Nashville's 5 Points intersection, 1108 Shops at Woodland is a good destination for one-of-a-kind goods you won't find at home. Expect locally made crafts, a bookstore with a local bent, home goods, vintage clothes for men and women, letterpress stationery, and more.

HILLSBORO VILLAGE
1808 21st Ave. S., http://hillsborovillage.com
HOURS: Vary by store
`Map 2`

Hillsboro Village, which runs several blocks along 21st Avenue South, is perhaps the city's best collection of boutiques, locally owned shops, and walkable option for a shopping outing. Hillsboro Village is located right next to the Vanderbilt campus and near Belmont's, so there is a student vibe. But the shops carry clothes, jewelry, books, gifts, cookware, and plenty of other stuff that wouldn't be at home in a dorm room. Hillsboro Village also has restaurants, bars, dessert spots, and the Belcourt Theatre.

MALL AT GREEN HILLS
2126 Abbott Martin Rd., 615/298-5478, www.themallatgreenhills.com
HOURS: Mon.-Sat. 10am-9pm, Sun. noon-6pm
`Map 6`

The finest shopping mall in Nashville is the Mall at Green Hills, an indoor mall located about a 15 minutes' drive south from downtown Nashville along Hillsboro Road. Stores include Macy's, Brooks Brothers, Tiffany & Co., and Nordstrom. The mall has spawned additional shopping opportunities nearby, including the upscale Hill Center, so this is a good place to head if you're in need of just about anything. Call the mall concierge (615/298-5478, ext. 22) to find out if your favorite store

is there. The parking lot can get packed on weekends, but the mall offers free valet service, which makes it tolerable.

NASHVILLE WEST
6716 Charlotte Pike, 615/352-5313
HOURS: Vary by store
`Map 6`

Nashville West is a better-than-average strip mall with chain shops like DSW, Costco, Marshall's, Target, and PetSmart. There's plenty of parking here and easy access to the I-40 expressway, so it is a reliable destination if you need something you forgot at home. Locals flock here for all the essentials, as well as to dine at **NY Pie** (615/915-1617, www.nypienashville.com, Sun.-Thurs. 11am-9pm, Fri.-Sat. 11am-9:30pm), one of the city's best pizza joints.

OPRY MILLS
433 Opry Mills Dr., 615/514-1000, www.simon.com/mall/oprymills
HOURS: Vary by store
`Map 4`

Shuttered for almost two years after the 2010 flood, the **Opry Mills** discount mall in Music Valley is the city's most-maligned favorite destination. Indeed, if upscale shopping is your thing, don't come here. But if good deals on name-brand merchandise appeal to you, or you are looking to kill time before a show at the Opry, Opry Mills is the mall for you. Brands include Old Navy, Disney, LEGO, Coach, Ann Taylor, and soon, H&M. There is also a 20-screen movie theater, IMAX, and Bass Pro Shop with all sorts of outdoor equipment.

SHOPPES ON FATHERLAND
Fatherland St. between 10th and 11th Sts., 615/227-8646, www.shoppesonfatherland.com
HOURS: Vary by store
`Map 3`

The tiny stores that comprise the Shoppes on Fatherland strip are hip to the point of humor.

It can be somewhat surreal, like an episode of *Portlandia*. But beyond silliness is a nice community of more than 20 local businesses primarily selling handmade goods and repurposed vintage items. There's a fun energy in these East Nashville businesses. Hours vary by store, but weekends are when you'll see locals strolling by and hanging out.

Western Wear

BOOT COUNTRY
304 Broadway, 615/259-1691
HOURS: Mon.-Thurs. 10am-10pm, Fri.-Sat. 10am-10:30pm, Sun. 11am-7pm
Map 1

It's all about the boots. Boot Country stocks a huge variety and organizes them by size. If you want boots, this is the place to go. If, in fact, you want three pairs of boots, this is the place to go, as they are always "buy one get two free." If you can't fit three pairs of boots in your luggage, organize a couple of friends and each get a pair.

KATY K DESIGNS RANCH DRESSING
2407 12th Ave. S., 615/297-4242, www.katyk.com
HOURS: Mon.-Fri. 11am-6pm, Sat. noon-6pm, Sun. 1pm-5pm
Map 2

Even without a ton of cash you can outfit yourself in some of the best Western designs at Katy K's. This is the showplace of designer Katy K's unique clothing line, which has been worn by the likes of Loretta Lynn and BR549. Ranch Dressing has a well-curated selection of vintage goods, plus clothing from other designers' lines. To find the shop, look for the giant cowgirl on the facade.

LUCCHESE
503 12th Ave. S., 615/242-1161, www.lucchese.com
HOURS: Mon.-Sat. 10am-7pm, Sun. noon-6pm
Map 1

A boot is not just a boot—at least not in Nashville, where boots are a status symbol as much as footwear. And in a town that loves boots, people really love Lucchese (pronounced

"Lu-K-C.") This brand has been around since 1883, but only since 2012 has it had its own retail shop in the Gulch. The boots (and belts and clothes) are made in the United States, and custom orders are taken.

MANUEL EXCLUSIVE CLOTHIER
1922 Broadway, 615/321-5444,
http://manuelamericandesigns.com
HOURS: Mon.-Fri. 10am-6pm, or by appointment
Map 2

The name says it all: Manuel Exclusive Clothier. Manuel Cuevas goes by just his first name, and he's the man who outfits all the stars with their stage-worthy clothing. The cowboy shirts start at $750 and jackets at more than $2,000, so this isn't the place for an impulse buy. This is the place to go when you've made it. You can stop by to admire the work even if you can't order your own Manuel suit. Yet.

TRAIL WEST
219 Broadway, 615/255-7030
HOURS: Mon.-Tues. 10am-8pm, Wed.-Sat. 10am-9pm, Sun. 11am-6pm
Map 1

Lots of the downtown boot shops are boots-only-type storefronts. Trail West is a one-stop shop for country attire, including hats, clothes, and, yes boots. The selection here runs the gamut, from bedazzled Western shirts with a yoke to cowboy boots that cost more than a planet ticket. There aren't a lot of locals who shop here, but if you want a Western-style souvenir to take back, the selection is ample and the staff friendly, although the prices are more touristy than bargain basement.

HOTELS

Locals sometimes lament Music City's status as a tourist mecca. But the upside of being a city that depends on visitors from out of town is that there is no shortage of places to stay and make your home base as you explore Nashville, whether you're in town for work, school, or fun.

Nashville has more than 33,000 hotel rooms, a number that increases annually, with options ranging from historic downtown hotels to standard chain motels to nontraditional places to sleep. Many hotels have unique Music City touches, such as recorded wake-up calls from country stars or guitar-shaped swimming pools.

CHOOSING A HOTEL

Because one of Nashville's drawbacks is lack of a robust public transportation system, that old saw—location, location, location—applies to selecting the right place to stay. If you're in town to see the Commodores play, you'll want to be near the Vanderbilt University campus. If you're attending a conference at the Gaylord Opryland, staying somewhere in Music Valley or near the airport will reduce your commute time by at least 20 minutes, but then you'll have a drive to see most of the city's attractions.

The bulk of hotels are concentrated in three areas: Downtown, Midtown (near Vanderbilt), and Music Valley (near Opryland), but there are options everywhere, from East Nashville to the airport. This chapter highlights a selection of top places to stay for every budget. For more options, plus a guide to nearby campgrounds, see www.visitmusiccity.com.

COURTESY UNION STATION HOTEL

HIGHLIGHTS

COURTESY NASHVILLE CONVENTION & VISITORS CORP.

For more than a century the Hermitage Hotel has been Nashville's hotel destination.

◀ **Most Historic Hotel:** Almost every elbow-rubber in Nashville's past has stayed at the **Hermitage Hotel** at some point, even Gene Autry's horse. You get a feel for the significance of this place by just walking in the lobby (page 140).

◀ **Best Place to Listen to Music without Leaving the Hotel:** The **Aloft West End** has a listening room in the lobby where better-than-average singer-songwriters play on weekday evenings (page 142).

◀ **Best Showers:** Ask anyone who stays at the swanky, eco-friendly **Hutton Hotel** and the first thing they'll mention are the showers.

The luxury stalls have showerheads in the ceiling with great water pressure and glassed-in cases that have to be seen to be appreciated (page 143).

◀ **Best Resort:** Other hotels in town, even the nice ones, are just that: hotels. The **Gaylord Opryland Hotel** is a resort, with enough attractions to allow you to fill a weekend without leaving the property. Set among the gardens are dozens of different restaurants and cafés, ranging from casual buffets to elegant steak houses. Hundreds of room balconies overlook the gardens, providing guests with views of the well-kept greenery (page 148).

HOTELS

PRICE KEY

$ Less than $150 per night

$$ $150-250 per night

$$$ More than $250 per night

Generally there are always hotel rooms available, but, as is the case anywhere, prices fluctuate based on the time of year. Summer and the Christmas holidays are in-demand times for Nashville hotel rooms. If you intend to come to town for the music extravaganza known as CMA Fest in June, book your rooms well in advance. Other music festivals can also put a strain on hotel availability, as can football (NFL and college) and college basketball games. The rates in this chapter are based on double occupancy in such high seasons.

Downtown and Germantown   Map 1

Downtown Nashville is small enough to be walkable, so wherever you pick in this area will be as close as you can get to attractions including the Country Music Hall of Fame and Broadway honky-tonks. Most of the city's official workings—the courthouse, offices, and the capitol building—are north of Broadway. The Hall of Fame, the symphony, and the new convention center are south.

COURTYARD BY MARRIOTT $$

179 4th Ave. N., 615/256-0900, www.marriott.com
This 181-room renovated hotel occupies a century-old downtown high-rise. It is located right next to Printer's Alley and is set midway between the downtown business district and Broadway's entertainment attractions. Guest rooms are tastefully decorated, with amenities including Web and cable TV, wired Internet access, coffeemakers, ironing boards, voicemail, and super-comfortable beds. There are two restaurants on-site, and guests can take advantage of valet parking.

DOUBLETREE HOTEL NASHVILLE $$$

315 4th Ave. N., 615/244-8200,
www.doubletree.hilton.com
Located just steps from the Tennessee State Capitol and near dozens of downtown office buildings, the Doubletree is a popular choice for business travelers. Rooms are spacious and bright, and even basic rooms have a comfortable desk and chair, coffeemaker, free Internet access, voice mail, and ironing boards. The hotel boasts a beautiful indoor swimming pool, business center, above-average fitness center, and on-site restaurant and coffee shop. Valet is the only option for parking at the Doubletree and costs $24 per day.

HERMITAGE HOTEL $$$

231 6th Ave., 615/244-3121, www.thehermitagehotel.com
The last of a dying breed of hotels, the Hermitage Hotel has been the first choice for travelers to downtown Nashville for more than a century. The 123-room hotel was commissioned by prominent Nashville citizens and opened for business in 1910, quickly becoming the favorite gathering place for the city's elite. Prominent figures including Al Capone, Gene Autry, and seven U.S. presidents have stayed at the Hermitage, not to mention some of country music's biggest names. Guests enjoy top-of-the-line amenities, including 24-hour room service, pet walking, valet parking, and laundry services. Rooms are furnished in an opulent style befitting a luxury urban hotel. Many rooms have lovely views of the capitol and city. With a nod to state pride, you can choose to have $2 from your room rate contributed to the Land Trust for Tennessee.

HILTON NASHVILLE DOWNTOWN $$

121 4th Ave. S., 615/620-1000, www.nashvillehilton.com
The all-suite Hilton Nashville is next door to the Country Music Hall of Fame, just south of

HISTORIC SLEEPS

Nashville is a city rich in heritage, with Civil War tales and musical history lore woven through its narrative. Fortunately, those stories aren't just reserved for tours and attractions. You can choose to stay somewhere that has a past.

Among the most famous historic picks for a hotel is downtown's **Hermitage Hotel.** Opened in 1910, the hotel has been at the center of historic events from the very beginning. In 1914 it hosted the National American Women's Suffrage Association's national convention, playing a role in women's right to vote. Presidents, senators, and movie and music stars have stayed there, and for eight years pool legend Minnesota Fats lived (and played) there.

You don't have to be famous to stay at the Hermitage, but having plenty of cash will help your cause. Rooms start at $300 a night, but check for last-minute specials on its website, when rates may dip to $200.

A restored 19th-century railroad station, **Union Station** is an example of Richardsonian-Romanesque elegance. Train schedules still adorn the lobby as decor, and the guest rooms have cathedral ceilings, stylish furnishings, and a subtle art deco touch, not to mention expansive marble vanities in the bathrooms. The track level of the hotel once held two alligator ponds, but today the luxury hotel is alligator-free.

Broadway's honky-tonks, and near the home of the Nashville Symphony. All of the hotel's 330 suites have two distinct rooms—a living room with sofa, cable television, microwave oven, refrigerator, and coffeemaker, and a bedroom with one or two beds. The rooms are appointed with modern, stylish furniture and amenities. An indoor pool, workout room, valet parking, and two restaurants round out the hotel's amenities.

HOLIDAY INN EXPRESS
NASHVILLE-DOWNTOWN ❸❸❸

902 Broadway, 615/244-0150, www.ihg.com

Located across Broadway from the Frist Center for the Visual Arts, the Holiday Inn Express offers a comfortable compromise between value and location. There is an on-site fitness room, free wireless Internet, a business center, and a guest laundry. Guest rooms have desks, coffeemakers, and two telephones. Suites have refrigerators and microwave ovens. All guests enjoy free continental breakfast, and on-site parking is available. The Holiday Inn is located about five blocks away from the Lower Broadway honky-tonk action.

HOTEL INDIGO DOWNTOWN ❸❸

301 Union St., 615/891-6000, www.ihg.com

Located in the restored historic American

Trust and Nashville Trust building, the Hotel Indigo is one of downtown Nashville's oft-overlooked hotels. This boutique hotel is on the north side of downtown, making it convenient to the Tennessee Performing Arts Center, the courthouse, and other government buildings. Financial problems have plagued the Indigo chain, but business travelers say this hotel meets their needs with high-speed Internet access and a nearby Fed-Ex business center. There's a small on-site fitness center, or guests can pay extra to use a nearby full gym.

OMNI NASHVILLE HOTEL ❸❸

250 5th Ave. S,
615/782-5300, www.omnihotels.com

Opened in early fall 2013, the Omni is the tall building adjacent to the new 1.2 million-square-foot Music City Convention Center. It is composed of more than 80,000 square feet of meeting and event space, more than 800 guest rooms, plus easy access to the convention center, the Hall of Fame, and other attractions south of Broadway. The hotel also features a rooftop pool with views of the city, a live music performance space, and the Mokara Spa, which offers several spa treatment options.

RENAISSANCE HOTEL ❸❸

611 Commerce St., 615/255-8400, www.marriott.com
The Renaissance is connected to what will soon be the old Nashville Convention Center by a raised and covered walkway. Located north of Broadway, it stands 25 stories, offering views of the city below. The Renaissance's 646 rooms offer Web TV, hair dryers, ironing boards, crisp linens, coffeemakers, and business services. High-speed wired Internet access and unlimited local and U.S. long-distance calls are available for a fee. The fitness center is next door to an indoor heated swimming pool, whirlpool, and sauna.

SHERATON DOWNTOWN NASHVILLE ❸❸

623 Union St., 615/259-2000,
www.sheratonnashvilledowntown.com
The Sheraton Downtown Nashville is a city landmark. The 472-room hotel stands tall above neighboring buildings, providing most guest rooms with views of the city below. Located in the middle of Nashville's bustling downtown business district, it is another good option for business travelers. The hotel has a fitness room, business center, indoor pool, and laundry and concierge services. Internet access and on-site parking are available for an additional fee.

UNION STATION ❸❸❸

1001 Broadway, 615/726-1001,
www.unionstationhotelnashville.com
One of Nashville's most notable downtown hotels is the Union Station, a 125-room hotel located in what was once the city's main train station. Distinctions include magnificent ironwork and molding, and an impressive marble-floored great hall that greets guests, contributing to what makes this one of the National Trust's Historic Hotels of America. One of Nashville's great old buildings, the hotel has high ceilings and lofty interior balconies, and amenities include a fitness center, wireless Internet, plasma televisions, complimentary morning newspapers, and room service. Travelers frequently make Union Station their home away from home.

Midtown and 12 South   Map 2

Coming to town for parents' weekend or a meeting with your record label? Then Midtown is where you want to stay, with hotels near Music Row and Vanderbilt and Belmont Universities. Music Row was once sleepy after five o'clock, but as the surrounding communities have grown up, this area offers easy access to the entertainment, dining, and shopping attractions of Hillsboro Village and its environs. The 12 South neighborhood is quaint, hip, and filled with restaurants and bars, shopping, parks, and ample parking spots. Accommodations, however, are more limited.

ⓚ ALOFT WEST END ❸❸

1719 West End Ave., 615/329-4200,
www.aloftnashvillewestend.com
This hotel has changed names and ownership over the years (it was once a Days Inn and then a Hotel Indigo), but it has remained a favorite of visitors to the Vanderbilt area. The lobby's café is more of a Nashville-style listening room than a traditional hotel lobby coffee shop. It hosts regular singer-songwriter nights, attracting locals who come to support their favorite musicians. The hotel offers free wireless Internet and amenities travelers welcome, such as dry cleaning and both self- and valet parking.

BEST WESTERN MUSIC ROW ❸

1407 Division St., 615/242-1631, www.bestwestern.com
This is a no-nonsense motel with an outdoor pool, free continental breakfast, Internet access, and indoor corridors. Rooms have cable TV, AM/FM alarm clocks, and coffeemakers. Pets are allowed for $10 a day, and parking is free (although it's typically easy to find in this neighborhood). The 75-room hotel is located a few steps away from the Music Row traffic

circle, *Musica* sculpture, and nearby restaurants and bars.

DAISY HILL B&B $

2816 Blair Blvd., 615/297-9795,
www.daisyhillbedandbreakfast.com

This 1925 Tudor home has a spot on the National Register of Historic Places. Tucked into a brick house near Hillsboro Village and the Vanderbilt and Belmont campuses are three guest rooms, each with its own European decor (Scottish, French, and Scandinavian). Amenities include fireplaces and a family-style breakfast. Cancellation policies differ during Titan game weekends and other big events, so check when making reservations during these times.

1501 LINDEN HOUSE BED AND BREAKFAST $

1501 Linden Ave., 615/298-2701,
www.nashville-bed-breakfast.com

Housed in a 19th-century Victorian house, this bed-and-breakfast has private baths in every room and other amenities that B&Bs sometimes lack, such as cable TV. This cheerful yellow-brick home on a corner lot has three guest rooms, each with stylish furniture and hardwood floors. One room has a private whirlpool, and another has a fireplace.

GUESTHOUSE INN AND SUITES $

1909 Hayes St., 615/329-1000,
www.nashvilleguesthouseinn.com

Located near Elliston Place and Vanderbilt University, the Guesthouse Inn is a pick of folks in town to take advantage of Nashville's great medical care. The hotel offers a free shuttle to nearby hospitals, including Baptist Hospital, Vanderbilt Medical Center, and the Veterans Administration Hospital. All rooms have microwave ovens, refrigerators, and coffeemakers, and guests enjoy free breakfast including made-to-order waffles. Suites include a sleeper couch.

HAMPTON INN VANDERBILT $$$

1919 West End Ave., 615/329-1144,
www.hamptoninnnashville.com

Free breakfast, free parking, and free wireless Internet make this chain hotel a popular choice for folks who want to stay near the Vanderbilt campus. Rooms are clean with good amenities for business travelers, and there's an outdoor pool for Nashville's summer nights.

HILTON GARDEN INN $$

1715 Broadway, 615/678-0149,
www.hiltongardeninn.hilton.com

Close to Music Row and Vanderbilt University, and just a quick drive to the Gulch or downtown, this hotel is appropriate for business or leisure travelers. Free wireless Internet, flat-screen TVs, and a 24-hour on-site convenience store means almost any need can be filled in a jiff. Suites are available, too.

◖ HUTTON HOTEL $$$

1808 West End Ave., 615/340-9333,
www.huttonhotel.com

Since its opening in 2009, the Hutton has become Nashville's eco-friendly darling. This swanky hotel near the Vanderbilt campus also offers an easy commute to Music Row and downtown, but regular visitors stay here less for the great location and more for the ambience. The lobby and guest rooms are stocked with well-edited art collections, and the entire hotel has an emphasis on sustainability, with biodegradable cleaning products and bamboo flooring. The bathrooms include sleek granite showers, which have a modern aesthetic and oversized, ceiling-mounted showerheads. Turn the water on, and you'll feel like you're in a serious rainstorm in the privacy of your well-appointed bathroom. The contemporary bathrooms also feature quality bath products and thick, fluffy towels. The pet-friendly property has all the expected amenities, such as flat-screen TVs and wireless Internet access. An added bonus is the likelihood of a celebrity sighting.

LOEWS VANDERBILT PLAZA $$$

2100 West End Ave., 615/320-1700,
www.loewshotels.com/Vanderbilt-Hotel

This luxurious 340-room hotel on West End Avenue close to Centennial Park and Hillsboro

HOTELS

COURTESY HUTTON HOTEL

Modern and eco-friendly, Midtown's Hutton Hotel is a 21st-century dream.

Village boasts 24-hour room service; luxurious sheets, towels, and robes; natural soaps; and spacious bathrooms. Guests enjoy in-room tea kettles and top-of-the-line coffee, evening turndown service, and free high-speed Internet access. Many rooms have views of the Nashville skyline; premium rooms provide guests with access to the concierge lounge, with continental breakfast and evening hors d'oeuvres and a cash bar. All guests can enjoy a fine fitness room, spa, art gallery, and gift shop. In 2013 the hotel underwent a massive renovation, which included public areas and guest rooms, as well as the addition of a new restaurant.

MARRIOTT NASHVILLE VANDERBILT ❸❸❸

2555 West End Ave., 615/321-1300,
www.marriottvanderbilt.com

You can't get closer to Vanderbilt University than the Marriott Nashville Vanderbilt. Set on the northern end of the university campus, the Marriott has 301 guest rooms, six suites, and plenty of meeting space. It is located across West End Avenue from Centennial Park, home of the Parthenon, and a few steps from Vanderbilt's football stadium. There is an indoor pool, full-service restaurant, concierge lounge, ATM, and business center. Plan ahead if you want a room during a Vanderbilt game weekend or parents' weekend.

MUSIC CITY HOSTEL ❸

1809 Patterson St., 615/692-1277,
www.musiccityhostel.com

The Music City Hostel is located among doctors' offices, restaurants, and commercial buildings in between downtown and Vanderbilt. The low-slung, 1970s-style building looks like nothing much on the outside, but inside it is cheerful, welcoming, and a comfortable home base for budget travelers. The hostel offers the usual dorm-style bunk-bed accommodations, as well as a handful of private apartments. You can also have a private bedroom with private bath plus shared kitchen and common room. Common areas include a large kitchen, dining room, reading room, cable TV room, computer with Internet access, and a coin laundry. Parking is free, and the hostel is within walking distance of restaurants, a bus stop, car rental agency, post office, and hospitals, but a bus or car would be best for getting downtown.

12 SOUTH INN ❻❺

918 Knox Ave., 615/260-8015, www.nashvillehouse.biz
This sweet B&B has suites, giving you lots of extra room with private porches, private entrances, and, in the case of the King Suite, a separate living room. Unlike some B&Bs that lack hotel-style amenities, the 12 South Inn has free wireless Internet, TV, refrigerators, and other perks, as well as the home-style digs that separate an inn from a traditional hotel. Discounted rates are available for extended stays.

East Nashville
Map 3

Just on the other side of the Cumberland River from downtown, East Nashville is better known for its hipster music venues, innovative restaurants, and quirky shopping than it is for its hotels. But there are a number of places to rest your head in this neighborhood. If you're looking for a Music City experience that is more local than tourist, check out one of the following accommodation options.

THE BIG BUNGALOW ❺

618 Fatherland St., 615/256-8375,
www.thebigbungalow.com
A Craftsman-style early-1900s town house, the Big Bungalow offers three guest rooms, each with its own private bath and television. Guests have shared access to a computer, microwave, and refrigerator. Common areas are comfortable and stylish, with tasteful decor and hardwood floors. Hostess Ellen Warshaw prepares breakfast for her guests and sometimes hosts in-the-round concerts in her living room. She is also a licensed masseuse and sometimes offers discounted massage rates with the room. This is a pet-free facility; children over 10 are welcome. It is located about seven blocks from the Shelby Street Pedestrian Bridge (seen often on ABC's *Nashville*), which takes you to the heart of downtown.

DAYS INN AT THE STADIUM ❺

211 N. 1st St., 615/254-1551, www.daysinnnashville.com
Located on the east bank of the Cumberland River, the Days Inn at the Stadium is near LP Field, where the Tennessee Titans play. The hotel's 180 rooms have clock radios, cable TV, and wireless Internet. Some have nice views of the Nashville skyline. Guests enjoy access to a fitness room, indoor pool, and laundry facilities, plus free breakfast. There is a bar and restaurant inside the hotel. While not within easy walking distance of downtown Nashville, the Days Inn is just across the river from the city's premier attractions. Free parking is a plus, particularly during events when downtown parking is at a premium.

THE EAST PARK INN ❺

822 Boscobel St., 615/226-8691
A brightly painted Queen Anne-style bed-and-breakfast in East Nashville's Edgefield neighborhood, the East Park Inn is at the heart of East Nashville goings-ons. Two guest suites offer private bathrooms and elegant furnishings. Guests also enjoy a relaxing terrace and garden, comfortable common rooms, and delicious breakfasts of fresh fruit, breads, quiche, waffles, and fresh-squeezed orange juice. Afternoon tea or wine is served on the front porch, which enjoys a pleasant view of the city skyline. The inn is within easy walking distance from coffee shops and restaurants.

RAMADA LIMITED AT THE STADIUM DOWNTOWN NASHVILLE ❺❺

303 Interstate Dr., 615/244-6690, www.ramada.com
The Ramada looks unassuming from the exterior, in a location literally sandwiched between the interstate and an LP Field parking lot. This hotel has seen better days: The

HOTEL ALTERNATIVES

Not every trip calls for a traditional hotel. Sometimes the best way to see Music City is by booking a guest room, condo, or even a room at a farm. These options are often more economical than a hotel, particularly for groups, who may appreciate having a kitchen and not eating every meal out. International websites Airbnb (airbnb.com) and VRBO (vrbo.com) list options across the city. Many of these locations have the advantage of being in neighborhoods where locals live, rather than in tourist-heavy areas. Parking is typically free.

For more specialized non-hotel options, check out **Nashville Farm Stay** (615/425-3616, www.nashvillefarmstay.com), just off the Natchez Trace Parkway. This is an option for cyclists and others who want to experience Nashville's great outdoors (and pet a goat while in town).

Scarritt-Bennett Center (1008 19th Ave. S., 615/340-7500, www.scarrittbennett.org, $50) is a religious conference center near both the Vanderbilt campus and Music Row. There are 87 spartan rooms in the facility that can be rented like hotel rooms, and many standard hotel amenities, including wireless Internet, are provided. However, bathrooms are shared with other guests. The real appeal of Scarritt-Bennett is the lovely grounds and the meditative vibe you get from just being there.

rooms are in need of upgrades and the amenities are just the most basic. Some guests have claimed that room cleanliness is lacking. But the hotel's proximity to the stadium makes it a favorite of football fans, who can tailgate and walk to Titans or TSU games. Parking is pricey for guests—more than $40—on game weekends, but the location is worth it to some. The hotel also boasts a guitar-shaped pool.

TOP O'WOODLAND ⑤
603 Woodland St., 888/288-368,
www.topofwoodland.com
You'll be happy to call Top O'Woodland home during your stay in Nashville. This redbrick home on a corner lot is distinctive and beautiful. Features include a spacious wraparound front porch, original stained-glass windows, a turret, a Steinway baby grand piano, and lots of period and original antiques. The bed-and-breakfast is within five blocks of restaurants and pubs, and a short drive over the Cumberland to downtown Nashville. Guests can choose to stay in the master suite, with a king-size four-poster bed, working fireplace, private bath, and private entrance, or in Mr. Green's Cottage, a detached cottage with kitchenette that can sleep up to six people. The home has wireless high-speed Internet access, and a generous continental breakfast is served at your convenience.

Music Valley   Map 4

The area surrounding the Opryland complex is known as "Music Valley," although if you say "Opryland," people will know what you mean. This area isn't the city's most picturesque. But if you are planning to attend a conference at Opryland, see the Grand Ole Opry, shop at Opry Mills, or play golf while in town, this might be the best place to decamp. The area is convenient to the airport and is a quick drive to downtown.

BEST WESTERN SUITES NEAR OPRYLAND ⑤
201 Music City Cir., 615/902-9940,
www.bestwestern.com
The all-suite Best Western Suites near Opryland is a comfortable compromise between the luxury of the Gaylord Opryland Hotel and the affordability of a motel. Each of the hotel's 100 suites has a couch, desk,

HOTELS

COURTESY GAYLORD OPRYLAND RESORT

It's always warm and sunny inside the atrium of the Gaylord Opryland Resort.

high-speed Internet access, coffee- and tea maker, microwave, ironing board, and refrigerator. Rooms with whirlpool tubs are available. Guests enjoy an on-site fitness room, 24-hour business center, outdoor pool, free continental breakfast, and weekday newspaper. The Best Western is located along a strip of motels and restaurants about one mile from the Grand Ole Opry and other Opryland attractions.

COMFORT INN OPRYLAND AREA ❸

2516 Music Valley Dr., 615/889-0086, www.comfortinn.com

Located about two miles from Opryland, Comfort Inn Opryland Area has 121 clean, comfortable guest rooms with cable TV, free HBO, wireless Internet, ironing board, hair dryer, and free daily newspaper. There is free outdoor parking, interior corridors, and an outdoor pool. Pets are permitted with an additional fee.

COURTYARD BY MARRIOTT OPRYLAND ❸

125 Music City Cir., 615/889-0086, www.marriott.com

This 87-room hotel offers all the basic amenities, as well as a few plusses: It is close to the mammoth Opryland complex and offers shuttles to and from the resort. Convention-goers and others who are on a budget but attending an event at Opryland can save by staying here. The lobby and bistro restaurant were renovated in 2012. The guest rooms are scheduled to be updated next. At press time they were clean and serviceable, if not fancy.

FIDDLER'S INN ❸

2410 Music Valley Dr., 615/885-1440, www.fiddlers-inn.com

If you're looking for a clean, comfortable room, look no further than the Fiddler's Inn. This 202-room hotel is seriously no-frills, but it offers a solid Tennessee welcome to its guests, who come in droves to see the Opry and enjoy other Music Valley attractions. It's right next to a restaurant, and there's plenty of parking for cars and tour buses. Guests enjoy cable TV, free coffee and pastries in the morning, an outdoor pool, and a gift shop stocked with perfectly kitschy Music City souvenirs.

◖ GAYLORD OPRYLAND HOTEL $$$

2800 Opryland Dr., 615/889-1000, www.gaylordhotels.com

Said to be the largest hotel without a casino in the United States, the Gaylord Opryland Hotel is more than just a hotel. Completely renovated after the 2010 flood, the 2,881-room luxury resort and convention center is built around a nine-acre indoor garden. Glass atriums invite sunlight, and miles of footpaths invite you to explore the climate-controlled gardens. Highlights include a 40-foot waterfall and flatboats that float along a river. Service is impeccable. Press the "consider it done" button on the phone in your room, and any of your needs will be met. Guests can buy onetime or daily passes on the downtown shuttle for about $15 a day, and the airport shuttle costs $35 round-trip. Parking is $24 a day.

HYATT PLACE NASHVILLE-OPRYLAND $$

220 Rudy's Cir., 615/872-0422, www.place.hyatt.com

After the Gaylord resort, this is perhaps Music Valley's nicest hotel property, and if you ask for a room that faces the resort, you may even be able to see Opryland's famous holiday lights in season. This hotel caters to folks who want to take in the Music Valley attractions, with free shuttles (and friendly shuttle drivers) to the Gaylord resort, Grand Ole Opry, and Opry Mills mall. For a small fee there's even a shuttle that will take you downtown. The hotel offers a 24-hour fitness center, free wireless Internet, 24-hour room service, HDTVs, and other better-than-average amenities.

Greater Nashville   Map 6

Assuming you have access to a car, staying outside of the hot tourist neighborhoods can be the best way to save some cash on your Music City vacation (which leaves more money for great meals, good drinks, and priceless souvenirs).

ALEXIS INN AND SUITES NASHVILLE AIRPORT $

600 Ermac Dr., 615/889-4466, www.nashvillealexishotel.com

The Alexis Inn and Suites Nashville Airport is a comfortable and convenient place to stay near the airport. Rooms have all the usual amenities, plus guests get free popcorn in the lobby, a free airport shuttle (daily 7am-9pm), and free continental breakfast. All rooms have refrigerators, and most have microwaves. There is a business center on-site.

DRURY INNS AND SUITES $

555 Donelson Pk., 615/902-0400, www.druryhotels.com

The Drury Inns and Suites offers guests an appealing array of extras, including a free hot breakfast, free evening beverages and snacks, a free airport shuttle, 60 minutes of free long-distance calls, and $7 daily park-and-fly parking for locals and others not staying at the hotel. There is both an indoor and outdoor pool and a fitness center.

HOTEL PRESTON $$

733 Briley Pkwy., 615/361-5900, www.hotelpreston.com

Hotel Preston is a boutique hotel near the airport. Youthful energy, modern decor, and up-to-date rooms set this property apart from the crowd. Rooms are stocked with Tazo tea and Starbucks coffee, and there's a 24-hour fitness center. The "You-Want-It-You-Got-It" button in each room beckons the 24-hour room service, and whimsical extras including a lava lamp, pet fish, and art kit are available by request when you check in. High-speed Internet is an extra add-on. Naughty packages—like the "Ooey Gooey Night Out" couple's getaway

COURTESY HOTEL PRESTON

The Hotel Preston is not the average airport-area hotel.

with late check-out, wine, and whipped cream on request—prove that this isn't your parents' motel, though the hotel caters equally to business travelers with meeting rooms and a business center. Two restaurants, including the Pink Skip bar and nightclub, which features a sculpture by local artist Herb Williams, provide food and entertainment. In 2011 the hotel revamped its entire food and beverage program.

MILLENNIUM MAXWELL HOUSE NASHVILLE ❸

2025 Rosa L. Parks Blvd., 615/259-4343, www.millenniumhotels.com

Located in MetroCenter, just off the interstate and north of downtown, the Maxwell House is one of Nashville's overlooked, but reliable, hotels. The common areas are light, airy, and clean. Amenities for the 287-room hotel include a fitness center and outdoor pool, a business center, and a free shuttle to most of the city's main attractions. Free parking is ample.

SHERATON MUSIC CITY ❸

777 McGavock Pike, 615/885-2200, www.starwoodhotels.com

The Sheraton Music City is another good option for business travelers who want to be in the Music Valley area but don't need (or want) the full-on amenities of the Gaylord resort. This is a large convention hotel, with plenty of meeting room space, plus amenities for leisure travel, like both indoor and outdoor swimming pools. Spa services are available, and there's a free shuttle to the airport, which is a nice perk. There is a charge for wireless Internet access.

SPRING HILL SUITES ❸

1100 Airport Center Dr., 615/884-6111, www.marriott.com

Perhaps not the flashiest or most updated hotel in Music City, this is an affordable, clean hotel near the airport. Rooms have microwaves and refrigerators, and recent upgrades added new TVs and other improvements. Free wireless Internet is speedy throughout the hotel. Perks include free breakfast and free shuttles to the airport.

HOTELS

EXCURSIONS FROM NASHVILLE

Nashville tourism pros often tout the city's geographic location (just one day's drive from about one-half of the country's population) as one of the reasons Music City is such a good car-trip destination for vacation goers. That's true, but it also means the inverse is true. Nashville is a great place to launch weekend and day trips. In almost every direction there's something worth seeing.

It is true that Middle Tennessee doesn't have the high-profile reputation of, say, eastern Tennessee's Smoky Mountains. But that doesn't mean you should skip this area of the state. Tennessee's midsection is a road trip waiting to happen. The landscape is rural and pure relaxation. If you're planning to be in Nashville for a week or more, take the time to get in the car and explore some nearby attractions.

Chief among these must-sees are suburban Franklin and Leipers Fork, upscale communities that are Mecca for both history buffs and shoppers (how many destinations can say that?), quaint Bell Buckle, and the recreation paradise of Land Between the Lakes. All of them are easily accessed from Nashville by car. Much of the drive is on interstates, but, of course, taking the back roads is often more interesting.

PLANNING YOUR TIME

Tennessee is a long state (this is a point that is reinforced when you are writing a guidebook on the region on deadline). From tip to tip, the Volunteer State stretches 432 miles, so if you're

COURTESY OF VISITFRANKLIN.COM

HIGHLIGHTS

LOOK FOR ◖ TO FIND RECOMMENDED SIGHTS, ACTIVITIES, DINING, AND LODGING.

© MARGARET LITTMAN

Honor the Civil War fallen at Carnton Plantation.

◖ **Most Updated Blast from the Past:** The 1937-era **Franklin Theatre** has been renovated with modern amenities, but that old-world charm remains (page 154).

◖ **Place to Honor the Fallen:** The cemetery for the Confederate dead at **Carnton Plantation** is a solemn reminder of the area's past (page 154).

◖ **Best Place to Find a Treasure Worth Shipping Home:** Leipers Fork's **Serenite Maison** is chock-full of drool-worthy antiques (page 164).

◖ **Most Unlike Home:** The annual summer **RC and Moon Pie Festival** features folks dressed up as soft drinks and tasty baked treats (page 166).

◖ **Driest Distillery:** The county where the **Jack Daniel's Distillery** is based is dry. You can learn all about this icon of the South, but you can't sample it here (page 167).

◖ **Best Chance for Seeing Wildlife:** Land Between the Lakes's **Elk and Bison Prairie** is a 700-acre plot of land where you are likely to see these magnificent beasts at close range (page 172).

EXCURSIONS

planning to visit more than just Nashville's surrounding areas, you'll want to gas up the car and download an audiobook or two.

If you have limited time to explore, no worries. Just one day is ample (although will leave you wanting more) to check out Franklin, Leipers Fork, and Bell Buckle. A two- or three-day weekend is perfect for Land Between the Lakes, with time for boating, fishing, hiking, and more.

Franklin

For much of its life, Franklin was just another small town in Tennessee. The bloody Battle of Franklin that took place in the fields surrounding the town on November 30, 1864, was probably the single most important event to take place in the town. Like other towns in the region, it took many years for Franklin to fully recover from the impact of the Civil War.

Starting in the 1960s, Franklin underwent a metamorphosis. Construction of I-65 near the town spurred economic development. Today, Franklin is a well-heeled bedroom community for Nashville professionals and music industry bigwigs. The city, whose population runs around 62,000, is the 10th largest in Tennessee and one of the wealthiest

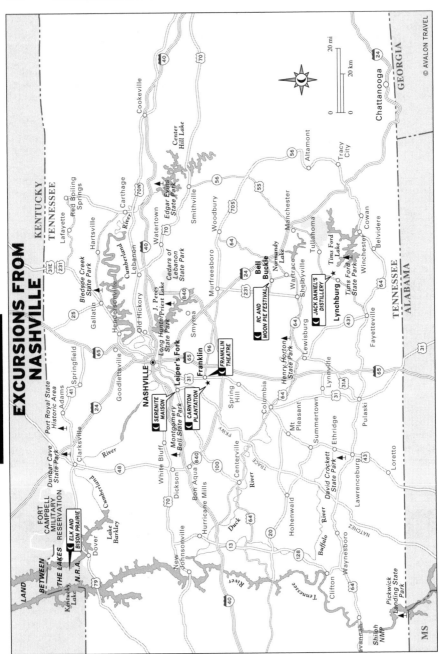

EXCURSIONS

EXCURSIONS FROM NASHVILLE

© AVALON TRAVEL

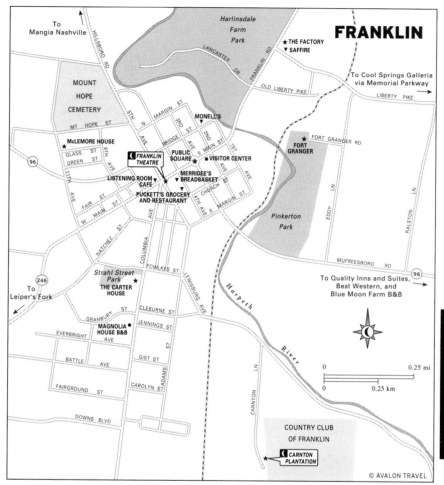

in the state. What sets Franklin apart from other small towns in the state is the efforts it has made to preserve and protect the historic downtown. The area is quaint and pedestrian-friendly. Its location only 20 miles from Nashville is also a major plus.

Franklin's attractions are all within a few miles of the city center, except for Cool Springs Galleria, a megamall located several miles out of town along the interstate.

SIGHTS
Historic Downtown

Franklin is one of the most picturesque small towns in Tennessee. Contained within four square blocks, downtown Franklin consists of leafy residential streets with old and carefully restored homes. The center of town is a traffic circle crowned by a simple white Confederate monument. The circle is fronted by banks, more offices, and the 1859 Williamson County courthouse.

The best way to explore downtown Franklin is on foot. Free parking is available along the streets or in two public garages, one on 2nd Avenue and one on 4th Avenue. Pick up a printed walking-tour guide from the visitors center on East Main Street, or download the free iPhone app.

The walking tour takes you past 39 different buildings, including the **Hiram Masonic Lodge** (115 2nd Ave. S.), the oldest Masonic lodge in Tennessee and also the building where Andrew Jackson in 1830 signed the treaty that led to the forced removal of thousands of Native Americans from Tennessee, Georgia, and other Southern states. You will also see the old city cemetery and the old **Franklin Post Office** (510 Columbia Ave.), as well as lots of beautiful old houses and churches, all of which remain in use today. The walking tour is a good way to become familiar with the town and to appreciate the different types of architecture. It takes 1-2 hours to complete.

Guided walking tours of Franklin are offered by **Franklin on Foot** (615/400-3808, www.franklinonfoot.com). The Classic Franklin tour provides an overview of the history of the town and its buildings. The *Widow of the South* tour is combined with admission to the Carnton Plantation and is a must for lovers of that popular novel. Other tours include a children's tour and the Haunted Franklin tour. Tours cost $5-18 per person.

Franklin Theatre

The newest gem in historic downtown Franklin is the **Franklin Theatre** (419 Main St., 615/538-2076, www.franklintheatre.com, box office Mon. noon-5pm, Tues.-Sat. 11am-6pm), a 1937 movie theater that had seen better days until it finally closed in 2007. In 2011 it reopened after an $8 million restoration funded primarily by donations from locals through the efforts of the Heritage Foundation. The renovation is spot on, bringing the theater, including its striking outdoor marquee, back to its former glory. Lush carpeting, detailed wallpaper, comfortable seats—everything about the theater evokes moviegoing in a different era.

But the Franklin Theatre isn't stuck in the past. It has many modern amenities that make it a great place to have a night out, complete with a concession stand that serves beer, wine, and spirits. Its menu delineates Jack Daniel's from bourbon and whiskey, as a nod to the locally made, favorite spirit. The Franklin Theatre hosts live concerts as well as films.

McLemore House

Five generations of the McLemore family lived in the white clapboard home at the corner of Glass Street and 11th Avenue in downtown Franklin. **McLemore House** was built in 1880 by Harvey McLemore, a former slave and farmer. Inside, a small museum has been created that documents the story of African Americans in Williamson County.

McLemore House is open by appointment only. Contact Mary Mills at 615/794-2270 or the convention and visitors bureau (615/591-8514) to arrange a tour ($5).

Carnton Plantation

When Robert Hicks's novel *The Widow of the South* became a best seller in 2005, the staff at the **Carnton Plantation** (1345 Carnton Ln., 615/794-0903, www.carnton.org, Mon.-Sat. 9am-5pm, Sun. noon-5pm, adults $15, seniors $12, children 6-12 $8, children under 5 free) noticed an uptick in the number of visitors. The novel is a fictionalized account of Carrie McGavock and how her home, the Carnton Plantation, became a Confederate hospital during the Battle of Franklin in the Civil War (how fictionalized is subject for discussion on the tours here).

The Carnton mansion was built in 1826 by Randal McGavock, a former Nashville mayor and prominent lawyer and businessman. Randal had died by the time of the Civil War, and it was his son, John, and John's wife, Carrie, who witnessed the bloody Battle of Franklin on November 30, 1864. Located behind the Confederate line, the Carnton Plantation became a hospital for hundreds of injured and dying Confederate soldiers.

FOR CIVIL WAR BUFFS

Fought on November 30, 1864, the Battle of Franklin was one of the biggest hits the Confederate Army took during the U.S. Civil War. By the time the fighting ended, more than 10,000 American soldiers had lost their lives, were wounded, or captured, all in about a five-hour period.

For those who want to learn all they can about the War Between the States, suburban Franklin is one of the best places to immerse oneself in all things Civil War. The history of the South comes alive, not only through occasional reenactments, but through cemeteries, former war hospitals, and other landmarks that help you understand the rigors of war.

Five of Franklin's Civil War highlights include **Carnton Plantation** (1345 Carnton Ln., 615/794-0903, www.carnton.org), **Fort Granger** (615/794-2103), **The Carter House** (1140 Columbia Ave., 615/791-1861, www.battleoffranklintrust.org), **Lotz House** (www.lotzhouse.com), and **McLemore House** (615/794-2270). Carnton Plantation, in particular, has accomplished guides who know enough to keep historians interested, but also can draw in those who aren't as familiar with the era.

As late as six months after the battle, the McGavock home remained a refuge for recovering veterans.

In the years that followed the battle, the McGavocks raised money, donating much of it themselves, to construct a cemetery for the Confederate dead, and donated two acres of land to the cause.

A new visitors center opened at Carnton in 2008, providing much-needed space for the museum and gift shop. Visitors to the Carnton Plantation can pay full price for a guided tour of the mansion and self-guided tour of the grounds, which include a smokehouse, slave house, and garden. You can also just pay $5

for the self-guided tour of the grounds. There is no admission charged to visit the cemetery.

Packages include discounts if you want admission to nearby Lotz House (www.lotzhouse.com), The Carter House, and Carnton Plantation. It's a good choice for hard-core history buffs but perhaps too much Civil War lore for one day for the average visitor.

Fort Granger

An unsung attraction, **Fort Granger** is a lovely and interesting place to spend an hour or so. Built between 1862 and 1863 by Union forces, the earthen fort is set on a bluff overlooking the Harpeth River just south of downtown Franklin. The fort was the largest fortification in the area built by Captain W. E. Merrill during the Federal occupation of Franklin. It saw action twice in 1863 and also in 1864 during the Battle of Franklin.

Many features of the fort remain intact for today's visitors. You can walk around portions of the breastworks. The interior of the fort is now a grassy field, perfect for a summer picnic or game of catch. An overlook at one end of the fort provides an unmatched view of the surrounding countryside.

You can reach Fort Granger two ways. One is along a short but steep trail departing Pinkerton Park on Murfreesboro Road east of town. Or you can drive straight to the fort by heading out of town on East Main Street. Turn right onto Liberty Pike, right onto Eddy Lane, and, finally, right again onto Fort Granger Drive.

The fort, which is maintained by the City of Franklin, is open during daylight hours only. While there is no office or visitors center at the fort, you may contact Franklin's parks department (615/794-2103) for more information.

The Carter House

Some of the fiercest fighting in the Battle of Franklin took place around the farm and house belonging to the Carter family, on the outskirts of town. The family took refuge in the basement while Union and Confederate soldiers fought right above them. Today, **The Carter**

House (1140 Columbia Ave., 615/791-1861, www.battleoffranklintrust.org, Mon.-Sat. 9am-5pm, Sun. noon-5pm, $15) is the best place to come for a detailed examination of the battle and the profound human toll that it exacted on both sides.

You will see hundreds of bullet holes, which help to illustrate the ferocity of the fight. Guides describe some of the worst moments of the battle and bring to life a few of the people who fought it. The house also holds a museum of Civil War uniforms and memorabilia, including photographs and short biographies of many of the men who were killed in Franklin. There is also a video about the battle, which shows scenes from a reenactment.

If you can't get enough Civil War history, consider one of the packages that offer discounts on joint admission to nearby **Lotz House** (www.lotzhouse.com), The Carter House, and Carnton Plantation.

RESTAURANTS

The best choice for baked goods, coffee, and light fare, including soups, salads, and sandwiches, is **Merridee's Breadbasket** (110 4th Ave., 615/790-3755, www.merridees.com, Mon.-Wed. 7am-5pm, Thurs.-Sat. 7am-9pm, $3-11). Merridee grew up in Minnesota and learned baking from her mother, a Swede. When Merridee married Tom McCray and moved to Middle Tennessee in 1973, she kept up the baking traditions she had learned as a child. In 1984, she opened Merridee's Breadbasket in Franklin. Merridee McCray died in 1994, but her restaurant remains one of Franklin's most popular. Come in for omelets, scrambled eggs, or sweet bread and fruit in the morning. At lunch choose from the daily soup, casserole, or quiche, or order a cold or grilled sandwich. Merridee's also bakes fresh bread daily; take home a loaf of the always-popular Viking bread. Merridee's attracts a variety of people—students, businesspeople, and families out on the town. The creaky wood floors and comfortable seating make it a pleasant and relaxing place to refuel.

Puckett's Grocery and Restaurant (120 4th Ave. S., 625/794-5527, Mon. 7am-3pm, Tues.-Sat. 7am-9pm, Sun. 7am-7pm, $7-10), the Leiper's Fork (4142 Old Hillsboro Rd., 615/794-1308) institution, has a second location in Franklin (and a third in Nashville). The Franklin shop offers traditional breakfasts with eggs, bacon, country ham, and biscuits, and plate lunches during the day. In the evening, order up a handmade burger (the locals swear that they're the best in town), a Southern dinner of fried catfish, or a traditional steak, chicken, or fish entrée. For vegetarians, they offer a veggie burger or a vegetable plate, as well as salads. Do not skip the fried green beans. The food is well prepared and the service friendly, and there's almost always a crowd, regardless of whether or not there's live music on tap.

The Cool Cafe coffee shop is transformed into **Mangia Nashville** (1110 Hillsboro Rd., 615/538-7456, Fri. 8pm and Sat. 6pm, $45), a New York-style Italian bistro, only on Friday and Saturday nights. You'll get an old-school five-course Italian dinner. There's a $5 corkage fee if you BYOB.

Always popular, award-winning **Saffire** (The Factory, 230 Franklin Rd., Bldg. 11, 615/599-4995, www.saffirerestaurant.com, Tues.-Thurs. and Sun. 11am-3pm and 5pm-9pm, Fri.-Sat. 11am-3pm and 5pm-10pm, $14-35) uses primarily organic and biodynamic ingredients. The menu sparkles with unique dishes such as the tender and flavorful Cuban roasted-pork appetizer plate or a simple salad of heirloom tomatoes. Entrées include upscale dishes like prime rib and ahi tuna. Their fried chicken is dusted with panko, topped with country ham gravy, and served with luscious macaroni and cheese. Saffire has an extensive wine and cocktail list, including organic choices. Take $4 off signature cocktails during happy hour (5pm-6pm), and on Tuesday night most bottles of wine go for half price. The lunch menu is casual, featuring sandwiches, salads, and lunch-size entrées. Or choose the "green plate" daily special, featuring local and organic ingredients. There is also a midday kids' menu with favorites like grilled cheese and chicken bites.

EXCURSIONS

Eat at award-winning Saffire.

boilerroomtheatre.com) is a professional theater company that performs seven or eight productions each year. Shows take place in a 120-seat theater at the Factory and range from light-hearted musical theater to dramas. The theater's season runs year-round.

Franklin's community theater is **Pull-Tight Players** (112 2nd Ave. S., 615/791-5007 or 615/790-6782, www.pull-tight.com). Performing in an intimate theater in downtown Franklin, Pull-Tight Players puts on about six productions each season, which runs September-June. Productions include many classic stage favorites.

Cinema

The restored **Franklin Theatre** (419 Main St., 615/538-2076, www.franklintheatre.com) shows classic black-and-white films as well as recent releases (although not first-run movies). Movie ticket prices are typically $5, and there are many kid-friendly flicks shown on the weekends.

Head to Cool Springs to find **Carmike Thoroughbred 20** (633 Frazier Dr., 615/778-0775), a 20-screen multiplex showing first-run movies.

FESTIVALS AND EVENTS
SPRING
The city's biggest festival of the year is the **Main Street Festival** (615/591-8500, www.historic-franklin.com) during the last full weekend of April. Local arts and crafts are the major draw of this showcase, which also includes food, music, theater, and children's activities.

The town's Rotary Club organizes the annual **Franklin Rodeo** (www.franklinrodeo.com), a weeklong event in May that includes a Rodeo Parade, Miss Tennessee Rodeo pageant, and a PRCA-sanctioned rodeo with steer wrestling and bronco and bull riding. It takes place at the Williamson County Ag Expo Park, and proceeds go to local service projects.

SUMMER
During the first full weekend of June you can join the Heritage Foundation on a **Town**

Set within an old warehouse, Saffire's dining room is spacious, with exposed brick and beams. The kitchen opens out onto the dining room, so you can watch the cooks work. With live music many nights, Saffire is a solid choice for excellent food in a pleasant and exciting environment.

NIGHTLIFE
Venues that sometimes offer live music include restaurants **Saffire** (The Factory, 230 Franklin Rd., Bldg. 11, 615/599-4995, www.saffirerestaurant.com), **Puckett's Grocery and Restaurant** (120 4th Ave. S., 625/794-5527), and **The Bunganut Pig** (1143 Columbia Ave., 615/794-4777). The **Franklin Theatre** (419 Main St., 615/538-2076, www.franklintheatre.com) has an impressive concert schedule, typically with affordable ticket prices.

THE ARTS
Theater
The **Boiler Room Theatre** (The Factory, 230 Franklin Rd., Bldg. 6, 615/794-7744, www.

EXCURSIONS

COURTESY VISITFRANKLIN.COM

The Factory is the place to shop and eat in Franklin.

and **Country Tour of Homes** (www.historic-franklin.com). Tours go to private and historic homes that are closed to the public during the rest of the year.

Franklin celebrates Independence Day with **Franklin on the Fourth** (www.tneventinfo.com), a patriotic family concert on the public square. The fireworks finale takes place near Mack Hatcher/Hillsboro Road.

During the last weekend in July the city celebrates **Bluegrass Along the Harpeth** (615/390-3588, www.bluegrassalongtheharpeth.com, free), a music festival featuring bluegrass, old-time string bands, and buck dancing.

The **Williamson County Fair** (www.williamsoncountyfair.org) starts on the first Friday in August and features agricultural exhibits, a midway, live entertainment, and competitions.

FALL

The **Franklin Jazz Festival** (www.franklinjazzfestival.com, free) is a two-day music festival that features jazz, Dixieland, and big-band acts in downtown Franklin. The festival takes place on the Sunday and Monday of Labor Day weekend.

WINTER

The Carter House organizes a **holiday tour of homes** during the first full weekend of December. During the second full weekend of the month, the city of Franklin is transformed into a bustling English Victorian town at **Dickens of a Christmas.** There are costumed characters, carolers, artisans, strolling minstrels, and unique foods.

The **Middle Tennessee Civil War Show** has become a favorite destination of history buffs each December.

RECREATION

Pinkerton Park (405 Murfreesboro Rd., 615/794-2103), just southeast of town off Murfreesboro Road, is a pleasant city park. Walking trails, playgrounds, and picnic tables draw dozens of town residents, who come to exercise or simply relax. A short hiking trail takes you to Fort Granger, overlooking the city. You can also take the Sue Douglas Berry Memorial pedestrian bridge over the Harpeth River and walk the six blocks to the town square.

Jim Warren Park (705 Boyd Mill Ave., 615/794-2103) is a large public park with baseball and softball fields, tennis courts, covered picnic areas, and 2.5 miles of walking trails.

Harlinsdale Farm

One of the most famous Tennessee Walking Horse breeding farms became a public park in 2007. **Harlinsdale Farm** (239 Franklin Rd., 615/794-2103) was a famed Franklin landmark for many years, thanks to a very famous horse. Midnight Sun, a stallion, was a world champion walking horse in 1945 and 1946, and all subsequent champions can trace their ancestry to him.

In 2004, Franklin bought the 200-acre farm for $8 million, and three years later the first 60 acres opened as a public park. It is a pleasant place to walk or picnic. There are plans for a visitors center, overlook, and extensive walking trails. For now, you can park, picnic, and look at the horses and the landscape.

Golf

Located a few miles southeast of Franklin, **Forrest Crossing Golf Course** (750 Riverview Dr., 615/794-9400, www.forrestcrossing.com, $35-50) is an 18-hole par 72 golf course designed by Gary Roger Baird. Just shy of 7,000 yards, the course rating is 77.8, and the slope is 135.

There are more golf courses in Cool Springs, a few miles north of Franklin. **Vanderbilt Legends Club** (1500 Legends Club Ln., 615/791-8100, www.legendsclub.com, $75-85) is a top-of-the-line golf club. There are two 18-hole courses at the club, as well as a complete array of club services, including a putting green and chipping green. Greens fees include a cart. Lower rates are available after 3pm. No blue jeans, T-shirts, or athletic shorts are allowed.

The **Fairways on Spencer Creek** (285 Spencer Creek Rd., 615/794-8223, www.fairwaysonspencercreek.net, $15-21) is a nine-hole alternative. The course rating is 64.6, and the slope is 105.

SHOPS

In many respects, shopping is Franklin's greatest attraction. Trendy downtown shops, the unique environment of the Factory, and proximity to a major mall make this a destination for shoppers. It is also one of Tennessee's most popular antiques shopping destinations.

Antiques

Franklin declares itself "the new antiques capital of Tennessee." Indeed, antiquing is one of the most popular pursuits of Franklin's visitors, and at least two dozen antiques shops serve to quench the thirst for something old. The town's antiques district is huddled around the corner of Margin Street and 2nd Avenue. Here you'll find no fewer than six major antiques stores. Other shops are found along Main Street in the downtown shopping district.

The best place to start antiquing is the **Franklin Antique Mall** (251 2nd Ave. S., 615/790-8593, Mon.-Sat. 10am-5pm, Sun. 1pm-5pm), located in the town's old icehouse. The mall is a maze of rooms, each with different goods on offer. Possibilities include books, dishware, quilts, furniture, knickknacks, and housewares. You can also follow 5th Avenue about two blocks south of downtown to find **Country Charm Mall** (301 Lewisburg Ave., 615/790-8998, www.countrycharmmall.com, summer Mon.-Sat. 10am-5pm, Sun. 1pm-5pm, winter Tues.-Sat. 10am-5pm, Sun. 1pm-5pm), whose three buildings house a vast array of furniture, quilts, glassware, china, and home decor.

Just outside the Franklin Antique Mall are at least five other antiques shops to roam through, including **J. J. Ashley's** (125 S. Margin St.,

615/791-0011, Mon.-Sat. 10am-5pm), which specializes in French and English country accessories, as well as European furniture. **Scarlett Scales Antiques** (212 S. Margin St., 615/791-4097, Mon.-Sat. 10am-5pm, Sun. 1pm-5pm), located in a 1900s shotgun house, has American country furnishings, accessories, and architectural elements arriving daily.

Downtown

Retail is alive and well in Franklin's downtown. West Main Street is the epicenter of the shopping district, although you will find stores scattered around other parts of downtown as well. Home decor, classy antiques, trendy clothes, and specialty items like candles, tea, and gardening supplies are just a few of the things you'll find in downtown Franklin.

Most shops in downtown Franklin are open by 10am, and many stay open until the evening to catch late-afternoon visitors. You can easily navigate the downtown shopping district on foot, although you may need to stow your parcels in the car now and then.

Bink's Outfitters (421 Main St., 615/599-8777, www.binksoutfitters.com, Mon.-Sat. 10am-9pm, Sun. 11am-7pm) sells outdoor clothing and equipment.

The city's best bookstore is **Landmark Booksellers** (114 E. Main St., 615/791-6400, daily 10am-5pm), found on the other side of the town square. They have a wide selection of used and new books, including many regional titles. It is friendly and welcoming, with fresh coffee for sale in the mornings.

Franklin Tea Merchant (430 Main St., 615/794-6311, www.franklintea.com, Mon.-Sat. 10am-5pm) has a wide selection of loose tea and various tea accessories. Toys old and new are on sale at **Main Street Toy Co.** (412 Main St., 615/790-4869, Mon.-Sat. 10am-6pm, Sun. noon-5pm). For the best in paper, gift wrap, and stationery, go to **Rock Paper Scissors** (317 Main St., 615/791-0150, www.rockpaperscissor.com, Mon.-Fri. 10am-6pm, Sat. 10am-5pm). **Heart and Hands** (418 Main St., 615/794-2537, www.heartandhandsonline.com, Mon.-Sat. 10am-5pm, Sun. noon-5pm) is one of several area shops specializing in crafts and home decor.

The Factory

Franklin's most distinctive retail center is **The Factory** (230 Franklin Rd., 615/791-1777, www.factoryatfranklin.com). A 250,000-square-foot complex of 11 different old industrial buildings, The Factory once housed stove factories and a textile mill. In the mid-1990s, Calvin Lehew bought the dilapidated eyesore and began the lengthy process of restoring the buildings and converting them to a space for galleries, retail shops, restaurants, and other businesses.

Today, The Factory is a vibrant commercial center for the city of Franklin. It houses a refreshing array of local independent retailers, including galleries, salons, candy shops, and a pet boutique. **The Little Cottage** (615/794-1405, http://thelittlecottagechildrensshop.com, Mon.-Thurs. 9:30am-5pm, Fri. 9:30am-6pm, Sat. 10am-6pm, Sun. noon-5pm) sells children's fashions.

There are also 11 different studios and learning centers, including **The Viking Store** (615/599-9617, www.vikingrange.com, Mon.-Sat. 10am-6pm, Sun. 11am-4pm), which offers cooking demonstrations and classes.

The **Franklin Farmer's Market** (The Factory, 230 Franklin Rd., www.franklinfarmersmarket.com, Sat. 8am-noon) is one of the finest small-town farmers markets in the state, featuring a wide variety of fruit and vegetable growers; cheese, milk, and meat sellers; as well as craftspeople and live music.

In addition to retail and learning centers, The Factory has four restaurants, a fish market, and free wireless Internet for your surfing needs.

Cool Springs Galleria

Cool Springs Galleria (1800 Galleria Blvd., Cool Springs, 615/771-2128, www.coolspringsgalleria.com, Mon.-Sat. 10am-9pm, Sun. noon-6pm) is a mall with 165 specialty stores, 5 major department stores, 20 restaurants, and a 500-seat food court. It is located a few miles north of Franklin, convenient to I-65. Shops include **Zales** (615/771-1886, www.zales.com), **Talbots** (615/771-1822, www.talbots.com), **Pier 1 Imports** (615/771-7884, www.pier1.com), **Pottery Barn** (615/771-0166, www.potterybarn.com), **Macy's** (615/771-2100, www.macys.com), and **JCPenney** (615/771-7743, www.jcpenney.com). The mall is found at exits 68B and 69 on I-65.

Near the mall is **Marti & Liz** (2000 Mallory Ln., 615/435-8125, www.martiandliz.com, Mon.-Sat. 9am-9pm), a shoe-shopper's bargain dream. **Happy reTales** (101 Creekside Crossing #700, Brentwood, 615/309-1835, www.happyretalesonline.com, Mon.-Sat. 10am-7pm, Sun. noon-4pm) is a dog and cat supply store that sends all profits to Happy Tales Rescue, a no-kill dog and cat rescue in Franklin. The store is staffed almost entirely with volunteers (the manager is employed). Besides all of the healthy food that one might expect at a boutique pet store, they also have a wide selection of pet and people clothing, a variety of dog treats for every purpose, and pet-inspired artwork.

Lebanon Prime Outlets

Bargain-lovers flock to **Lebanon Prime Outlets** (One Outlet Village Blvd., Lebanon, 615/444-0433, www.premiumoutlets.com, Mon.-Sat. 10am-9pm, Sun. 10am-7pm) for deals on designer goods. This mall includes 60 outlets, many of which are those of major brands, including **Gap** (615/453-9686), **Loft** (615/444-1158), and **Brooks Brothers** (615/453-3636).

HOTELS

Franklin has two types of accommodations: cozy bed-and-breakfast inns and chain motels. The bed-and-breakfasts are located in downtown Franklin and the surrounding countryside. The chain motels are located around exit 65 off I-65, about two miles from the city center. The bed-and-breakfast accommodations are far more congruous with Franklin's charm than the interstate motels.

Cool Springs Galleria is a local shopping destination.

Under $100

Several chain motels surround the interstate near Franklin. Closest to town are the 89-room **Quality Inn and Suites** (1307 Murfreesboro Rd., 615/794-7591, $65-110) and the 142-room **Best Western** (1308 Murfreesboro Rd., 615/790-0570, $55-70). Both offer wireless Internet, free continental breakfast, and an outdoor pool. The Quality Inn is pet friendly with a mere $10 fee.

$100-150

The **Magnolia House Bed and Breakfast** (1317 Columbia Ave., 615/794-8178, www.bbonline.com/tn/magnolia, $140-155) is less than a mile from downtown Franklin, near The Carter House. A large magnolia tree shades the early-20th-century Craftsman home. There are four carpeted guest rooms, each with a private bath. Three house queen-size beds; the fourth has two twin beds. Common areas include a polished sitting room, cozy den, and sunroom that looks out on the quiet residential neighborhood. Hosts Jimmy and Robbie Smithson welcome guests and prepare homemade breakfasts according to your preferences.

A more hip, urban-feeling hotel option is **Aloft/Cool Springs** (7109 South Springs Dr., 615/435-8700, www.aloftnashvillecoolsprings.com, $124-149). The hotel boasts a saltwater pool, a better-than-average hotel bar, and a good location for business or recreation in Franklin.

Over $200

Designed for couples, **Blue Moon Farm Bed and Breakfast** (4441 N. Chapel Rd., 800/493-4518, www.bluemoonfarmbb.com, $350-475) is a three-room cottage complete with kitchen, spa-style bathroom, and master bedroom. The art deco decor is unique among country bed-and-breakfasts, as is the sophistication of the welcome. Touches like spa robes, an ultra-luxurious tub, and a decadently dressed king-size bed make this a real getaway. The kitchen is stocked with drinks, snacks, and the ingredients for light meals. A "Grocery Bag Breakfast" is left in the refrigerator for you and your companion to enjoy when you want, and in privacy. During waking hours, you can stroll the grounds or take advantage of wireless Internet access. Hosts Susan and Bob Eidam will also be happy to recommend and arrange activities for your stay in the Franklin area. Children older than one year are welcome at a cost of $20 extra per night.

INFORMATION AND SERVICES

The **Williamson County Convention and Visitors Bureau** (615/791-7554 or 866/253-9207, www.visitwilliamson.com) publishes guides and maintains a website about Franklin and the surrounding area. They also operate the **Williamson County Visitor Center** (209 E. Main St., 615/591-8514, Mon.-Fri. 9am-4pm, Sat. 10am-3pm, Sun. noon-3pm).

The **Williamson Medical Center** (Hwy. 96 E., 615/435-5000) is a 185-bed full-service medical facility with a 24-hour emergency room.

King Neptune (1533 Columbia Ave., 615/790-7682) is a clean and comfortable laundry open 24 hours a day. A single wash costs $1.50.

GETTING THERE AND AROUND

Traffic can be heavy in and around Franklin. As a bedroom community for commuters working in Nashville, the morning and afternoon rush hours are to be avoided. The City of Franklin offers a **trolley bus service** around the town and to outlying areas, including Cool Springs Galleria, Williamson Medical Center, Watson Glen Shopping Center, and Independence Square. The trolleys run three different routes 6am-6pm. It can take anywhere from 30 minutes to an hour to get to downtown Franklin from downtown Nashville, depending on traffic. You can pick up a full schedule and route map from the visitors center or download it from www.tmagroup.org. Fares for the Cool Springs Galleria bus are $3 for a one-way trip and $5 for a round-trip.

If you need a taxi, call **Brentwood Taxi** at 615/373-4950.

Leiper's Fork

Part bucolic small town, part yuppified enclave, Leiper's Fork is a pleasant place to spend a few hours. It is located about a 15 minutes' drive from Franklin and near milepost 420 on the Natchez Trace Parkway. The town runs for several miles along Leiper's Fork, a tributary of the West Harpeth River. Beautiful old farmhouses line Old Hillsboro Road, which serves as the main thoroughfare through town.

One of the earliest settlers of the area was the Benton family, including Thomas Hart Benton, who would go on to become a U.S. senator from Missouri. For many years, Leiper's Fork was called Hillsboro after Hillsborough, North Carolina, where many of its early settlers came from. There is another Hillsboro in Coffee County, Tennessee, however, so when this Hillsboro petitioned for a post office in 1818, the U.S. Postal Service insisted that it change its name. Leiper's Fork was born.

Acclaimed furniture maker Dick Poyner was from the Leiper's Fork area. Poyner, a former slave, was famous for his sturdy ladder-back wooden chairs, one of which is on display at the Tennessee State Museum in Nashville.

Leiper's Fork is a pleasant community, with a die-hard group of locals who are proud of their town. Art galleries and antiques shops line the short main drag. Unusually good food can be found at local restaurants, and a laid-back let's-laugh-at-ourselves attitude prevails. Many music powerhouses live here; if you see a celebrity, don't make a fuss. That's why they choose to live in Leiper's Fork.

Bed-and-breakfast inns in the area make it a viable destination or a pleasant pit stop during a tour of the region.

RESTAURANTS
Puckett's Grocery (4142 Old Hillsboro Rd., 615/794-1308, www.puckettsgrocery. com, summer Mon.-Thurs. 6am-7pm, Fri.-Sat. 6am-10:30pm, Sun. 6am-6pm, Dec.-Feb. reduced hours, $6-25) is the heartbeat of Leiper's Fork. An old-time grocery with a small dining room attached, Puckett's serves breakfast, lunch, and dinner to the town faithful and visitors alike. The original country store opened about 1950. In 1998, Andy Marshall bought the store and expanded the restaurant offerings. Solid country breakfasts are the order of the day in the mornings, followed by plate lunches. The pulled pork is a favorite, as is the Puckett Burger. Dinner specials include catfish nights, family nights, and a Saturday-night seafood buffet. Friday night the grocery turns upscale with a supper club and live music. Reservations are essential for Friday night. Puckett's hours vary by the season, so it is best to call ahead, especially for dinner arrangements. A second Puckett's Grocery location in Franklin (120 4th Ave. S., 625/794-5527) offers a more varied menu.

For a casual sandwich, decadent pastry, or cup of coffee, head to the **Backyard Cafe** (4150 Old Hillsboro Rd., 615/790-4003, Mon.-Sat. 11am-3pm, Sun. noon-3pm).

NIGHTLIFE
Friday night is songwriter night at **Puckett's Grocery** (4142 Old Hillsboro Rd., 615/794-1308, www.puckettsgrocery.com). For $30 you can enjoy a dressed-up dinner—fresh seafood, poultry, and steak are usually among the options—at 7pm and an in-the-round performance from Nashville singer-songwriters starting at 8:30pm. If you prefer, pay $15 for the concert only. Reservations are essential for either, so call ahead. Check the website to find out who is performing.

THE ARTS
Jailhouse Industries operates the Leiper's Fork **Lawn Chair Theatre** behind Leiper's Creek Gallery (4144 Old Hillsboro Rd., May-Sept.). Bring your lawn chair or blanket and enjoy classic movies and kids' favorites on Friday and Saturday nights, plus concerts. Call 615/477-6799 for more information, or just ask around.

EXCURSIONS

© AMY WHIDBY

Puckett's Grocery is a music and food institution.

RECREATION

The Leiper's Fork District of the Natchez Trace National Scenic Trail runs for 24 miles, starting near milepost 427 and ending at milepost 408, where State Highway 50 crosses the parkway. The trail follows the old Natchez Trace through rural countryside. The best access point is from Garrison Creek Road, where there is parking, restrooms, and picnic facilities. You can also access the trail from Davis Hollow Road.

SHOPS

Leipers Fork's retailers are open Wednesday-Saturday 10am-5pm and Sunday 1pm-5pm.

Opening its doors in 2007, **R Place** (4154 Old Hillsboro Rd., 615/794-8592) sells the artwork of Anne Goetz, the handmade furniture of Reed Birnie, and used books curated by Renee Armand. You can also get homemade pie and coffee if you need sustenance while you browse the shop, housed in an old home.

The **Leiper's Creek Gallery** (4144 Old Hillsboro Rd., 615/599-5102, www.leiperscreekgallery.com) is the finest gallery in town. It shows a wide selection of paintings by local and regional artists, and hosts a variety of arts events year-round.

Neena's Primitive Antiques (4158 Old Hillsboro Rd., 615/790-0345) specializes in primitive antiques, linens, home decor items, and leather goods.

ⓒ Serenite Maison

The 3,000-square-foot **Serenite Maison** (4149 Old Hillsboro Pike, 615/599-2071, www.serenitemaison.com) houses a well-edited inventory thanks to the smart design sense of Alexandra Cirimelli. A California transplant, Cirimelli has appeared on an episode of *American Pickers* and is known for finding her well-heeled clients the perfect farm table or pie safe for their kitchen. Don't overlook the pickin' corner, where locals stop in to play the antique guitars, banjos, and mandolins that hang on the walls.

INFORMATION

The **Leiper's Fork Merchant's Association** (615/972-2708, www.leipersforkvillage.com) promotes the town, maintains a listing of local businesses, and publishes an annual calendar of events.

Bell Buckle

A tiny town nestled in the northern reaches of the Walking Horse region, Bell Buckle is a charming place to visit. Founded in 1852 and once a railroad town, Bell Buckle has successfully become a destination for antiques shopping, arts and crafts, small-town hospitality, and country cooking. The town's single commercial street faces the old railroad tracks; handsome old homes—some of them bed-and-breakfast inns—spread out along quiet residential streets.

What makes Bell Buckle so appealing is the sense of humor that permeates just about everything that happens here. T-shirts for sale on the main street proclaim "Tokyo, Paris, New York, Bell Buckle," and the town's quirky residents feel free to be themselves. Tennessee's poet laureate, Margaret "Maggi" Britton Vaughn, who operates the Bell Buckle Press and had an office on Main Street for many years, once told an interviewer that William Faulkner "would have killed" for a community with the ambience, and characters, of Bell Buckle.

Bell Buckle's name is derived from Bell Buckle Creek, named thus because a cow's bell was found hanging in a tree by the creek, attached by a buckle.

The town's annual RC and Moon Pie Festival in June attracts thousands to the small town, and the well-respected Webb School Arts and Crafts Festival in October is one of the finest regional arts shows in the state. This is also home to the annual Tennessee Shakespeare Festival each summer.

SIGHTS

Bell Buckle is noted as the home of the elite and well-regarded **Webb School** (319 Webb Rd. E., 888/733-9322, www.thewebbschool.com). Founded in 1870 and led by William Robert Webb until his death in 1926, Webb School has graduated 10 Rhodes scholars, several governors and attorneys general, and numerous successful academics. The school now has about 300 students in grades 8-12 from around the country and the world. While it was all male for many years of its life, Webb School now admits both male and female students. Its athletic mascot is the "Webb Feet."

The Webb campus is about three blocks north of downtown Bell Buckle. You can visit the main administrative office during regular business hours, where there are photographs and school memorabilia on display. Pay attention as you drive by; the speed limit in this school zone is considerably lower than that on all the nearby country roads.

RESTAURANTS

There's no debate about where to eat in Bell Buckle. The **Bell Buckle Cafe** (Railroad Sq., 931/389-9693, Mon. 10:30am-2pm, Tues.-Thurs. 10:30am-8pm, Fri.-Sat. 10:30am-9pm, Sun. 11am-5pm, $5-15) is not

© HANNAH COFFEY

The Bell Buckle Cafe is local favorite.

only a Bell Buckle institution, but it is also one of the only games in town. The menu is Southern, with a few refined touches (like ostrich burgers and spinach-strawberry salad) you won't find at most small-town cafés. The menu is also mighty diverse, with seafood, pasta, and sandwiches in addition to the usual plate lunches and dinner entrées. The large dining room fills up quick, especially for lunch, so there's no shame in coming a bit early. The Bell Buckle Cafe takes care of your entertainment needs, too. There's always live music on Thursday, Friday, and Saturday nights, usually bluegrass or country. Local radio station WLIJ broadcasts a musical variety show from the café on Saturday 1pm-3pm, which is a great reason to come to the café for lunch.

If you managed to pass up homemade dessert at the Bell Buckle Cafe, then head to **Bluebird Antiques and Ice Cream Parlor** (15 Webb Rd., 931/389-6549, Mon.-Sat. 9am-5pm, Sun. noon-5pm). Here you'll find a turn-of-the-20th-century soda fountain with hand-dipped ice cream and homemade waffle cones. Come in the morning to see (and smell) them making the cones.

FESTIVALS AND EVENTS
C RC and Moon Pie Festival

Bell Buckle's biggest annual event is the **RC and Moon Pie Festival** (931/389-9663) in mid-June, a nod to one of the South's favorite culinary combos. This hilarious weekend event includes country and bluegrass music, Moon Pie games (such as the Moon Pie toss), arts and crafts booths, the crowning of a Moon Pie King and Queen, and a 10-mile run. You can also witness the cutting of the world's largest Moon Pie (and if you are willing to join the mob, you can taste it, too). In case you're wondering why Bell Buckle has rights to the Moon Pie festival, it's because they asked for it. June in Tennessee is almost always oppressively hot at the Moon Pie Festival, which is a good excuse to drink another RC.

Webb School Arts and Crafts Festival

The **Webb School Arts and Crafts Festival** (931/389-9663, www.bellbucklechamber.com) in October brings hundreds of artisans to town. It is one of the finest arts and crafts shows in the region, attracting fine and folk artists from Tennessee and beyond.

Since 2008 the Webb School also has hosted the Tennessee Shakespeare Festival (www.tennesseeshakespearefestival.com) each summer. This open-air performance brings in actors from across the country to perform one of the Bard's works each season, led by artistic director Lane Davies (of NBC's *Santa Barbara* fame). Tickets are typically a reasonable $5-15.

SHOPS

The single most popular pursuit in Bell Buckle is shopping. Antiques are the main attraction, but arts and crafts are a close second. Several Nashville interior designers and antiques dealers have booths in shops in Bell Buckle because of the goods found here. You can spend an entire day rummaging through these shelves, although it is generally too crowded to do so the day of the Moon Pie Festival.

The **Bell Buckle Pottery Place** (26 Railroad Sq., 931/389-0101, www.paintedclaystudio.com, Mon.-Sat. 10am-8pm, Sun. noon-6pm) sells a wide selection of artwork, from pottery and sculpture to paintings. Most pieces here have a fresh, modern appeal.

The **Froggie Went a Shoppin'** (6 Railroad Sq., 931/813-3034, Mon. 11am-4pm, Tues.-Thurs. 11am-5pm, Fri.-Sat. 10:30am-6pm, Sun. noon-5pm) and **Doodle Bug Too** (14 Railroad Sq., 931/389-9009, www.doodlebugtoo.net, Mon. 10:30am-4pm, Tues.-Thurs. 10:30am-5pm, Fri.-Sat. 10am-7pm, Sun. noon-5pm) are sister shops that sell jewelry, housewares, gifts, and folk art.

For antiques try the **Bell Buckle Antique Mall** (112 Main St., 931/389-6174, www.bellbuckleantiquemall.com, Mon.-Sat. 9am-5pm, Sun. 1pm-5pm).

HOTELS

Host and hostess James and Ina Mingle run the **Mingle House Bed and Breakfast** (116 Main St., 931/389-9453, www.theminglehouse.blogspot.com, $80-85) in a restored 1898 Victorian home. Rooms are furnished with antiques, and guests can fuel up with a country-style breakfast of eggs, sausage, bacon, and more in the morning.

INFORMATION

The **Bell Buckle Chamber of Commerce** (931/389-9663, www.bellbucklechamber.com) publishes brochures, promotes the town, and operates as a clearinghouse for information.

Lynchburg

A 1.5-hour drive southeast of Nashville, Lynchburg was once a town with a population of 361. It has been transformed by the popularity of Jack Daniel's Tennessee Whiskey, which is made a few blocks from the town square. No other small town in Tennessee sees as many visitors from as many different places as this one.

Critics may object to the tour buses and crowds, but for now, the town has managed to survive its success with relative grace. It has maintained its small-town feel, and it offers its guests a hospitable and heartfelt welcome.

Lynchburg is centered on the Moore County courthouse, a modest redbrick building. Souvenir shops, restaurants, and a few local businesses line the square. Outside of this, Lynchburg is quiet and residential. The Jack Daniel's Distillery is about three blocks away from the town square; a pleasant footpath connects the two.

◖ JACK DANIEL'S DISTILLERY

As you drive into Lynchburg, or walk around the town, you might notice some odd-looking gray warehouses peeking out above the treetops. These are barrel houses, where Jack Daniel's Distillery ages its whiskey. Around Moore County there are 74 of these warehouses, and each one holds about one million barrels of whiskey.

Thousands of whiskey drinkers make the pilgrimage every year to **Jack Daniel's Distillery** (280 Lynchburg Hwy./Hwy. 55, 931/759-4221, www.jackdaniels.com, 9am-4:30pm, free) to see how Jack Daniel's is made. And what they find is that, aside from the use of electricity, computers, and the sheer scale of the operation, things have not changed too much since 1866 when Jack Daniel registered his whiskey still at the mouth of Cave Spring near Lynchburg.

Jack Daniel was an interesting man. He stood just five feet, two inches tall and liked to wear three-piece suits. He was introduced to the whiskey business by a Lutheran lay preacher named Dan Call, who sold the distillery to Daniel shortly after the Civil War. In 1866, Daniel had the foresight to register his distillery with the federal government, making his the oldest registered distillery in the United States. He never married and had no known children.

Daniel died of gangrene in 1911. He got it from kicking a metal safe in frustration after he couldn't get it open, and breaking his toe. After Daniel died, the distillery passed to his nephew, Lem Motlow. The distillery remained in the Motlow family until it was sold in 1957 to the Brown-Forman Corporation of Louisville, Kentucky.

The one-hour tour of the distillery begins with a video about the master distillers—Jack Daniel's has had seven in its lifetime—who are the final authority on all facets of the product. You then board a bus that takes you up to the far side of the distillery, and from here you'll walk back to the visitors center, stopping frequently to be told about the key steps in the process. The highlight of the tour for some is seeing Cave Spring, where the distillery gets its iron-free spring water. Others enjoy taking a potent whiff of the sour mash and the mellowing whiskey.

See how Tennessee whiskey is made at Jack Daniel's Distillery.

The tour ends back at the visitors center, where you are served free lemonade and coffee. Moore County, where Lynchburg is located, is a dry county, and for 86 years the irony was that Jack Daniel's could not sell any of its whiskey at the distillery. In 1995, however, the county approved a special exemption that allows the distillery to sell souvenir bottles of whiskey at its visitors center. That is all they sell, however; you have to buy other Jack Daniel's merchandise at one of the other gift shops in town.

OTHER SIGHTS

A stately two-story brick building on the southwest corner of the square is the **Moore County Old Jail Museum** (231 Main St., 931/993-1791, www.lynchburgtn.com, Mar.-mid-Dec. Tues.-Sat. 11am-3pm, $1 adults, free for children under 16), which served as the sheriff's residence and the county jail until 1990. The building is now a museum and is operated by the local historical society. You can see law-enforcement memorabilia, old newspaper

clippings, and vintage clothes. Go upstairs to see the prisoners' cells.

Just down Main Street is the **Tennessee Walking Horse Museum** (Public Sq., 931/759-5747, www.twhbea.com/TWHMuseum. htm, Tues.-Sat. 9am-5pm, free). The museum was originally located in Shelbyville, heart of Walking Horse country, but moved to Lynchburg in the early 2000s to take advantage of the bustling tourist trade here.

The Walking Horse Museum displays photographs, trophies, and other memorabilia from walking horse champions. You can admire both show and posed photographs of top horses, and watch a video that explains what makes the walking horse so special. The films include show footage of the breed's distinctive flat walk, fast walk, and canter.

RESTAURANTS

The most popular place to eat in Lynchburg is **Miss Mary Bobo's Boarding House** (295 Main St., 931/759-7394, seating Mon.-Fri. 1pm, Sat. 11am and 1pm). Miss Mary's started life as the home of Thomas Roundtree, the founder of Lynchburg. It later became the home of Dr. E. Y. Salmon, a Confederate captain, who maintained an office there and rented out rooms to boarders. In 1908, Lacy Jackson Bobo and his wife, Mary Evans Bobo, bought the house and continued to operate it as a boardinghouse until the 1980s. Over the years, word of Mary Bobo's legendary home-cooked meals spread, and this boardinghouse became one of the region's best-known eating houses. Today, Miss Mary's is no longer a boardinghouse, and the restaurant is operated by Miss Lynne Tolley, who has worked hard to keep up the traditions established by Miss Mary. The restaurant is owned by the Jack Daniel's Distillery, and servers are hired from the local community college. A meal at Miss Mary's will easily be the most unique of your trip. Guests should arrive at least 15 minutes early so they can check in, pay, and be assigned to a dining room. When the dinner bell rings, you will be taken to your dining room by a hostess, who stays with you throughout the meal. Everyone sits family-style around a big table. The meal served at Miss Mary's is a traditional Southern dinner. You'll find no less than six side dishes and two meats, plus iced tea (unsweetened), dessert, coffee, and bread. Almost every meal features fried chicken. Side dishes may include green beans, mashed potatoes, fried okra, carrot slaw, and corn bread. Your hostess will make sure that everyone has enough to eat, answer questions about the food, and tell you some stories about the restaurant—if you ask. Be sure to call well ahead to make your reservations. Meals are fully booked weeks and even months in advance, especially during the busy summer months and on Saturdays.

For a more low-key meal, go to the **Bar-B-Que Caboose Cafe** (217 Main St., 931/759-5180, bbqcaboose.com, Mon.-Thurs. 11am-4:30pm, Fri. 11am-8pm, Sat. 10am-4:30pm, Sun. noon-4:30pm). The menu offers pulled-pork barbecue sandwiches, jambalaya, red beans and rice, and hot dogs. You can also get pizzas. On Friday nights (Apr.-Oct. 6:30pm-8pm), you can get a barbecue plate dinner ($9) while you listen to live music. On Saturday mornings (10am-11am), a live country music radio show is broadcast from the Caboose Cafe.

There are a handful of other restaurants in Lynchburg, all on the town square. **Elk River Coffee** (12 Short St., 931/759-5552, Mon.-Wed. 7am-5:30pm, Thurs.-Sat. 7am-8pm) sells lighter fare, including wraps and salads.

Be prepared: It is next to impossible to get an evening meal in Lynchburg; by 6pm the place is a ghost town.

FESTIVALS AND EVENTS

Spring in the Hollow is an arts, crafts, and music festival that takes place in early May. At the end of May, the **Spotted Saddle Horse Show,** a horse show held twice a year, takes place.

Frontier Days in mid- to late June is a weekend celebration of early settlers where costumed performers and traders evoke bygone days. July sees the **Tennessee Walking Horse Show** and August features the **Spotted Saddle Horse Show**.

The biggest event of the year in Lynchburg is the **Jack Daniel's World Champion Invitational Barbecue,** which takes place the last weekend of October. Teams must qualify to take part—they must have won another large barbecue tournament—and even then teams must be invited. Despite serious competition, the event is a whole lot of fun. Spectators compete in bung tossing and butt bowling. There is clogging and bluegrass music, and lots of county fair-type food is sold. The barbecue competition takes place at Wiseman Park on the outskirts of the town square. An arts and crafts festival takes place at the town square.

Christmas in Lynchburg livens up an otherwise quiet time in town with seasonal performances and decorations.

For information about any events, contact the Metropolitan Lynchburg Moore County Chamber of Commerce at 931/759-4111, www.lynchburgtn.com.

HOTELS

The **Tolley House** (1253 Main St., 931/759-7263, www.tolleyhouse.com, $100-150) is located about a mile from the town square, and is a pleasant country retreat. A handsome antebellum farmhouse once owned by Jack Daniel's master distiller Lem Motlow, the Tolley House provides touches of luxury. Rooms have private baths, television, and wireless Internet access, and are furnished tastefully with antiques. Hosts Frank and Karen Fletcher provide your choice of a full country or light continental breakfast. Discounts are available for stays of two or more nights.

The closest thing to a motel in Lynchburg is the **Lynchburg Country Inn** (423 Majors Blvd., 931/759-5995, www.lynchburgcountryinn.com, $55-65). Its 25 rooms are each furnished with a microwave, refrigerator, and cable TV. There's a pool out back and rocking chairs on the front and back porches. The building is modern, built in 2003, but the decor is pure country.

INFORMATION

The **Lynchburg Welcome Center** (182 Lynchburg Hwy./Hwy. 55, 931/759-6357, www.lynchburgtenn.com) is open daily at the intersection of Majors Boulevard and Mechanic Street. The welcome center has public restrooms and information about local businesses and attractions.

Land Between the Lakes

This narrow finger of land that lies between the Cumberland and Tennessee Rivers is a natural wonderland. Comprising 170,000 acres of land and wrapped by 300 miles of undeveloped river shoreline, the **Land Between the Lakes National Recreation Area** (100 Van Morgan Dr., Golden Pond, 270/924-2000, www.lbl.org) has become one of the most popular natural areas in this region of the country. Split between Tennessee and Kentucky, the area provides unrivaled opportunities to camp, hike, boat, play, or just simply drive through quiet wilderness.

Land Between the Lakes is about a 1.5-hour drive northwest from Nashville. The area lies between what is now called Kentucky Lake (the Tennessee River) and Lake Barkley (the Cumberland River). At its narrowest point, the distance between these two bodies of water is only one mile. The drive from north to south is 43 miles. About one-third of the park is in Tennessee; the rest is in Kentucky. It is managed by the U.S. Forest Service, an agency of the U.S. Department of Agriculture.

History

Land Between the Lakes was not always a natural and recreational area. Native Americans settled here, drawn to the fertile soil, proximity to the rivers, and gentle terrain. European settlers followed, and between about 1800 and the 1960s the area, then called Between the Rivers, saw thriving small settlements. Residents farmed and traded along the rivers, which were served by steamboats.

In many respects, settlers in Between the Rivers were even more isolated than those in other parts of what was then the western frontier of the United States. They did not necessarily associate with one state or another, instead forming a distinct identity of their own. During the Civil War, it was necessary to finally determine the border between Tennessee and Kentucky, since this line also marked the border between the Union and the Confederacy.

It was during another period of upheaval in the United States that the future of the Between the Rivers region changed forever. In the midst of the Great Depression, Congress created the Tennessee Valley Authority, which improved soil conditions, eased flooding, brought electricity, and created jobs in Tennessee. One of TVA's projects was the Kentucky Dam, which was built between 1938 and 1944 and impounded the Tennessee River. In 1957, work

BONNAROO: THE TENNESSEE MUSIC FESTIVAL

Bonnaroo Music and Arts Festival (www. bonnaroo.com) started out in 2002 as a jam band music festival, but diversification has made this summertime mega event *the* destination for all types of music fans. Bonnaroo takes place over four days in June on a rural farm in Manchester. Between 75,000 and 90,000 people come each year.

Bonnaroo has a hippie heart with a slightly hard edge. Place names are Suessian—the music tents are called, from largest to smallest, What Stage, Which Stage, This Tent, That Tent, and The Other Tent. Activities run the gamut from a Mardi Gras parade to kids' art activities. Of course, it's the music that really draws the crowds: reggae, rock, Americana, jam bands, world, hip-hop, jazz, electronic, folk, gospel, and country. The event is truly a feast for the ears.

In 2007, the Police were reunited at Bonnaroo. In 2008, headliners included Kanye West, Willie Nelson, and Pearl Jam. But quality permeates every echelon of the stage. Unknowns and barely knowns routinely wow audiences, including names like The Civil Wars, Moon Taxi, and Feist. There is an emphasis on world artists and folk music. A jazz tent provides nightclub ambience, and there's even a comedy tent.

A few things to know about Bonnaroo: First, it's huge. The event takes place on a 700-acre farm, and the list of offerings is seemingly endless: four stages of music, whole villages dedicated to the arts, a 24-hour movie tent, yoga studio, salon, music-industry showcase, food vendors, and a whole lot more.

Second, Bonnaroo has above-average logistics. Organizers seem to consider everything, including the basics: drinking water, medical care, parking, traffic control, and a general store where you can buy necessities. Food vendors sell Tennessee barbecue, veggie burgers, and just about everything in between. A shuttle service between the Nashville airport and the Bonnaroo helps minimize traffic. Rules about camping, RVs, reentry, and security are common-sense and easy to follow.

All that said, you can't turn up with the clothes on your back and expect to have much fun. It's important to pack well: A good camping tent, folding chairs, and water bottles are important. It is June in the south. It will be unspeakably hot. If it rains, it will be muddy. If it doesn't, it will be dusty. Even if you plan to buy most of your food at the festival, at least pack some snacks. There are ATMs at the Bonnaroo, but lines can be very long, so bringing plenty of cash is also a good idea (but not so much that you attract trouble). Also bring garbage bags, sunscreen, and hot-weather, comfortable clothes.

Beer—including good microbrews—are sold, and consumed generously. Plenty of Bonnaroo fans take the opportunity to do a lot of drinking and drugs, partly because they're somewhere they don't have to drive for four days.

Most people buy a four-day pass to the festival, but day-pass tickets are available, too. Four-day passes cost $200 and up; a limited number of reduced-price early-bird tickets go on sale in January each year. Regular tickets go on sale in the spring, after the lineup has been announced, typically in February. VIP packages are pricier, but offer amenities that are priceless, such as VIP restroom and shower facilities.

began on Barkley Dam, which impounded the Cumberland River and put an end to floods that damaged crops and destroyed property along the river.

About 25 years later, President John F. Kennedy announced that the U.S. government would buy out residents of the land between the Cumberland and Tennessee Rivers to create a new park, which would serve as an example of environmental management and recreational use. The project was to bring much-needed economic development to the area by attracting visitors to the park.

The project was not without opponents, who objected to the government's use of eminent domain to take over lands that were privately owned. Residents lamented the loss of unique communities in the lake region. More than 2,300 people were removed to create Land Between the Lakes (LBL). In all, 96,000 of the 170,000 acres that make up LBL were purchased or taken from private hands.

Over time, however, the controversy of the creation of the park has faded, and the Land Between the Lakes has become well loved. It is the third most-visited park in Tennessee, behind only the Smoky Mountains and Cherokee National Forest.

Planning Your Time

Some of the best attractions at Land Between the Lakes charge admission. If you are planning to visit all or most of them, consider one of the packages offered by the Forest Service. The discount package allows you to visit each attraction once over a seven-day period at a 25 percent discount. Another option is the $30 LBL Fun Card, which gives you 10 admissions to any of three attractions. It does not expire. You can buy packages at either the north (Kentucky) or south (Tennessee) welcome station or the Golden Pond Visitor Center.

During certain summer weekends there are free two-hour tours of Lake Barkley's Power Plant and Navigation Lock (270/362-4236). You must call in advance to reserve a spot and complete a registration form. The tours restarted in 2012; they had been on hold since the events of September 11, 2001.

SIGHTS
Great Western Iron Furnace

About 11 miles inside the park is the **Great Western Iron Furnace,** built by Brian, Newell, and Company in 1854. If you have traveled around this part of Tennessee much, you will have come to recognize the distinctive shape of the old iron furnaces that dot the landscape in the counties between Nashville and the Tennessee River. Like the Great Western Furnace, these plants were used to create high-quality iron from iron ore deposits in the earth.

The Great Western Furnace operated for less than two years. By 1856 panic over reported slave uprisings and the coming of the Civil War caused the plant to shut down. It would never make iron again.

The Homeplace

Just beyond the furnace is **The Homeplace** (Apr.-Oct. Mon.-Sat. 9am-5pm, Sun. 10am-5pm, Mar. and Nov. Wed.-Sat. 9am-5pm, Sun. 10am-5pm, $4 ages 13 and up, $2 children 5-12, free for children 4 and under), a living-history museum that depicts life in Between the Rivers in about 1850. At the middle of the 19th century, Between the Rivers was home to an iron ore industry and hundreds of farmers. These farmers raised crops and livestock for their own use, as well as to sell where they could. In 1850, about 10,000 people lived in Between the Rivers, including 2,500 slaves and 125 free blacks.

The Homeplace re-creates an 1850 farmstead. Staff dress in period clothes and perform the labors that settlers would have done: They sow seeds in the spring, harvest in the summer and fall, and prepare the fields for the next year in the winter. The farm includes a dogtrot cabin, where you can see how settlers would have lived, cooked, and slept. Out back there is a small garden, a plot of tobacco, pigs, sheep, oxen, and a barn. You may see farmers splitting shingles, working oxen, sewing quilts, making candles, or another of the dozens of tasks that settlers performed on a regular basis.

The Homeplace publishes a schedule that announces when certain activities will take place, such as canning, shearing of sheep, or harvesting tobacco. Even if you come when there is no special program, you will be able to see staff taking on everyday tasks, and you can ask them about any facet of life on the frontier.

◖ Elk and Bison Prairie

Archaeological evidence shows that elk and bison once grazed in Tennessee and Kentucky, including the area between the rivers. Settlers quickly destroyed these herds, however. Both bison and elk were easy to hunt, and they were desirable for their meat and skins. By 1800, bison had been killed off, and about 50 years later elk were gone, too.

When Land Between the Lakes was created, elk and bison were reintroduced to the area. The South Bison Range across the road from The Homeplace is one of the places where bison now live. The bison herd that roams on about 160 acres here can sometimes be seen from the main road, or from side roads bordering the range.

You can see both bison and elk at the **Elk and Bison Prairie,** a 700-acre restoration project located near the midpoint of the Land Between the Lakes. In 1996, 39 bison were relocated here from the south prairie, and 29 elk were transported from Canada. Since then, the population of both animals has grown.

Visitors may drive through the range along a one-mile loop. Admission is $5 per vehicle. You are advised to take your time, roll down your windows, and keep your eyes peeled for a sign of the animals. The best time to view elk and bison is in the early morning or late afternoon. At other times of day, you may just enjoy the sights and sounds of the grassland. Pay attention to the road as well as the animals, as the car in front of you may slow to take photos of one of these magnificent creatures. You may also see some bison from the Natchez Trace en route.

Golden Pond Visitor Center and Planetarium

For the best overview of the history, nature, and significance of the Land Between the Lakes, stop at the **Golden Pond Visitor Center and Planetarium** (Natchez Trace and U.S. Hwy. 68/SR 80, 270/924-2000, daily 9am-5pm, visitors center free, planetarium $4 adults, $2 children 5-12, free for children 4 and under). The visitors center is home to a small museum about the park, where you can also watch a video about the elk that have been restored on the Elk and Bison Prairie. There is also a gift shop, restrooms, and picnic area.

The planetarium screens at least four programs daily about astronomy and nature, with more during the holidays. On Saturday and Sunday at 1pm, you can get a sneak peak at the night sky above.

Golden Pond was the name of Land Between the Lakes's largest town before the park was created. Golden Pond, also called Fungo, was a vibrant town that, at its peak, had a hotel, bank, restaurants, and other retail outlets. During Prohibition, farmers made moonshine in the woods and sold it in Golden Pond. Golden Pond whiskey was sought after in back-alley saloons as far away as Chicago. When Land Between the Lakes was created in 1963, Golden Pond had a population of about 200 people. Families moved their homes and relocated to communities outside the park. In 1970, when the historical society unveiled a marker at the site of Golden Pond, the strains of "Taps" rang out over the hills.

You can visit the site of Golden Pond by driving a few miles east of the visitors center on Highway 80. There is a picnic area.

Woodlands Nature Station

The final major attraction in Land Between the Lakes is the **Woodlands Nature Station** (north of the visitors center on the Trace, 270/924-2020, Apr.-Oct. Mon.-Sat. 9am-5pm, Sun. 10am-5pm, Nov. and Mar. Wed.-Sat. 9am-5pm, Sun. 10am-5pm, $4 ages 13 and up, $2 children 5-12, free for children 4 and under). Geared to children, the nature station introduces visitors to animals including bald eagles, coyotes, opossum, and deer. There are also opportunities for staff-led hiking trips. Special events and activities take place nearly every weekend, and during the week in summertime.

Center Furnace

You can see the ruins **Center Furnace,** once the largest iron furnace in the Land Between the Lakes, along the Center Furnace Trail. Along the short (three-tenths of a mile) walk you will see signs that describe the process of making iron and explain why it was practiced in Between the Rivers.

Center Furnace was built between 1844 and 1846. It continued to operate until 1912, much longer than any other furnace in the area.

EXCURSIONS

RESTAURANTS

There are no restaurants in Land Between the Lakes. There are vending machines with snacks and sodas at The Homeplace, Golden Pond Visitor Center, and the Woodlands Nature Station. Picnic facilities abound.

There is a McDonald's at the southern entrance to the park. Dover, five miles east, has a number of fast-food and local eateries. Twenty miles to the west, Paris has dozens of different restaurants.

RECREATION

Promoting outdoor recreation is one of the objectives of Land Between the Lakes. Visitors can enjoy hiking, biking, paddling, or horseback riding; hunting and fishing; and camping. There is even an area specially designated for all-terrain vehicles.

Trails

There are 200 miles of hiking trails in Land Between the Lakes. Some of these are also open for mountain biking and horseback riding.

The **Fort Henry Trails** are a network of 29.3 miles of trails near the southern entrance to the park, some of which follow the shoreline of Kentucky Lake. The intricate network of trails allows hikers to choose anywhere from a three-mile loop to something much longer.

Driving south to north along the scenic main road, or Trace, that runs along the middle of the park, you will find the major attractions within Land Between the Lakes.

Access the trails from the south welcome station, or from the Fort Henry Trails parking area, at the end of Fort Henry Road. These trails crisscross the grounds once occupied by the Confederate Fort Henry. They are for hikers only.

The **North-South Trail** treks the entire length of the Land Between the Lakes. From start to finish, it is 58.6 miles. Three backcountry camping shelters are available along the way for backpackers. The trail crosses the main road in several locations. Portions of the trail are open to horseback riders, and the portion from the Golden Pond Visitor Center to the northern end is also open to mountain bikers.

The 2.2-mile **Honker Lake Loop Trail** begins at the Woodlands Nature Station. This trail is open to hikers only. Sightings of fallow deer and giant Canada geese are common along this trail. The banks of nearby Hematite Lake are littered with bits of blue stone, remnants of slag from the Center Iron Furnace.

Finally, at the northern end of the park are the **Canal Loop Trails,** a network of hike/bike trails that depart from the north welcome station. These trails meander along the shores of both Kentucky Lake and Lake Barkley. The entire loop is 14.2 miles, but connector trails enable you to fashion a shorter hike or ride if you want.

A detailed map showing all hiking, biking, and horseback trails can be picked up at any of the park visitors centers. You can rent bikes at Hillman Ferry and Piney Campgrounds.

Off-Highway Vehicles

There are more than 100 miles of trail for off-highway vehicles (OHVs). OHV permits are available for $15 for 1-3 days, $30 for 7 days, and $60 for an annual pass; passes may be purchased at any Land Between the Lakes visitors center. Call 270/924-2000 in advance to find out if any of the trails are closed due to bad weather or poor conditions.

Fishing and Boating

Land Between the Lakes offers excellent fishing. The best season for fishing is spring, April-June, when fish move to shallow waters to spawn. Crappie, largemouth bass, and a variety of sunfish may be caught at this time.

Summer and fall offer good fishing, while winter is fair. A fishing license from the state in which you will be fishing is required; these may be purchased from businesses outside the park. Specific size requirements and open dates may be found at any of the visitors centers.

There are 19 different lake access points where you can put in a boat. Canoe rentals are available at the Energy Lake Campground, which is over the border in Kentucky. Energy Lake is a no-wake lake.

Hunting

Controlled hunting is one of the tools that the Forest Service uses to manage populations of wild animals in Land Between the Lakes. Hunting also draws thousands of visitors each year. The annual spring turkey hunt and fall deer hunts are the most popular.

Specific rules govern each hunt, and in many cases hunters must apply in advance for a permit. Hunters must also have a $20 LBL Hunter Use Permit, as well as the applicable state licenses. For details on hunting regulations, call the park at 270/924-2065.

Camping

There are nine campgrounds at Land Between the Lakes. All campgrounds have facilities for tent and trailer camping.

Most campgrounds are open March 1-November 1, although some are open year-round. There's a complicated formula for figuring out the price of campsites, based on which campground it is, the day of the week, and the month of the year. In general costs range $12-13 per night; RV sites range $6-32, depending on whether there is access to electricity, water, and sewer services.

Reservations are accepted for select campsites at Piney, Energy Lake, Hillman Ferry, and Wrangler Campgrounds up to six months in advance. Call the LBL headquarters in Kentucky at 270/924-2000 or visit the website at www.lbl.org to make a reservation.

PINEY CAMPGROUND

Located on the southern tip of Land Between the Lakes, Piney Campground is convenient to visitors arriving from the Tennessee side of the park, and, as a result, can be one of the most crowded campgrounds in LBL. Piney has more than 300 campsites; 281 have electricity; 44 have electricity, water, and sewer; and 59 are primitive tent sites.

There are also nine rustic one-bedroom camping shelters with a ceiling fan, table and chairs, electric outlets, and large porch. Sleeping accommodations are one double bed and a bunk bed. Outside there is a picnic table and fire ring. There are no bathrooms; shelter guests use the same bathhouses as other campers. Camp shelters cost $35-37 per night and sleep up to four people.

Piney's amenities include a camp store, bike rental, archery range, playground, swimming beach, boat ramp, and fishing pier.

ENERGY LAKE CAMPGROUND

Near the midpoint of Land Between the Lakes, Energy Lake Campground has tent and trailer campsites, electric sites, and group camp facilities. It tends to be less crowded than some of the other campgrounds and has nice lakeside sites, with a swimming area, volleyball, and other kid-friendly activities.

HILLMAN FERRY CAMPGROUND

Located near the northern end of Land Between the Lakes, Hillman Ferry has 380 tent and RV campsites. It is nestled on the shores of Kentucky Lake, between Moss Creek and Pisgah Bay.

Electric and nonelectric sites are available. There is a dumping station, bathhouses with showers and flush toilets, drinking water, a camp store, swimming area, coin-operated laundry, and bike rentals.

Boat and Horse Camping

In addition to the campgrounds already listed, Land Between the Lakes operates five lakeside camping areas that are designed for boaters who want to spend the night. Rushing Creek/Jones Creek is the most developed of these camping areas; it has 40 tent or RV sites and a bathhouse with showers and flush toilets. Other campsites, including Birmingham Ferry/Smith Bay, Cravens Bay, Fenton, and Gatlin Point, have chemical toilets, tent camping sites, and grills.

LBL also has Wrangler's Campground, designed for horseback riders. In addition to tent and RV sites, there are camping shelters and horse stalls. Amenities include a camp store, bathhouses, coin laundry, and playground.

Backcountry Camping

Backcountry camping is allowed year-round

in Land Between the Lakes. All you need is a backcountry permit and the right gear to enjoy unlimited choices of campsites along the shoreline or in the woodlands.

INFORMATION

The Forest Service maintains a useful website about Land Between the Lakes at www. lbl.org. You can also call 270/924-2000 to request maps and information sheets. The park headquarters is located at the Golden Pond Visitor Center.

When you arrive, stop at the nearest welcome or visitors center for up-to-date advisories and activity schedules. All of the welcome centers and the visitors center are open daily 9am-5pm.

The **Land Between the Lakes Association** (800/455-5897, www.friendsoflbl.org) organizes volunteer opportunities and publishes a detailed tour guide to the park, which includes historical and natural anecdotes.

BACKGROUND

The Setting

The Cumberland River winds its way through Nashville, bending and turning through its neighborhoods and skyline. The river and its banks provide Music City with the water for its lush, green open spaces. It's also responsible for some of the traffic congestion, as streets curve along its meanders. Often heading to the next neighborhood requires finding a bridge.

That said, Nashville's location in the Cumberland River basin is part of its appeal. The river gives even Music City's most urban areas a bucolic quality. The neighborhoods are full of hustle and bustle, but it doesn't take much effort to escape when you need some R&R.

GEOGRAPHY

Middle Tennessee is home to Tennessee's capital city, Nashville, and some of its most fertile farmland. Before the Civil War, great plantation mansions dotted the countryside south of Nashville. Today, Tennessee Walking Horse farms, new industries, and the economic success of Nashville continue to make Middle Tennessee prosperous.

Geographically, Middle Tennessee begins with the Cumberland Plateau, which rises to about 2,000 feet above sea level and lies west of East Tennessee's Great Valley. Despite its name, the plateau is not flat; there are a number of

steep valleys in the plateau, the largest being the Sequatchie Valley.

The Highland Rim is a region of hills, valleys, and fertile farmland that lies west of the plateau. The largest physical region of Tennessee, the Highland Rim contains 10,650 square miles of land, or almost 25 percent of the state. Almost entirely surrounded by the Highland Rim is the Central Basin, a low, flat, and fertile region in north-central Tennessee. Nashville is located in the Central Basin.

Nashville itself sits at 550 feet above sea level. It is the U.S. city with the second-largest land mass: more than 500 square miles.

CLIMATE

Nashville enjoys a relatively mild climate, with average temperatures ranging from 38°F to 80°F. Summer days can feel very hot, however, and a run of humid 100°F days in August is not unusual. A few flakes of snow may fall in the winter, and the city essentially shuts down when there is any accumulation, although that is rare. Generally, an evening's snowfall has evaporated by mid-morning.

The city receives an average of 45 inches of rain per year. Long springs and falls mean a long season for beautiful flowers, but also a long season for allergy sufferers.

Floods

The devastating flood in Nashville and Middle Tennessee in May 2010 brought the issue of global climate changes, combined with man-made development and water management, to the forefront of the minds of city planners and residents. The flood caused more than $1.5 billion of damage to the Music City. At press time, most of the commercial public repairs to the city had been made, but residential redevelopment continues.

History

THE FIRST TENNESSEANS

The first humans settled in what is now Tennessee 12,000-15,000 years ago. Descended from people who crossed into North America during the last ice age, these Paleo-Indians were nomads who hunted large game animals, including mammoth, mastodon, and caribou. Remains of these extinct mammals have been found in West Tennessee, and the Indians' arrowheads and spear points have been found all over the state. The ice age hunters camped in caves and under rock shelters but remained predominantly nomadic.

About 10,000 years ago, the climate and vegetation of the region changed. The deciduous forest that still covers large parts of the state replaced the evergreen forest of the fading ice age. Large game animals disappeared, and deer and elk arrived, attracted to the forests of hickory, chestnut, and beech. Descendants of the Paleo-Indians gradually abandoned the nomadic lifestyle of their ancestors and established settlements, often near rivers. They hunted deer, bear, and turkey; gathered nuts and wild fruit; and harvested freshwater fish and mussels. They also took a few tentative steps toward cultivation by growing squash and gourds.

This Archaic Period was replaced by the Woodland Period about 3,000 years ago. The Woodland Indians adopted the bow and arrow for hunting and—at the end of their predominance—began cultivating maize and beans as staple crops. Ceramic pottery appeared, and ritualism took on a greater importance in the society. Pinson Mounds, burial mounds near Jackson in West Tennessee, date from this period, as does the wrongly named Old Stone Fort near Manchester, believed to have been built and used for ceremonies by the Woodland Indians of the area.

The development of a more complex culture continued, and at about AD 900 the Woodland culture gave way to the Mississippian Period, an era marked by population growth, an increase in trade and warfare, the rise of the chieftain, and cultural accomplishments. The Mississippian era is best known for the impressive large pyramid mounds that were left behind in places such as Etowah and Toqua in Tennessee and Moundville in Alabama. Mississippian Indians also created beautiful ornaments and symbolic objects including combs, pipes, and jewelry.

EUROPEANS ARRIVE

Having conquered Peru, the Spanish nobleman Hernando de Soto embarked on a search for gold in the American southeast in 1539. De Soto's band wandered through Florida, Georgia, and the Carolinas before crossing into what is now Tennessee, probably in June 1540. His exact route is a source of controversy, but historians believe he made his way through parts of East Tennessee before heading back into Georgia.

It was more than 100 years until another European was reported in the Tennessee wilderness, although life for the natives was already changing. De Soto and his men brought firearms and disease, and there was news of other whites living to the east. Disease and warfare led to a decline in population for Tennessee's Indians during the presettlement period. As a result, Indian communities formed new tribes with each other: The Creek Confederacy and Choctaws were among the tribes that were formed. In Tennessee, the Shawnee moved south into the Cumberland River country—land previously claimed as hunting ground by the Chickasaw Nation. Also at this time, a new tribe came over the Smoky Mountains from North Carolina, possibly to escape encroachment of European settlers, to form what would become the most important Indian group in modern Tennessee: the Overhill Cherokees.

In 1673 European scouts entered Tennessee at its eastern and western ends. Englishmen James Needham, Gabriel Arthur, and eight hired Indian guides were the first European party to enter East Tennessee. Needham did not last long; he was killed by his Indian guides early in the outing. Arthur won over his traveling companions and joined them on war trips and hunts before returning to Virginia in 1674. Meanwhile, on the western end of the state, French explorers Father Jacques Marquette and trader Louis Joliet came down the Mississippi River and claimed the surrounding valley for the French.

THE LONG HUNTERS

The first Europeans to carve out a foothold in the unknown frontier of Tennessee were traders who made journeys into Indian territory to hunt and trade. These men disappeared for months at a time into the wilderness and were therefore known as long hunters. They left with European-made goods and returned with animal skins. They led pack trains of horses and donkeys over narrow, steep, and crooked mountain trails and through sometimes-hostile territory. It was a lonely, hard life, full of uncertainty. Some of the long hunters were no better than crooks; others were respected by both the Indians and Europeans.

The long hunters included men like Elisha Walden, Kasper Mansker, and Abraham Bledsoe. Daniel Boone, born in North Carolina, was in present-day Washington County in northeastern Tennessee when, in 1760, he carved on a beech tree that he had "cilled" a "bar" nearby. Thomas Sharp Spencer became known as Big Foot and is said to have spent the winter in a hollowed-out sycamore tree. Another trader, a Scotch-Irish man named James Adair, traded with the Indians for years and eventually wrote *A History of the American Indian,* published in London in 1775 and one of the first such accounts.

The animal skins and furs that were the aim of these men's exploits were eventually sold in Charleston and exported to Europe. In 1748 alone, South Carolina merchants exported more than 160,000 skins worth $250,000. The trade was profitable for merchants and, to a lesser extent, the traders themselves. But it was rarely profitable for the Indians, and it helped to wipe out much of Tennessee's native animal life.

THE FRENCH AND INDIAN WAR

In 1754 the contest between the French and the British for control of the New World boiled over into war. Indian alliances were seen as critical to success, and so the British set out to win the support of the Cherokee. They did this by agreeing to build a fort in the land over the mountain from North Carolina—territory that came to be known as the Overhill country. The Cherokee wanted the fort to protect their women and children from French or hostile Indian attack while the men were away. The fort was begun in 1756 near the fork of the Little Tennessee and Tellico Rivers, and it was named Fort Loudoun after the commander of British forces in America. Twelve cannons were transported over the rough mountain terrain by horse to defend the fort from enemy attack.

The construction of Fort Loudoun did not prove to be the glue to hold the Cherokee and British together. In fact, it was not long before relations deteriorated to the point where the Cherokee chief Standing Turkey directed an attack on the fort. A siege ensued. Reinforcements were called for and dispatched, but the British colonel and 1,300 men turned back before reaching the fort. The English inside the fort were weakened by lack of food and surrendered. On August 9, 1760, 180 men, 60 women, and a few children marched out of Fort Loudoun, the first steps of a 140-mile journey to the nearest British fort. The group had been promised to be allowed to retreat peacefully, but on the first night of the journey the group was ambushed: killed were 3 officers, 23 privates, and 3 women. The rest were taken prisoner. The Indians said they were inspired to violence upon finding that the British had failed to surrender all of their firepower as promised.

The Cherokee's action was soon avenged. A year later, Col. James Grant led a party into the Lower Cherokee territory, where they destroyed villages, burnt homes, and cut down fields of corn.

The French and Indian War ended in 1763, and in the Treaty of Paris the French withdrew any claims to lands east of the Mississippi. This result emboldened European settlers and land speculators who were drawn to the land of the Overhill country. The fact that the land still belonged to the Indians did not stop the movement west.

EARLY SETTLERS

With the issue of French possession resolved, settlers began to filter into the Overhill country. Early settlers included William Bean, on the Holston River; Evan Shelby, at Sapling Grove (later Bristol); John Carter, in the Carter Valley; and Jacob Brown, on the Nolichucky River. By 1771 the settlers at Watauga and Nolichucky won a lease from the Cherokee, and the next year, they formed the Watauga Association, a quasi government and the first such in Tennessee territory.

The settlers' success in obtaining land concessions from the Indians was eclipsed in 1775 when the Transylvania Company, led by Richard Henderson of North Carolina, traded £10,000 of goods for 20 million acres of land in Kentucky and Tennessee. The agreement, negotiated at a treaty conference at Sycamore Shoals, was opposed by the Cherokee Indian chief Dragging Canoe, who warned that the Cherokee were paving the way for their own extinction. Despite his warning, the treaty was signed.

Dragging Canoe remained the leader of the Cherokee's resistance to European settlement. In 1776 he orchestrated assaults on the white settlements of Watauga, Nolichucky, Long Island, and Carter's Valley. The offensive, called by some the Cherokee War, had limited success at first, but it ended in defeat for the natives. In 1777 the Cherokee signed a peace treaty with the settlers that ceded more land to the Europeans.

Dragging Canoe and others did not accept the treaty and left the Cherokee as a result. He and his followers moved south, near Chickamauga Creek, where they became known as the Chickamauga tribe. Over time, this tribe attracted other Indians whose common purpose was opposition to white settlement.

The Indians could not, however, overpower the increasing tide of European settlers, who brought superior firepower and greater numbers. Pressure on political leaders to free up more and more land for settlement made relations with the Indians and land agreements with them one of the most important features of political life on the frontier.

In the end, these leaders delivered. Europeans obtained Indian land in Tennessee through a series of treaties and purchases, beginning with the Sycamore Shoals purchase in 1775 and continuing until 1818 when the Chickasaw ceded all control to land west of the Mississippi. Negotiating on behalf of the settlers were leaders including William Blount, the territorial governor, and Andrew Jackson, the first U.S. president from Tennessee.

Nashville itself was settled on Christmas Day in 1796.

INDIAN REMOVAL

Contact with Europeans had a significant impact on the Cherokee's way of life. Christian missionaries introduced education, and in the 1820s Sequoyah developed a Cherokee alphabet, allowing the Indians to read and write in their own language. The Cherokee adopted some of the Europeans' farming practices, as well as some of their social practices, including slavery. Adoption of the European lifestyle was most common among the significant number of mixed-race Cherokee. In 1827 the Cherokee Nation was established, complete with a constitutional system of government and a capital in New Echota, Georgia. From 1828 until 1832, its newspaper, the *Cherokee Phoenix,* was published in both English and Cherokee.

The census of 1828 counted 15,000 Cherokee remaining in Tennessee. They owned 1,000 slaves, 22,400 head of cattle, 7,600 horses, 1,800 spinning wheels, 700 looms, 12 sawmills, 55 blacksmith shops, and 6 cotton gins.

Despite these beginnings of assimilation, or because of them, the Cherokee were not welcome to remain in the new territory. Settlers pushed for a strong policy that would lead to the Cherokee's removal, and they looked over the border to Georgia to see that it could be done. There, in 1832, authorities surveyed lands owned by Cherokee and disposed of them by lottery. Laws were passed to prohibit Indian assemblies and bar Indians from bringing suit in the state. The majority of Tennessee settlers, as well as Georgia officials, pushed for similar measures to be adopted in Tennessee.

The Cherokee were divided in their response: Some felt that moving west represented the best future for their tribe, while others wanted to stay and fight for their land and the Cherokee Nation. In the end, the Cherokee leaders lost hope of remaining, and on December 29, 1835, they signed the removal treaty. Under the agreement, the Cherokee were paid $5 million for all their lands east of the Mississippi, and they were required to move west within two years. When that time expired in 1838 and only a small number of the Cherokee had moved, the U.S. Army evicted the rest by force.

STATEHOOD

Almost as soon as settlers began living on the Tennessee frontier there were movements to form government. Dissatisfied with the protection offered by North Carolina's distant government, settlers drew up their own governments as early as the 1780s. The Watauga Association and Cumberland Compact were early forms of government. In 1785, settlers in northeastern Tennessee seceded from North Carolina and established the State of Franklin. The experiment was short-lived, but foretold that in the future the lands west of the Smoky Mountains would be their own state.

Before Tennessee could become a state, however, it was a territory of the United States. In 1789 North Carolina ratified its own constitution and in doing so ceded its western lands, the Tennessee country, to the U.S. government. These lands eventually became known as the Southwest Territory, and in 1790 President George Washington appointed William Blount its territorial governor.

Blount was a 41-year-old land speculator and businessman who had campaigned actively for the position. A veteran of the War for Independence, Blount knew George Washington and was one of the signers of the U.S. Constitution in 1787.

At the time of its establishment, the Southwest Territory was 43,000 square miles in area. The population of 35,000 was centered in two main areas: the northeastern corner and the Cumberland settlements near present-day Nashville.

Tennessee's request to become a state was being debated in Washington, where finally, on June 1, 1796, President Washington signed the statehood bill and Tennessee became the 16th state in the Union.

FRONTIER LIFE

The new state of Tennessee attracted settlers who were drawn by cheap land and the opportunity it represented. Between 1790 and 1800 the state's population tripled, and by 1810 Tennessee's population had grown to 250,000. The expansion caused a shift in power as the middle and western parts of the state became more populated. The capital moved from Knoxville to Nashville in 1812. It was made the permanent capital of the state in 1843.

Life during the early 19th century in Tennessee was largely rural. For the subsistence farmers who made up the majority of the state's population, life was a relentless cycle of hard work. Many families lived in one- or two-room cabins and spent their days growing food and the fibers needed to make their own clothes; raising animals that supplied farm power, meat, and hides; building or repairing buildings and tools; and cutting firewood in prodigious quantities.

Small-hold farmers often owned no slaves. Those who did only owned one or two and worked alongside them.

Children provided valuable labor on the Tennessee farm. Boys often plowed their first furrow at age nine, and girls of that age were expected to mind younger children, help cook, and learn the skills of midwifery, sewing, and gardening. While women's time was often consumed with child rearing, cooking, and sewing, the housewife worked in the field alongside her husband when she was needed.

EDUCATION AND RELIGION

There were no public schools on the frontier, and the few private schools that existed were not accessible to the farming class. Religious missionaries were often the only people who could read and write in a community, and the first schools were established by churches. Presbyterian, Methodist, and Baptist ministers were the first to reach many settlements in Tennessee.

Settlements were spread out, and few had established churches. As a result, the camp meeting became entrenched in Tennessee culture. The homegrown spirituality of the camp meeting appealed to Tennesseans' independent spirit, which looked suspiciously at official religion and embraced the informal and deeply personal religion of the camp meeting.

The meetings were major events drawing between a few hundred and thousands of people. Wilma Dykeman writes:

> From distances as far as 40, 50 and more miles, they came in wagons, carriages, a wide array of vehicles, and raised their tents...They spent the summer days and nights surrounded by seemingly endless expanse of green forest, supplied with a bounty of cold pure water, breathing that acrid blue wood smoke from rows of campfires and the rich smells of food cooking over glowing red coals, listening to the greetings of old friends, the voices of children playing, crying, growing drowsy, a stamping of the horses, and the bedlam of the meeting itself once the services had begun.

Camp services were passionate and emotional, reaching a feverish pitch as men and women were overtaken by the spirit. Many camp meetings attracted both black and white participants.

THE WAR OF 1812

Tennesseans were among the "War Hawks" in Congress who advocated for war with Great

Britain in 1812. The conflict was seen by many as an opportunity to rid their borders once and for all of all Indians. The government asked for 2,800 volunteers, and 30,000 Tennesseans offered to enlist. This is when Tennessee's nickname as the Volunteer State was born.

Nashville lawyer, politician, and businessman Andrew Jackson was chosen as the leader of the Tennessee volunteers. Despite their shortage of supplies and lack of support from the War Department, Jackson's militia prevailed in a series of lopsided victories. Given command of the southern military district, Andrew Jackson led U.S. forces at the Battle of New Orleans on January 8, 1815. The ragtag group inflicted a crushing defeat on the British, and despite having occurred after the signing of the peace treaty with Great Britain, the battle was a victory that launched Jackson onto the road to the presidency.

GROWTH OF SLAVERY

The state's first settlers planted the seed of slavery in Tennessee, and the state's westward expansion cemented the institution. In 1791 there were 3,400 blacks in Tennessee—about 10 percent of the general population. By 1810, blacks were more than 20 percent of Tennessee's people. The invention of the cotton gin and subsequent rise of King Cotton after the turn of the 19th century also caused a rapid expansion of slavery.

Slavery was most important in West Tennessee; eastern Tennessee, with its mountainous landscape and small farms, had the fewest slaves. In Middle Tennessee the slave population was concentrated in the Central Basin, in the counties of Davidson, Maury, Rutherford, and Williamson. By 1860, 40 percent of the state's slave population was in West Tennessee, with the greatest concentration in Shelby, Fayette, and Haywood Counties, where cotton was grown on plantations somewhat similar to those of the Deep South.

As slavery grew, slave markets were established in Nashville and Memphis. The ban on the interstate sale of slaves was virtually ignored.

From 1790, when the territory was established, until 1831, Tennessee's slave code was relatively lenient. The law recognized a slave as both a chattel and a person, and slaves were entitled to expect protection against the elements and other people. Owners could free their slaves for any reason, and many did, causing growth in Tennessee's free black population in the first half of the 1800s. These free blacks concentrated in eastern and Middle Tennessee, and particularly the cities of Nashville, Memphis, and Knoxville, where they worked as laborers and artisans.

There were vocal opponents to slavery in Tennessee, particularly in the eastern part of the state. The first newspaper in the United States devoted to emancipation was established in 1819 in Jonesborough by Elihu Embree. Charles Osborne, a Quaker minister, preached against slavery shortly after the turn of the 19th century in Tennessee. Emancipationists formed societies in counties including Washington, Sullivan, Blount, Grainger, and Cocke. Many of these early abolitionists opposed slavery on religious grounds, arguing that it was incompatible with the spirit of Christianity.

These abolitionists often argued for the gradual end of slavery and sometimes advocated for the removal of freed slaves to Africa.

SLAVE EXPERIENCES

There was no single slave experience for Tennessee's slaves. On the farm, a slave's experience depended on the size of the farm, the type of crops that were grown, and the number of slaves on the farm.

Most Tennessee slaves lived on small- or medium-sized farms. The 1860 census showed that only one person in the state owned more than 300 slaves, and 47 owned more than 100. More than 75 percent of all slave owners had fewer than 10 slaves. Work assignments varied, but almost all slaves were expected to contribute to their own subsistence by keeping a vegetable garden. Slaves with special skills in areas like carpentry, masonry, blacksmithing, or weaving were hired out.

Urban slaves were domestics, coachmen,

house painters, laundresses, and midwives. In cities, many families owned just one or two slaves, and it was common for slaves to be hired out to others in order to provide a source of income for the slave owner. It became customary in some cities for a market day to be held on New Year's Day, where employers bargained for slave labor over the coming year.

Slaves sought to overcome their circumstances by building close-knit communities. These communities acted as surrogate families for slaves whose own spouse, parents, siblings, and children were often sold, causing lifelong separation.

Religion also served as a survival mechanism for Tennessee's slaves. Methodist and Baptist churches opened their doors to slaves, providing a space where slaves could be together. The musical tradition that resulted is today's gospel music. Religion also provided a vehicle for some slaves to learn how to read and write.

THE CIVIL WAR

In the 1830s, Tennessee's position on slavery hardened. The Virginia slave uprising led by Nat Turner frightened slave owners, who instituted patrols to search for runaway slaves and tightened codes on slave conduct. In 1834, the state constitution was amended to bar free blacks from voting, a sign of whites' increasing fear of the black people living in their midst.

The division between East and West Tennessee widened as many in the east were sympathetic with the antislavery forces that were growing in Northern states. In the west, the support for slavery was unrelenting.

Despite several strident secessionists, including Tennessee governor Isham Harris, Tennessee remained uncertain about secession. In February 1861, the state voted against a convention on secession. But with the attack on Fort Sumter two months later, followed by President Abraham Lincoln's call for volunteers to coerce the seceded states back to the Union, public opinion shifted. On June 8, 1861, Tennesseans voted 105,000 to 47,000 to secede.

A BORDER STATE

Tennessee was of great strategic importance during the Civil War. It sent an estimated 186,000 men to fight for the Confederacy, more than any other state. Another 31,000 are credited with having joined the Union army.

Tennessee had resources that both the Union and Confederacy deemed important for victory, including agricultural and manufacturing industries, railroads, and rivers. And its geographic position as a long-border state made it nearly unavoidable.

TENNESSEE BATTLES

Some 454 battles and skirmishes were fought in Tennessee during the war. Most were small, but several key battles took place on Tennessee soil.

The first of these was the Union victory at Forts Henry and Donelson in January 1862. Gen. Ulysses S. Grant and 15,000 Union troops steamed up the Tennessee River and quickly captured Fort Henry. They then marched overland to Fort Donelson, and, 10 days later, this Confederate fort fell as well. The battle of Fort Donelson is where U. S. Grant earned his sobriquet: He was asked by the Confederate general the terms of capitulation, and he replied, "unconditional surrender."

The Battle of Shiloh was the bloodiest and largest to take place in Tennessee. The battle happened near Pittsburgh Landing (the Federal name for the struggle), on the Mississippi River about 20 miles north of the Mississippi state line. More than 100,000 men took part in this battle, and there were more than 24,000 casualties.

The battle began with a surprise Confederate attack at dawn on April 6, 1862, a Sunday. For several hours, victory seemed in reach for the Southern troops, but the Union rallied and held. They built a strong defensive line covering Pittsburgh Landing, and on April 7 they took the offensive and swept the Confederates from the field. The Confederates' loss was devastating, and Shiloh represented a harbinger of the future bloodletting between Blue and Gray.

Another important Tennessee battle was at Stones River, near Murfreesboro, on December

31, 1862. Like at Shiloh, the early momentum here was with the Confederates, but victory belonged to the Union. The Battle of Chickamauga Creek, fought a few miles over the state line in Georgia, was a rare Confederate victory. It did not come cheaply, however, with 21,000 members of the Army of Tennessee killed.

Federal forces retreated and dug in near Chattanooga, while Confederates occupied the heights above the town. Union reinforcements led by General Grant drove the Confederates back into Georgia at the Battle of Lookout Mountain, also known as the "Battle Above the Clouds," on November 25, 1863.

WARTIME OCCUPATION

Battles were only part of the wartime experience in Tennessee. The Civil War caused hardship for ordinary residents on a scale that many had never before seen. There was famine and poverty. Schools and churches were closed. Harassment and recrimination plagued the state, and fear was widespread.

In February 1863, one observer described the population of Memphis as "11,000 original whites, 5,000 slaves, and 19,000 newcomers of all kinds, including traders, fugitives, hangers-on, and negroes."

Memphis fell to the Union on June 6, 1862, and it was occupied for the remainder of the war. The city's experience during this wartime occupation reversed decades of growth and left a city that would struggle for years.

Those who could fled the city. Many of those who remained stopped doing business (some of these because they refused to pledge allegiance to the Union and were not permitted). Northern traders entered the city and took over many industries, while blacks who abandoned nearby plantations flooded into the city.

While the military focused on punishing Confederate sympathizers, conditions in Memphis deteriorated. Crime and disorder abounded, and guerrilla bands developed to fight the Union occupation. The Federal commander responsible for the city was Maj. Gen. William T. Sherman, and he adopted a policy of collective responsibility, which held civilians responsible for guerrilla attacks in their neighborhoods. Sherman destroyed hundreds of homes, farms, and towns in the exercise of this policy.

The war was equally damaging in other parts of Tennessee. In Middle Tennessee, retreating Confederate soldiers after the fall of Fort Donelson demolished railroads and burned bridges so as not to leave them for the Union. Union troops also destroyed and appropriated the region's resources. Federals took horses, pigs, cows, corn, hay, cotton, fence rails, firearms, and tools. Sometimes this was carried out through official requisitions, but at other times it amounted to little more than pillaging.

Criminals took advantage of the loss of public order, and bands of thieves and bandits began roaming the countryside.

The experience in East Tennessee was different. Because of the region's widespread Union sympathies, it was the Confederacy that first occupied the eastern territory. During this time hundreds of alleged Unionists were charged with treason and jailed. When the Confederates began conscripting men into military service in 1862, tensions in East Tennessee grew. Many East Tennesseans fled to Kentucky, and distrust, bitterness, and violence escalated. In September 1863 the tables turned, however, and the Confederates were replaced by the Federals, whose victories elsewhere enabled them to now focus on occupying friendly East Tennessee.

THE EFFECTS OF THE WAR

Tennessee lost most of a generation of young men to the Civil War. Infrastructure was destroyed, and thousands of farms, homes, and other properties were razed. The state's reputation on the national stage had been tarnished, and it would be decades until Tennessee had the political power that it enjoyed during the Age of Jackson. But while the war caused tremendous hardships for the state, it also led to the freeing of 275,000 black Tennesseans from slavery.

RECONSTRUCTION

Tennessee was no less divided during the years following the Civil War than it was during the conflict. The end to the war ushered in a period where former Unionists—now allied with the Radical Republicans in Congress—disenfranchised and otherwise marginalized former Confederates and others who had been sympathetic with the Southern cause.

They also pushed through laws that extended voting and other rights to the newly freed blacks, changes that led to a powerful backlash and the establishment of such shadowy groups as the Ku Klux Klan.

The greatest legacy of the Civil War was the emancipation of Tennessee's slaves. Following the war, many freed blacks left the countryside and moved to cities, including Memphis, Nashville, Chattanooga, and Knoxville, where they worked as skilled laborers, domestics, and more. Other blacks remained in the countryside, working as wage laborers on farms or sharecropping in exchange for occupancy on part of a former large-scale plantation.

The Freedmen's Bureau worked in Tennessee for a short period after the end of the war, and it succeeded in establishing schools for blacks. During this period the state's first black colleges were established: Fisk, Tennessee Central, LeMoyne, Roger Williams, Lane, and Knoxville.

As in other states, blacks in Tennessee enjoyed short-lived political power during Reconstruction. The right to vote and the concentration of blacks in certain urban areas paved the way for blacks to be elected to the Tennessee House of Representatives, beginning with Sampson Keeble of Nashville in 1872. In all, 13 blacks were elected as representatives between 1872 and 1887, including James C. Napier, Edward Shaw, and William Yardley, who also ran for governor.

Initially, these pioneers met mild acceptance from whites, but as time progressed whites became uncomfortable sharing political power with black people. By the 1890s, racist Jim Crow policies of segregation, poll taxes, secret ballots, literacy tests, and intimidation prevented blacks from holding elected office—and in many cases, voting—in Tennessee again until after the civil rights movement of the 1960s.

The Republican Party saw the end of its influence with the end of the Brownlow governorship. Democrats rejected the divisive policies of the Radical Republicans, sought to protect the racial order that set blacks at a disadvantage to whites, and were less concerned about the state's mounting debt than the Republicans.

ECONOMIC RECOVERY

The social and political upheaval caused by the Civil War was matched or exceeded by the economic catastrophe that it represented for the state. Farms and industry were damaged or destroyed, public infrastructure was razed, schools were closed, and the system of slavery that underpinned most of the state's economy was gone. During this period Nashville flourished, as the city become an essential business hub. The Nashville population skyrocketed from less than 17,000 in 1860 to more than 80,000 just 40 years later. In Nashville, new distilleries, sawmills, paper mills, stove factories, and an oil refinery led the way to industrialization.

The economic setback was seen as an opportunity by proponents of the "New South," who advocated for an industrial and economic revival that would catapult the South to prosperity impossible under the agrarian and slavery-based antebellum economy. The New South movement was personified by carpetbagging Northern capitalists who moved to Tennessee and set up industries that would benefit from cheap labor and abundant natural resources. Many Tennesseans welcomed these newcomers and advocated for their fellow Tennesseans to put aside regional differences and also welcome the Northern investors. Mines were opened in Cleveland, flour mills in Jackson, and textile factories in Tullahoma and other parts of the state.

WORLD WAR I

True to its nickname, Tennessee sent a large number of volunteer troops to fight in World War I. Most became part of the 30th "Old Hickory" Division, which entered the war on August 17, 1918. The most famous Tennessee veteran of World War I was Alvin C. York, a farm boy from the Cumberland Mountains who staged a one-man offensive against the German army after becoming separated from his own detachment. Reports say that York killed 20 German soldiers and persuaded 131 more to surrender.

WOMEN'S SUFFRAGE

The movement for women's suffrage had been established in Tennessee prior to the turn of the 20th century, and it gained influence as the century progressed. The Southern Woman Suffrage Conference was held in Memphis in 1906, and a statewide suffrage organization was established. State bills to give women the right to vote failed in 1913 and 1917, but support was gradually growing. In the summer of 1920, the 19th Amendment had been ratified by 35 states, and one more ratification was needed to make it law. Tennessee was one of five states yet to vote on the measure, and on August 9, Governor Roberts called a special sitting of the legislature to consider the amendment.

Furious campaigning and public debate led up to the special sitting. The Senate easily ratified the amendment 25 to 4, but in the House of Representatives the vote was much closer: 49 to 47. Governor Roberts certified the result and notified the secretary of state: Tennessee had cast the deciding vote for women's suffrage.

THE DEPRESSION

The progress and hope of the 1920s was soon forgotten with the Great Depression. Tennessee's economic hard times started before the 1929 stock market crash. Farming in the state was hobbled by low prices and low returns during the 1920s. Farmers and laborers displaced by this trend sought work in new industries like the Dupont plant in Old Hickory, Eastman-Kodak in Kingsport, or the Aluminum Company of America in Blount County. But others, including many African Americans, left Tennessee for northern cities such as Chicago.

The Depression made bad things worse. Farmers tried to survive, turning to subsistence farming. In cities, unemployed workers lined up for relief. Major bank failures in 1930 brought most financial business in the state to a halt.

President Roosevelt's New Deal provided some relief for Tennesseans. The Civilian Conservation Corps, Public Works Administration, and Civil Works Administration were established in Tennessee. Through the CCC, more than 7,000 Tennesseans planted millions of pine seedlings, developed parks, and built fire towers. Through the PWA, more than 500 projects were undertaken, including bridges, housing, water systems, and roads. Hundreds of Tennesseans were employed by the CWA to clean public buildings, landscape roads, and do other work.

But no New Deal institution had more impact on Tennessee than the Tennessee Valley Authority. Architects of TVA saw it as a way to improve agriculture along the Tennessee River, alleviate poverty, and produce electrical power. The dam system would also improve navigation along what was then an often dangerous river. The law establishing TVA was introduced by Senator George W. Norris of Nebraska and passed in 1933. Soon after, dams were under construction, and trade on the river increased due to improved navigability. Even more importantly, electric power was now so cheap that even Tennesseans in remote parts of the state could afford it. By 1945, TVA was the largest electrical utility in the nation, and new industries were attracted by cheap energy and improved transportation. Tourists also came to enjoy the so-called Great Lakes of the South.

WORLD WAR II

Tennessee, like the rest of the country, was changed by World War II. The war effort transformed the state's economy and led to a migration to the cities unprecedented in Tennessee's history. The tiny mountain town of Oak Ridge became the state's fifth-largest city almost overnight, and it is synonymous with the atomic bomb that was dropped on Hiroshima at the final stage of the war.

More than 300,000 Tennesseans served in World War II, and just under 6,000 died. During the war, Camps Forrest, Campbell, and Tyson served as prisoner-of-war camps. Several hundred war refugees settled in Tennessee, many in the Nashville area.

POSTWAR TENNESSEE

Tennessee's industrialization continued after the war. By 1960 there were more city dwellers than rural dwellers in the state, and Tennessee was ranked the 16th most industrialized state in the United States. Industry that had developed during the war transformed to peacetime operation.

Ex-servicemen were not content with the political machines that had controlled Tennessee politics for decades. In 1948 Congressman Estes Kefauver won a U.S. Senate seat, defeating the candidate chosen by Memphis mayor Ed Crump. The defeat signaled an end to Crump's substantial influence in statewide elections. In 1953 Tennessee repealed the state poll tax, again limiting politicians' ability to manipulate the vote. The tide of change also swept in Senator Albert Gore Sr. and Governor Frank Clement in 1952. Kefauver, Gore, and Clement were moderate Democrats of the New South.

CIVIL RIGHTS IN TENNESSEE

The Nashville lunch counter sit-ins of 1960 were an important milestone in both the local and national civil rights movements. Led by students from the city's black universities, the sit-ins eventually forced an end to racial segregation of the city's public services. Over two months, hundreds of black students were arrested for sitting at white-only downtown lunch counters. Black consumers' boycott of downtown stores put additional pressure on the business community. On April 19, thousands of protesters marched in silence to the courthouse to confront city officials, and the next day Rev. Martin Luther King Jr. addressed Fisk University. On May 10, 1960, several downtown stores integrated their lunch counters, and Nashville became the first major city in the South to begin desegregating its public facilities.

MODERN TENNESSEE

The industrialization that began during World War II has continued in modern-day Tennessee. In 1980 Nissan built what was then the largest truck assembly plant in the world at Smyrna, Tennessee. In 1987 Saturn Corporation chose Spring Hill as the site for its $2.1 billion automobile plant.

At the same time, however, the state's older industries—including textiles and manufacturing—have suffered losses over the past three decades, due in part to the movement of industry outside of the United States.

During the 1950s and beyond, Tennessee developed a reputation as a hotbed of musical talent. The Grand Ole Opry in Nashville was representative of a second musical genre that came to call Tennessee home: country music. Country legend Roy Acuff helped put the city and its music scene on the map. He founded one of the city's first music publishing companies and later ran for governor of the state.

Nashville is still home to North America's largest-volume vinyl pressing plant. This, literally, is where the music is made.

NASHVILLE SIT-INS

Greensboro, North Carolina, is often considered as the site of the first sit-ins of the American civil rights movement. But, in truth, activists in Nashville carried out the first "test" sit-ins in late 1959. In these test cases, protesters left the facilities after being refused service and talking to management about the injustice of segregation. In between these test sit-ins and the moment when Nashville activists would launch a full-scale sit-in campaign, students in Greensboro took that famous first step.

The Nashville sit-ins began on February 13, 1960, when a group of African-American students from local colleges and universities sat at a downtown lunch counter and refused to move until they were served. The protesting students endured verbal and physical abuse, and were arrested.

Community members raised money for the students' bail, and black residents of the city began an economic boycott of downtown stores that practiced segregation. On April 19, the home of Z. Alexander Looby, a black lawyer who was representing the students, was bombed. Later the same day, students led a spontaneous, peaceful, and silent march through the streets of downtown Nashville to the courthouse. Diane Nash, a student leader, asked Nashville mayor Ben West if he thought it was morally right for a restaurant to refuse to serve someone based on the color of his or her skin. Mayor West said, "No."

The march was an important turning point for the city. The combined effect of the sit-ins, the boycott, and the march caused, in 1960, Nashville to be the first major Southern city to experience widespread desegregation of its public facilities. The events also demonstrated to activists in other parts of the South that non-violence was an effective tool of protest.

The story of the young people who led the Nashville sit-ins is told in the book *The Children* by David Halberstam. In 2001, Nashville resident Bill King was so moved by the story of the protests that he established an endowment to fundraise for a permanent civil rights collection at the Nashville Public Library. In 2003, the Civil Rights Room at the Nashville Public Library was opened. It houses books, oral histories, audiovisual records, microfilm, dissertations, and stunning photographs of the events of 1960. The words of one student organizer, John Lewis, who went on to become a congressman from Georgia, are displayed over the entryway: "If not us, then who; if not now, then when?"

Government

Tennessee is governed by its constitution, unchanged since 1870 when it was revised in light of emancipation, the Civil War, and Reconstruction.

Tennessee has a governor who is elected to four-year terms, a legislature, and court system. The lieutenant governor is not elected statewide; he or she is chosen by the Senate and also serves as its speaker.

The legislature, or General Assembly, is made up of the 99-member House of Representatives and the 33-member Senate. The Tennessee State Supreme Court is made up of five members, no two of whom can be from the same Grand Division. The Supreme Court chooses the state's attorney general.

The executive branch consists of 21 cabinet-level departments, which employ 39,000 state workers. Departments are led by a commissioner who is appointed by the governor and serves as a member of his or her cabinet.

Tennessee has 95 counties; the largest is Shelby County, which contains Memphis. The smallest county by size is Trousdale, with 113 square miles; the smallest population is in Pickett County.

The state has 11 electoral college votes in U.S. presidential elections.

MODERN POLITICS

Like other Southern states, Tennessee has seen a gradual shift to the political right since the 1960s. The shift began in 1966 with Howard Baker's election to the U.S. Senate, and it continued with Tennessee's support for Republican presidential candidate Richard Nixon in 1968 and 1972. Despite a few exceptions, the shift has continued into the 21st century, although Nashville, Memphis, and other parts of Middle and West Tennessee remain Democratic territory.

East Tennessee holds the distinction as one of a handful of Southern territories that has consistently supported the Republican Party since the Civil War. Today, Republicans outpoll Democrats in this region by as much as three to one.

The statewide trend toward the Republican party continued in 2008, with Tennessee being one of only a handful of states where Democrat Barack Obama received a lesser proportion of votes than did Senator John Kerry four years earlier. State Republicans also succeeded in gaining control of both houses of the state legislature. The general shift to the right has continued in the governor's office. Previous governor Phil Bredesen is a Democrat, but he was succeeded by Republican Bill Haslam. Since 1967, no party has been able to keep the governor's seat for more than two terms.

Andrew Jackson may still be the most prominent Tennessean in American political history, but Tennessee politicians continue to play a role on the national stage. Albert Gore Jr., elected to the U.S. House of Representatives in 1976, served as vice president under President Bill Clinton from 1992 until 2000, and he lost the highly contested 2000 presidential contest to George W. Bush. Gore famously lost his home state to Bush, further evidence of Tennessee's move to the right. Gore went on to champion global climate change and win the Nobel Peace Prize, and he is often seen around Nashville.

Lamar Alexander, a former governor of Tennessee, was appointed secretary of education by the first President Bush in 1990. Alexander—famous for his flannel shirts—ran unsuccessfully for president and was later elected senator from Tennessee. Bill Frist, a doctor, was also elected senator and rose to be the Republican majority leader during the presidency of George W. Bush, before quitting politics for medical philanthropy.

The most recent Tennessean to seek the Oval Office was former senator and *Law and Order* star Fred Thompson, from Lewisburg in Middle Tennessee.

One of the most persistent political issues for Tennesseans in modern times has been the state's tax structure. The state first established a 2 percent sales tax in 1947, and it was increased incrementally over the years, eventually reaching 7 percent in 2013. With local options, it is one of the highest sales tax rates in the country. (The state sales tax on food is 5.5 percent.) At the same time, the state has failed on more than one occasion—most recently during the second term of Republican governor Donald Sundquist in the late 1990s—to establish an income tax that would provide greater stability to the state's revenues.

Like much of the country, in 2008 Tennessee faced a serious budget crunch that led to the elimination of thousands of state jobs, cutbacks at state-funded universities, and the scaling back of the state health insurance program. Nashville and Davidson County have a consolidated government, and half a century ago were the first municipalities to choose this government structure. The system, which celebrated its 50th anniversary in 2013, is often thought of as being more efficient and reducing redundancy.

Economy

Tennessee has the 18th-largest economy in the United States. Important industries include health care, education, farming, electrical power, and tourism. In the past few years, most job growth has been recorded in the areas of leisure, hospitality, education, and health care. Manufacturing, mining, and construction jobs have declined. Despite the overall decline in manufacturing, there was good news in 2008 when Volkswagen announced that it chose Chattanooga as home for a new $1 billion plant, expected to bring 2,000 jobs to the state in the coming years.

Tennessee's unemployment rate fluctuates but generally sits a half point above the national average. In 2010, the jobless rate was about 9.4 percent.

About 16.5 percent of Tennessee families live in poverty, roughly 3 percent higher than the nationwide average. The median household income in 2011 was $38,686—75 percent of the U.S. median income. All of Tennessee's cities have poverty rates higher than the state or national average.

AGRICULTURE

Farming accounts for 14.2 percent, or $38.5 billion, of the Tennessee economy. More than 42 percent of the state's land is used in farming; 63.6 percent of this is cropland.

Soybeans, tobacco, corn, and hay are among Tennessee's most important agricultural crops. Cattle and calf production, chicken farming, and cotton cultivation are also important parts of the farm economy.

Greene County, in northeastern Tennessee,

is the leading county for all types of cow farming; Giles and Lincoln Counties, in the south-central part of the state, rank second and third. The leading cotton producer is Haywood County, followed by Crockett and Gibson, all three of which are located in West Tennessee. Other counties where agriculture figures largely into the economy are Obion, Dyer, Rutherford, and Robertson.

Tennessee ranks sixth among U.S. states for equine production, and walking or quarter horses account for more than half of the state's estimated 210,000 head of equine. The state ranks third for tomatoes, fourth for tobacco, and seventh for cotton.

Some farmers have begun converting to corn production in anticipation of a biofuel boom.

TOURISM

According to the state tourism department, the industry generated $14.1 billion in economic activity in 2010. More than 170,000 Tennessee jobs are linked to tourism. The state credits the industry with generating more than $1 billion in state and local tax revenue. More than 50,000 Nashville jobs are tied to the hospitality industry. The Nashville Convention and Visitors Bureau estimates than in 2011, 11 million visitors came to the city, bringing in $4 million in revenues.

In addition to tourism, people typically assume that music is job number one in Nashville. It is true that the music industry is important to the city, but health care, real estate, and education are bigger industries in Music City.

People and Culture

DEMOGRAPHICS

Nashville's populationas of 2011 was 609,644 people, according to the US Census. Approximately 60 percent of Tennesseans are white, 27 percent are African American, and 8 percent are Latino or Hispanic. Nashville's foreign-born population tripled during the decade between 1990 and 2000, and 11 percent of the city's population was born outside of the United States. This includes large populations from Mexico, Vietnam, Laos, and Somalia. Nashville is also home to more than 11,000 Iraqi Kurds.

RELIGION

Nashville is unquestionably part of the U.S. Bible Belt; the conservative Christian faith is both prevalent and prominent all over the state. Fifty-eight percent of Nashvillians call themselves Christians, and 27 percent identify as Baptist. Nashville is the headquarters of the Southern Baptist Convention, the National Baptist Convention, and the United Methodist Church. The city has growing populations that practice Judaism and Islam.

Non-Christians will feel most comfortable in urban areas, where numbers of religious minorities have grown in recent years and where the influence of the local churches is not as great.

One practical effect of Tennessee's Christian bent is that alcohol is not sold on Sunday in stores, but it can be served in restaurants and bars.

LANGUAGE

Nashvillians speak English, of a kind. Many have a Tennessee drawl, although with transplants from across the world, there's not really a Music City accent.

Speech patterns have been documented throughout the state, outlined by Michael

FAMOUS NASHVILLIANS

Since its earliest days, Nashville's siren song has attracted those who wanted to see (or more likely, hear) their name in lights. The wannabe famous come here to get their break, and they stay here because, for the most part, it is an easy place to be famous. Uber-stars like Keith Urban and Nicole Kidman can shop at Whole Foods and take their kids to the library without being harassed by paparazzi.

- Tons of the music industry's elite call Nashville (or, more often than not, suburban Leipers Fork and Franklin) home. In addition to Urban, Taylor Swift, Brad Paisley, Robert Plant, Ben Folds, The Black Keys and the Kings of Leon, Jack White, and Peter Frampton live here at least part of the year.

- But it isn't just the musicians who can be seen around town. Since ABC's drama *Nashville* started airing, its actors can be seen here, too, including Connie Britton. Finance guru Dave Ramsey's office is located in suburban Brentwood. Travis Stork, of *The Bachelor* and *The Doctors* fame is often sighted in the 12 South neighborhood.

- Al Gore Jr., though born in Washington D.C., and raised in Carthage, Tennessee, is closely associated with Nashville. After the Vietnam War he attended Vanderbilt University for one year and then spent five years as a reporter for the *Tennessean*. The former U.S. vice president has had a home in Nashville for many decades.

- Remember that celebrities like to live here because they get a chance to be "normal." Use discretion when asking for autographs or taking photos. And, most important, don't overlook seeing the next soon-to-be-star by searching only for the big-name celebs.

Montgomery of the University of South Carolina in the *Tennessee Encyclopedia of History and Culture.* Montgomery writes that Tennesseans tend to pronounce vowels in the words *pen* and *hem* as *pin* and *him;* they shift the accent to the beginning of words, so *Tennessee* becomes *TIN-isee;* they clip or reduce the vowel in words like *ride* so it sounds more like *rad;* and vowels in other words are stretched, so that a single-syllable word like *bed* becomes *bay-ud.*

Local speech patterns are not limited to word pronunciation. Tennesseans also speak with folksy and down-home language. Speakers often use colorful metaphors, and greater value is placed on the quality of expression than the perfection of grammar.

ESSENTIALS

Getting There

Thanks to a friendly, accessible airport, easy access to several interstates, reliable bus services, and a plethora of rental cars, getting to Music City shouldn't be a hassle (although no guarantees about the rush-hour traffic once you get here).

Many visitors to Nashville drive their own cars. The highways are good, distances are manageable, and many, if not most, destinations in the city and surrounding area are not accessible by public transportation.

If you're coming to Nashville for a weekend getaway or a conference, and staying downtown or in Music Valley, you may be able to manage without a car. Many of the major attractions are within walking distance of downtown, and the Music Valley hotels have shuttles. But the lack of wheels will limit your ability to visit attractions outside the main tourist areas. If you will have significant time outside your conference room, consider bringing or renting a car.

BY AIR

The recently renovated **Nashville International Airport** (BNA, http://

flynashville.com) brings back some of the pleasure to air travel. Despite shuttling 10 million passengers annually, it is easy to navigate, affordable to park at, and rarely overwhelmingly crowded. BNA offers email updates that tell travelers when to expect congestion, so they can plan accordingly.

The four-runway airport is filled with local art and live music and comfortable waiting areas for those picking up in-bound passengers. There's even a health clinic for routine medical care.

At the Nashville International Airport, you can exchange currency at SunTrust Bank near A/B concourse or at the Business Service Center (Wright Travel, 615/275-2658) near C/D concourse.

Many of the major hotels offer shuttles from the airport; there's a kiosk on the lower level of the terminal to help you find the right one.

Gray Line Transportation (615/883-5555, www.graylinenashville.com) offers regular shuttle service from the airport to downtown, West End, and Music Valley hotels. The shuttle departs from the airport every 15-20 minutes between 4am and 11pm; reservations are not required. Call ahead to book your hotel pickup at the end of your trip. Fare is $14 one way and $25 round-trip.

BY BUS

Greyhound (709 5th Ave. S., www.greyhound.com) fully serves Music City, with daily routes that crisscross the state in nearly every direction. In 2012 the city opened a new, LEED-certified depot. The environmentally friendly building has parking for picking up passengers, a restaurant, vending area, and ample space for buses coming and going. Service goes to major cities in most directions, including Atlanta, Chattanooga, Memphis, and Louisville.

Budget-friendly **Megabus** (http://us.megabus.com) also leaves from the same station. Megabus boasts free Wi-Fi on board and, perhaps because of that, attracts a younger clientele.

BY CAR

If you don't bring your own car, a dozen different major rental agencies have a fleet of cars, trucks, and SUVs at the airport. Agencies include **Alamo** (615/361-7467, www.alamo.com), **Avis** (615/361-1212, www.avis.com), and **Hertz** (615/361-3131, www.hertz.com). For the best rates, use an online travel search tool, such as Expedia (www.expedia.com) or Travelocity (www.travelocity.com), and book the car early, along with your airline tickets.

Getting Around

DRIVING

A reliable road map or GPS is essential for exploring Nashville by car. The city is only vaguely laid out on a grid, and even then, the numeric grid is a suggestion, rather than the rule. Roads frequently change names and merge into other roads (even numbered streets that seem like they ought to be parallel). Locals know this and are more than willing to give directions, but they often do so using landmarks ("Turn left where the Shoney's used to be") rather than street names.

The interstates are a little easier to navigate than side streets. I-65 and I-24 create a tight inner beltway that encircles the heart of the city. I-440 is an outer beltway that circles the southern half of the city, while I-40 runs horizontally, from east to west. Briley Parkway, shown on some maps as Highway TN-155, is a highway that circles the north and east perimeters of the city.

City residents use the interstates not just for long journeys but for short cross-town jaunts as well. Most businesses give directions according to the closest interstate exit.

Non-interstate thoroughfares emanate out from Nashville like spokes in a wheel. Many are named for the communities that they eventually run into. Murfreesboro Pike runs southeast from the city; Hillsboro Pike (Rte. 431) starts out as 21st Avenue South and takes you to Hillsboro Village and Green Hills.

the Nashville skyline

Broadway becomes West End Avenue and takes you directly to Belle Meade and, eventually, the Loveless Cafe. It does not take long to realize that roads in Nashville have a bad habit of changing names all of a sudden, so be prepared and check the map to avoid getting too confused.

For real-time traffic advisories and road construction closures, dial 511 from any touchtone phone, or go to www.tn511.com.

PARKING
There is metered parking on most downtown streets, but some have prohibited-parking signs effective during morning and afternoon rush hours. Always read the fine print carefully.

There is plenty of off-street parking in lots and garages. Expect to pay about $10 a day for garage parking. Park It! Downtown (parkit-downtown.com) is a great resource for finding downtown parking deals, plus information about the shuttle that transports parkers to LP Field during downtown events.

TRAFFIC REPORTS
Nashville traffic is among the worst in the nation. For current traffic and road reports, including weather-related closures, construction closures, and traffic jams, dial 511 from any mobile or landline. You can also log on to www.tn511.com.

TAXIS
Licensed taxicabs will have an orange driver permit, usually displayed on the visor or dashboard.

Several reliable cab companies are **Allied Cab Company** (615/244-7433 or 625/320-9083, www.nashvillecab.com), **Checker Cab** (615/256-7000), **Music City Taxi Inc.** (615/865-4100, www.musiccitytaxi.com), and **United Cab** (615/228-6969). Taxi rates are $2.10 per mile.

If cruising around in a stretch limo is more your style, call **Basic Black Limo** (615/430-8157, www.basicblacklimo.net). The rate is $125 per hour on Saturday nights; the limo seats up to 14 passengers.

© MARGARET LITTMAN

PUBLIC TRANSPORTATION

Nashville's **Metropolitan Transit Authority** operates city buses. Pick up a map and schedule from either of the two downtown visitors centers, or online at www.nashvillemta.org.

Improvements to the city's public transport system have made it easier to use, but few tourists ride the buses because they can be difficult to understand if you're new to the city. One favorite is the Music City Circuit, a free bus that runs between downtown and the Gulch. These Blue and Green Circuit buses stop at 75 different spots on three different routes. One route that is helpful, however, is the Opry Mills Express that travels from downtown Nashville to Music Valley, home of the Grand Ole Opry, Opryland Hotel, and Opry Mills, the shopping mall. The Opry Mills Express departs the Bridgestone Arena 13 times a day on weekdays. Fare is $1.70 one way; $0.85 for senior citizens. You can pick up a detailed route timetable from either of the two downtown visitors centers or online.

On Tennessee Titans' game days, the MTA offers its End Zone Express. Park at either Greer Stadium (where the Nashville Sounds play) or the state employee lot at 4th Avenue North and Harrison, and for just $6 you get shuttled straight to LP Field.

COMMUTER RAIL

In 2006 Nashville debuted the **Music City Star Rail** (501 Union St., 615/862-8833, www.musiccitystar.org), a commuter rail system designed to ease congestion around the city. With service Monday-Friday, several times a day, trains connect Donelson, Hermitage, Mount Juliet, and Lebanon to downtown Nashville. There is often additional service during special events, such as the 4th of July celebration downtown. More routes are planned for the future.

One-way tickets can be purchased for $5 each from vending machines at any of the stations. You can pre-purchase single-trip tickets, 10-trip packs, and monthly passes at a discount online. For a complete list of ticket outlets, contact the railway.

BICYCLING

Riding a bike as transportation, rather than exercise, is still a growing pursuit in Nashville, with more activity in some neighborhoods than others.

Many roadways lack dedicated bike lanes, and while some businesses have bike racks out front, many do not. That said, both those who want to ride their own bikes and those who want to rent will discover that two wheels are a good way to see Music City. The Arts and Leisure chapter of this book highlights places to rent, ride, and repair bikes. If you're looking for more information on biking around Nashville and recommended routes in the surrounding countryside, check out www.nashvillecyclist.com, an online community of bikers.

The **Harpeth Bike Club** (www.harpethbikeclub.com) is Nashville's largest bike club. It organizes weekend and weekday group rides April-October, plus races and social events where you can meet other bike enthusiasts.

Tips for Travelers

TRAVELING WITH CHILDREN

It is hard to imagine a place better for family vacations than Music City. There are museums and kid-friendly exhibits at most of the major attractions. And don't forget the zoo or railroad excursions. Nearby state parks provide numerous places to camp, hike, swim, fish, and explore.

Many hotels and inns offer special discounts for families, and casual restaurants almost always have a children's menu with lower-priced, kid-friendly choices.

SENIOR TRAVELERS

Elderhostel (800/454-5768, www.elderhostel.org), which organizes educational tours for people over 55, offers tours in Memphis and Nashville.

For discounts and help with trip planning, try the **AARP** (800/687-2277, www.aarp.org), which offers a full-service travel agency, trip insurance, a motor club, and the AARP Passport program, which provides you with senior discounts for hotels, car rentals, and other things.

Persons over 55 should always check for a senior citizen discount. Most attractions and some hotels and restaurants have special pricing for senior citizens.

GAY AND LESBIAN TRAVELERS

Tennessee's gay, lesbian, bisexual, and transgender people have a mixed bag. On one hand, this is the Bible Belt, a state where not long ago a bill was introduced that would have banned teachers from even saying the word *gay* in the classroom. (This is often referred to as the "Don't Say Gay" bill.) On the other hand, there has been no better time to be gay in Tennessee. More and more social, civic, and political organizations are waking up to the gay community, and there are vibrant gay scenes in many Nashville neighborhoods.

Three different publications cover the gay, lesbian, bisexual, and transgender community in Nashville. *InsideOut Nashville* (www.insideoutnashville.com) is a free weekly; *Out and About* (www.outandaboutnewspaper.com) is a free monthly newsmagazine.

In Nashville, the **Doubletree Hotel Nashville** (315 4th Ave. N., 615/244-8200, www.doubletree.hilton.com) welcomes lesbian and gay guests. They also offer commitment ceremonies. **International Travel Inc.** (4004 Hillsboro Rd., 615/385-1222) is a Nashville-based gay-friendly travel agency.

Several specific guidebooks and websites give helpful listings of gay-friendly hotels, restaurants, and bars. The Damron guides (www.damron.com) offer Tennessee listings; the International Gay and Lesbian Travel Association (IGLTA, www.iglta.org) is a trade organization with listings of gay-friendly hotels, tour operators, and much more. San Francisco-based Now, Voyager (www.nowvoyager.com) is a gay-owned and gay-operated travel agency that specializes in gay tours, vacation packages, and cruises.

TRAVELERS WITH DISABILITIES

More people with disabilities are traveling than ever before. The Americans with Disabilities Act requires most public buildings to make provisions for disabled people, although in practice accessibility may be spotty.

When you make your hotel reservations, always check that the hotel is prepared to accommodate you. Airlines will also make special arrangements for you if you request help in advance. To reduce stress, try to travel during off-peak times.

Several national organizations have information and advice about traveling with disabilities. The **Society for Accessible Travel and Hospitality** (www.sath.org) publishes links to major airlines' accessibility policies and publishes travel tips for people with all types of disabilities, including blindness, deafness, mobility disorders, diabetes, kidney disease, and arthritis. The society publishes *Open World,* a magazine about accessible travel.

Wheelchair Getaways (800/642-2042, www.wheelchairgetaways.com) is a national chain specializing in renting vans that are wheelchair accessible or otherwise designed for disabled drivers and travelers. Wheelchair Getaways has locations in Memphis (901/795-6533 or 866/762-165), Knoxville (865/622-6550 or 888/340-8267), and Nashville (615/451-2900 or 866/762-1656), and they will deliver to other locations in the state.

Avis offers **Avis Access,** a program for travelers with disabilities. Call the dedicated 24-hour toll-free number (888/879-4273) for help renting a car with features such as transfer boards, hand controls, spinner knobs, and swivel seats.

INTERNATIONAL TRAVELERS

Foreign travelers will find a warm welcome. Those in the music and tourist trades are used to working with people from all over the world and will be pleased that you have come from so far away to visit their home. If you are not a native English speaker, it may be difficult to understand the local accent at first. Just smile and ask the person to say it again, a bit slower. Good humor and a positive attitude will help at all times.

Most citizens of a foreign country require a visa to enter the United States. There are many types of visas, issued according to the purpose of your visit. Business and pleasure travelers apply for B-1 and B-2 visas, respectively. When you apply for your visa, you will be required to prove that the purpose of you trip is business, pleasure, or for medical treatment; that

you plan to remain in the United States for a limited period; and that you have a place of residence outside the United States. Apply for your visa at the nearest U.S. embassy. For more information, contact the U.S. Citizenship and Immigration Service (www.uscis.gov).

Nationals of 36 countries may be able to use the Visa Waiver Program, operated by Customs and Border Protection. Presently, these 36 countries are Andorra, Australia, Austria, Belgium, Brunei, Czech Republic, Denmark (including Greenland and Faroe Islands), Estonia, Finland, France, Germany, Greece, Hungary, Iceland, Ireland, Italy, Japan, Latvia, Liechtenstein, Lithuania, Luxembourg, Malta, Monaco, the Netherlands (including Aruba, Bonaire, Curacao, Saba, and Sint Maarten), New Zealand, Norway, Portugal (including Azores and Madeira), San Marino, South Korea, Singapore, Slovenia, Spain, Sweden, Switzerland, and the United Kingdom.

Take note that in recent years the United States has begun to require visa-waiver participants to have upgraded passports with digital photographs and machine-readable information. They have also introduced requirements that even visa-waiver citizens register in advance before arriving in the United States. For more information about the Visa Waiver Program, contact the Customs and Border Protection Agency (www.travel.state.gov).

All foreign travelers are now required to participate in U.S. Visit, a program operated by the Department of Homeland Security. Under the program, your fingerprints and photograph are taken—digitally and without ink—as you are being screened by the immigration officer.

Health and Safety

Nashville is a safe city, with the regular concerns of any urban area. Locals, both native and otherwise, are at-the-ready with Southern hospitality, and willing to help a visitor who has lost his or her way.

In general, if you stay alert, you should feel free to explore the city's neighborhoods. For the most part, the neighborhoods highlighted in this guide, those that are chockful of attractions, are safe to venture out in, although crimes that take place in high-tourist areas, like pickpocketing, do happen. Lock your valuables out of sight in your car, don't carry large amounts of cash, pay attention to your surroundings, and you'll be fine.

HOSPITALS AND PHARMACIES

Because healthcare is such a big industry in Nashville, there are a lot of hospitals. Should you need emergency medical care, the majority of the hospitals are clustered in the Midtown neighborhood, near Vanderbilt. The **Monroe Carell Jr. Children's Hospital** at Vanderbilt (2200 Children's Way, 615/936-1000, www. childrenshospital.vanderbilt.org) is among the best in the country. **Baptist Hospital** (2000 Church St., 615/284-5555, www.baptisthospital.com) is another major player in this area.

Skyline Medical Center (3441 Dickerson Pike, 615/769-2000, tristarskyline.com) is the closest hospital to Music Valley and parts of East Nashville. Others include **St. Thomas Health** (4220 Harding Rd., 615/222-2111, www.sths.com) and **Centennial Medical Center** (2300 Patterson St., 615/342-1000, tristarcentennial.com).

Rite Aid, CVS, Walgreens, and the major grocery store chains have drugstores all over Nashville. Try the **CVS** (426 21st Ave. S., 615/321-2590, www.cvs.com). If you need a 24-hour option, try **Walgreens** (5555 Edmondson Pike, 615/333-2722, www.walgreens.com).

EMERGENCY SERVICES

Dial 911 for police, fire, or ambulance in an emergency. The local number for "urgency without emergency" is 615/862-8600. For help with a traffic accident, call the Tennessee Highway Patrol at 615/741-3181. The concierge at major hotels can also help direct you in the event of an emergency.

Nashville Veterinary Specialists (2971 Sidco Dr., 615/386-0107, www.nashvillevet-specialists.com) has an emergency staff ready and waiting for anything that happens to your pet while you are traveling.

Communications and Media

INTERNET SERVICES

You can go online free at the **Nashville Public Library** (615 Church St., 615/862-5800). There is free wireless access at the visitors center located at 5th and Broadway. Many local restaurants, coffee shops, and hotels also offer free wireless Internet.

MAIL SERVICES

The **United States Post Office** (800/742-5877, www.ups.com) maintains a branch is almost every Nashville neighborhood. Search for specific locations at www.usps.gov. If you need to mail a letter or buy stamps while downtown, you have a few options. The post offices at 901 Broadway is found on the basement level of the **Frist Center for the Visual Arts,** which itself used to be a post office before it was renovated for the museum space. There is also a post office in the downtown Arcade and at 1718 Church Street.

Both **FedEx** (800/463-3333, www.fedex.com) and **UPS** have several locations downtown and drop boxes in local hotels and businesses.

RADIO AND TELEVISION

The Nashville dial is chock-a-block with the usual commercial radio prospects (what else would you expect in Music City?). There are a few radio stations worth mentioning, however. **WSM 650 AM** is the legendary radio station that started it all when it put a fiddler on the air in 1925. Still airing the Grand Ole Opry after all these years, WSM plays country music at other times.

Nashville Public Radio has two stations: **WPLN 90.3 FM and 91.1 FM.** The first plays National Public Radio news and talk; the second is all classical music. **WPLN 1430 AM** is a companion station with all-day news and talk, including BBC broadcasts. Nashville's only community radio station is **Radio Free Nashville** (107.1 FM, www.radiofreenashville.org).

WKDA 900 AM is Nashville's Spanish-language radio station. **WAMB 1160 AM** plays big-band music, and **WNAH 1360 AM** plays old-fashioned Southern gospel.

Several Nashville universities liven up the radio dial. Fisk's **WFSK 88.1 FM** plays jazz. Middle Tennessee State University has **WMTS 88.3 FM,** the student-run station, and **WMOT 89.5 FM,** a jazz station.

Nashville's network affiliates offer local news morning and night. These include **WKRN** (Channel 2 ABC), **WSMV** (Channel 4 NBC), **WTVF** (Channel 5 CBS), and **WZTV** (Channel 17 FOX).

The local public-television station is **WNPT** (Channel 8 PBS).

Remember that since Nashville is in the central time zone; most nationally televised programs air one hour earlier than they do on the East and West Coasts.

Information and Services

BANKS

Dozens of local and regional banks are found in Nashville. Most banks will cash travelers checks, exchange currency, and send wire transfers. Banks are generally open weekdays 9am-4pm, although some are open later and on Saturday. Automatic Teller Machines (ATMs) are ubiquitous at grocery stores, live-music venues, and elsewhere, and many are compatible with bank cards bearing the Plus or Cirrus icons. Between fees charged by your own bank and the bank that owns the ATM you are using, expect to pay $2-5 extra to get cash from an ATM that does not belong to your own bank.

SALES TAX

Sales tax is charged on all goods, including food and groceries.

The sales tax you pay is split between the state and local governments. Tennessee's sales tax is 5.5 percent on food and groceries and 7 percent on all other goods. Cities and towns add an additional "local use tax" of 1.5-2.75 percent.

TIPPING

You should tip waiters and waitresses 15-20 percent in a sit-down restaurant. You can tip 5-10 percent in a cafeteria or restaurant where you collect your own food from the counter.

Tip a bellhop or bag handler $1 per bag, or more if they went out of their way to help you.

TIME ZONES

Middle Tennessee is in the central time zone. The time zone line runs a slanted course from Signal Mountain in the south to the Big South Fork National River and Recreation Area in the north. The time zone line falls at mile marker 340 along I-40, just west of Rockwood and a few miles east of Crossville. Chattanooga, Dayton, Rockwood, Crossville, Rugby, Fall Creek Falls State Park, the Catoosa Wildlife Management Area, and Big South Fork lie close to or on the time zone line, and visitors to these areas should take special care to ensure they are on the right clock.

RESOURCES

Suggested Reading

PHOTOGRAPHY AND ART

Escott, Colin. *The Grand Ole Opry: The Making of an American Icon.* Nashville: Center Street, 2006. An authorized (and somewhat sanitized) look at the Grand Ole Opry. Lots of pictures, reminiscences, and short sidebars make it an attractive coffee-table book.

McGuire, Jim. *Nashville Portraits: Legends of Country Music.* Guilford, CT: The Lyons Press, 2007. Sixty stunning photographs of country music legends including Johnny Cash, Waylon Jennings, Doc Watson, and Dolly Parton. The companion book to an eponymous exhibit that debuted in 2007.

Sherraden, Jim, Paul Kingsbury, and Elek Horvath. *Hatch Show Print: The History of a Great American Poster Shop.* San Francisco: Chronicle Books, 2001. A fully illustrated, beautiful book about Hatch Show Print, the Nashville advertising and letter press founded in 1897.

Wood, Nicki Pendleton. *Nashville Yesterday and Today.* West Side Publising, 2010. This is an illustrated guide of what makes Music City tick, written by a local former newspaper writer, restaurant critic, and cookbook author.

GUIDES

Brandt, Robert. *Touring the Middle Tennessee Backroads.* Winston-Salem, NC: John F. Blair Publisher, 1995. Robert Brandt is a Nashville judge and self-professed "zealot" for Middle Tennessee. His guidebook details 15 driving tours through backroads in the heartland of Tennessee. Brandt's knowledge of local history and architecture cannot be surpassed, and his enthusiasm for his subject shines through the prose. While some of the entries are now dated, the guide remains an invaluable source of information about small towns in the region.

Van West, Carroll. *Tennessee's Historical Landscapes: A Traveler's Guide.* Knoxville: University of Tennessee Press, 1995. The editor of the *Tennessee Historical Quarterly* and a professor of history at Middle Tennessee State University, Carroll Van West guides readers along highways and byways, pointing out historical structures and other signs of history along the way. A good traveling companion, especially for students of architecture and landscape.

The WPA Guide to Tennessee. Knoxville: University of Tennessee Press, 1986. The Works Progress Administration guide to Tennessee, written in 1939 and originally published by Viking Press, is a fascinating portrait of Depression-era Tennessee. Published as part of a New Deal project to employ writers and document the culture and character of the nation, the guide contains visitor information, historical sketches, and profiles of the state's literature, culture, agriculture, industry, and more. The guide, republished as part of Tennessee's "Homecoming '86," is a delightful traveling companion.

GENERAL HISTORY

Bergeron, Paul H. *Paths of the Past: Tennessee, 1770-1970.* Knoxville: University of Tennessee Press, 1979. This is a concise, straight-up history of Tennessee, with a few illustrations and maps.

Corlew, Robert E. *Tennessee: A Short History.* Knoxville: University of Tennessee Press, 1990. The definitive survey of Tennessee history, this text was first written in 1969 and has been updated several times by writers including Stanley J. Folmsbee and Enoch Mitchell. This is a useful reference guide for a serious reader.

Dykeman, Wilma. *Tennessee.* New York: W. W. Norton & Company and the American Association for State and Local History, 1984. Novelist and essayist Wilma Dykeman says more about the people of Tennessee and the events that shaped the modern state in this slim and highly readable volume than you would find in the most detailed and plodding historical account. It becomes a companion, and a means through which to understand the Tennessee spirit and character.

SPECIALIZED HISTORY

Egerton, John. *Speak Now Against the Day: The Generation Before the Civil Rights Movement in the South.* Chapel Hill: University of North Carolina Press, 1995. Nashville native John Egerton tells the relatively unacknowledged story of Southerners, white and black, who stood up against segregation and racial hatred during the years before the civil rights movement.

Egerton, John. *Visions of Utopia.* Knoxville: University of Tennessee Press, 1977. An accessible and fascinating portrait of three intentional Tennessee communities: Ruskin in Middle Tennessee, Nashoba in West Tennessee, and Rugby in East Tennessee. Egerton's usual sterling prose and sensitive observations make this volume well worth reading.

Sword, Wiley. *The Confederacy's Last Hurrah: Spring Hill, Franklin and Nashville.* Lawrence: University Press of Kansas, 2004. This is a well-written and devastating account of John Bell Hood's disastrous campaign through Middle Tennessee during the waning months of the Confederacy. It was a campaign that cost the South more than 23,000 men. With unflinching honesty, Sword describes the opportunities lost and poor decisions made by General Hood.

MUSIC

Carlin, Richard. *Country Music.* New York: Black Dog and Leventhal Publishers, 2006. This is a highly illustrated, well-written, and useful reference for fans of country music. It profiles the people, places, and events that contributed to country's evolution. With lots of graphic elements and photographs, it is a good book to dip into.

Chapman, Marshall. *They Came to Nashville.* Vanderbilt University Press, 2010. Singer-songwriter Chapman tells her tales, as well as those of many others, as they came to Music City and set about hitting the big time.

Escott, Colin. *Hank Williams The Biography.* Back Bay Books, 2004. No country star had a bigger impact on Nashville's evolution to Music City than Hank Williams. This detailed history shares his failings, downfall, and remarkable legacy.

Kingsbury, Paul, ed. *Will the Circle Be Unbroken: Country Music in America.* London: DK Adult, 2006. An illustrated collection of articles by 43 writers, including several performing artists, this book is a useful reference on the genre's development from 1920 until the present.

Kossner, Michael. *How Nashville Became Music City: 50 Years of Music Row.* Milwaukee: Hal Leonard, 2006. Forget about the stars and the singers, this profile of country music focuses on the people you've never heard of: the executives, songwriters, and behind-the-scenes technicians who really make the music happen. An interesting read for fans who don't mind seeing how the sausage is made; a good introduction for people aspiring to be a part of it.

Wolfe, Charles K. *Tennessee Strings.* Knoxville: University of Tennessee Press, 1977. This slim, easy to read volume is the definitive survey of Tennessee musical history.

Zimmerman, Peter Coats. *Tennessee Music: Its People and Places.* San Francisco: Miller Freeman Books, 1998. This nicely illustrated book tries, and succeeds, to do the impossible: tell the varied stories of Tennessee music all the way from Bristol to Memphis.

REFERENCE

Van West, Carroll, ed. *The Tennessee Encyclopedia of History and Culture.* Nashville: Tennessee Historical Society and Rutledge Hill Press, 1998. Perhaps the most valuable tome on Tennessee, this 1,200-page encyclopedia covers the people, places, events, and movements that defined Tennessee history and the culture of its people. Dip in frequently and you will be all the wiser.

FICTION

Burton, Linda, ed. *Stories from Tennessee.* Knoxville: University of Tennessee Press, 1983. An anthology of Tennessee literature, the volume begins with a story by David Crockett on hunting in Tennessee and concludes with works by 20th-century authors such as Shelby Foote, Cormac McCarthy, and Robert Drake.

Hicks, Rover. *Widow of the South.* Grand Central Publishing, 2006. Tour guides at Carton Plantation gripe about the poetic license taken with some facts in this fictional tale. But it offers a moving story of the Battle of Franklin and the high emotional costs of the Civil War.

Taylor, Peter. *Summons to Memphis.* New York: Knopf Publishing Group, 1986. Celebrated and award-winning Tennessee writer Peter Taylor won the Pulitzer Prize for fiction for this novel in 1986. Phillip Carver returns home to Tennessee at the request of his three older sisters to talk his father out of remarrying. In so doing, he is forced to confront a troubling family history. This is a classic of American literature, set in a South that is fading away.

FOOD

Lewis, Edna, and Scott Peacock. *The Gift of Southern Cooking: Recipes and Revelations from Two Great American Cooks.* New York: Knopf Publishing Group, 2003. Grande dame of Southern food Edna Lewis and son-of-the-soil chef Scott Peacock joined forces on this seminal text of Southern cuisine. It demystifies, documents, and inspires. Ideal for those who really care about Southern foodways.

Lundy, Ronnie, ed. *Cornbread Nation 3.* Chapel Hill: University of North Carolina Press, 2006. The third in a series of collections on Southern food and cooking. Published in collaboration with the Southern Foodways Alliance, which is dedicated to preserving and celebrating Southern food traditions, the Cornbread Nation collection is an ode to food traditions large and small. Topics include paw-paws, corn, and pork. *Cornbread Nation 2* focused on barbecue. *Cornbread Nation 1* was edited by restaurateur and Southern food celebrant John Egerton.

Stern, Jane, and Michael Stern. *Southern Country Cooking from the Loveless Cafe: Biscuits, Hams, and Jams from Nashville's Favorite Café.* Nashville: Rutledge Hill Press, 2005. Road-food aficionados wrote the cookbook on Nashville's most famous pit stop: the Loveless Cafe. Located at the northern terminus of the Natchez Trace Parkway, the Loveless is quintessential Southern cooking: delectable biscuits, country ham, and homemade preserves. Now you can take some of that down-home flavor home with you.

Internet and Digital Resources

Tennessee State Parks
www.state.tn.us/environment/parks
An online directory of all Tennessee state parks, this site provides useful details, including campground descriptions, cabin rental information, and the lowdown on activities.

Tennessee Department of Tourism Development
www.tnvacation.com
On Tennessee's official tourism website you can request a visitors guide, search for upcoming events, or look up details about hundreds of attractions, hotels, and restaurants. This is a great resource for suggested scenic drives.

Tennessee Encyclopedia of History and Culture
www.tennesseeencyclopedia.net
The online edition of an excellent reference book, this website is a great starting point on all topics Tennessee. Articles about people, places, and events are written by hundreds of different experts. Online entries are updated regularly.

Nashville Convention and Visitors Bureau
www.visitmusiccity.com
The official tourism website for Nashville, this site offers concert listings, hotel booking services, and useful visitor information. You can also order a visitors guide and money-saving coupons.

The Tennessean
www.tennessean.com
Nashville's major newspaper posts news, entertainment, sports, and business stories online. Sign up for a daily newsletter of headlines from Music City, or search the archives.

The Nashville Scene
www.nashvillescene.com
Nashville's alternative weekly has a great website. The dining guide is fabulous, the stories interesting and archived, and the entertainment calendar is the best in town. Go to Our Critics' Picks for a rundown on the best shows in town. The annual manual, reader's choice awards, and other special editions are useful for newcomers and old-timers alike.

Nashville Essential Guide
sutromedia.com/apps/
Nashville_Essential_Guide
Digital iPhone app written by the author of this book. Includes regularly updated Nashville highlights, plus links to music to downtown, Twitter and Facebook information for key sites, and more.

Eat Drink Smile
www.eat-drink-smile.com
A fun blog about what to eat (and drink) in Music City.

TVA Lake Info
This free iPad and iPhone app lists recreational dam release schedules for across the state.

Tennessee Civil War 150
A free app for iPhones and iPads provides quick-hit history lessons about Civil War battle sites, plus information about visiting them.

VisitSouth
Weekly blog postings on what to do in Southern cities, including Nashville, Memphis, Chattanooga, Knoxville, as well as the Smoky Mountains.

Index

Restaurants Index

Nightlife Index

Shops Index

Hotels Index

Acknowledgments

Even in the face of looming deadlines, stacks of photo-filled jump drives on the desk, and marked-up maps littering the floor, I'm convinced I have the world's best job. I have a legitimate, work-related excuse to throw my tent in the station wagon, strap the paddleboard to the top, and head to Land Between the Lakes for a weekend. Or to call a few friends and ask them to help me check out Nashville's honky-tonks. Or taste-test the newest variety of Moon Pie.

I'm grateful to many people who helped me synthesize what I've heard, seen, and experienced into something coherent that others could use. First and foremost, thanks go to DG Strong, who encouraged me to move back to Tennessee after many years away and who indulges (and sometimes even enables) my whims to drive for miles to see a new boat launch or try a new hot chicken place.

Perhaps the only person to love Music City more than I do is Jenny Steuber of the Nashville Convention and Visitors Bureau. She's always available for brainstorming and, of course, providing photos (with the help of Dana W. McDowell).

Other essential photographers include Hannah Coffey, DG Strong, Griffin Norman, and Liz Littman.

Emily Moe is an excellent editorial assistant, verifying the alphabet soup of phone numbers and URLs, and tracking down photos and permissions.

I first worked with the crackerjack staff of Avalon Travel on *The Dog Lover's Companion to Chicago* and while other authors may complain about their publishers, I've never felt like mine was anything less than an invaluable partner in this process. Particular thanks, again, this time around to Grace Fujimoto, Leah Gordon, Domini Dragoone, and Albert Angulo. Many thanks to those who worked on previous editions of *Moon Tennessee* and *Moon Nashville*, including Susanna Henighan Potter and Jeff Bradley.

As always, I am grateful for the help and support of my family and friends, who tolerate my working long hours on "vacation" and dragging them to sightsee wherever we are, not to mention my soundtrack of bluegrass and country music, and the ever-expanding wardrobe of cowboy boots.

www.moon.com

DESTINATIONS | ACTIVITIES | BLOGS | MAPS | BOOKS

MOON.COM is ready to help plan your next trip! Filled with fresh trip ideas and strategies, author interviews, informative travel blogs, a detailed map library, and descriptions of all the Moon guidebooks, Moon.com is all you need to get out and explore the world—or even places in your own backyard. While at Moon.com, sign up for our monthly e-newsletter for updates on new releases, travel tips, and expert advice from our on-the-go Moon authors. As always, when you travel with Moon, expect an experience that is uncommon and truly unique.

f �="" KEEP="" UP="" WITH="" MOON="" ON="" FACEBOOK="" AND="" TWITTER="" join="" the="" moon="" photo="" group="" on="" flickr<="" p="">

MAP SYMBOLS

▦ Expressway	⬤ Highlight	✗ Airfield	⚓ Golf Course
▦ Primary Road	○ City/Town	✗ Airport	▣ Parking Area
▦ Secondary Road	◉ State Capital	▲ Mountain	⬟ Archaeological Site
▦ Unpaved Road	⊛ National Capital	✛ Unique Natural Feature	▮ Church
┄ Trail	★ Point of Interest		▮ Gas Station
⋯ Ferry	• Accommodation	⚑ Waterfall	Glacier
▦ Railroad	▼ Restaurant/Bar	▲ Park	Mangrove
▦ Pedestrian Walkway	■ Other Location	◲ Trailhead	Reef
▦ Stairs	⋀ Campground	⛷ Skiing Area	Swamp

CONVERSION TABLES

°C = (°F − 32) / 1.8
°F = (°C x 1.8) + 32
1 inch = 2.54 centimeters (cm)
1 foot = 0.304 meters (m)
1 yard = 0.914 meters
1 mile = 1.6093 kilometers (km)
1 km = 0.6214 miles
1 fathom = 1.8288 m
1 chain = 20.1168 m
1 furlong = 201.168 m
1 acre = 0.4047 hectares
1 sq km = 100 hectares
1 sq mile = 2.59 square km
1 ounce = 28.35 grams
1 pound = 0.4536 kilograms
1 short ton = 0.90718 metric ton
1 short ton = 2,000 pounds
1 long ton = 1.016 metric tons
1 long ton = 2,240 pounds
1 metric ton = 1,000 kilograms
1 quart = 0.94635 liters
1 US gallon = 3.7854 liters
1 Imperial gallon = 4.5459 liters
1 nautical mile = 1.852 km

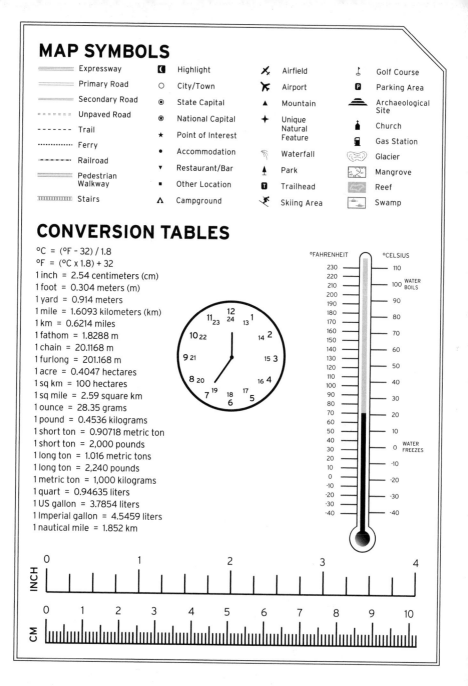

MOON NASHVILLE

Avalon Travel
a member of the Perseus Books Group
1700 Fourth Street
Berkeley, CA 94710, USA
www.moon.com

Editor: Leah Gordon
Series Manager: Erin Raber
Copy Editor: Ann Seifert
Graphics and Production Coordinator:
  Domini Dragoone
Cover Designer: Domini Dragoone
Map Editor: Albert Angulo
Cartographers: Stephanie Poulain, Chris Henrick

ISBN-13: 978-1-61238-518-1
ISSN: 2330-4952

Printing History
1st Edition — January 2014
5 4 3 2 1

Text © 2013 by Margaret Littman and Avalon Travel.
Maps © 2013 by Avalon Travel.
All rights reserved.

Some photos and illustrations are used by permission
and are the property of the original copyright
owners.

Front cover photo: Nashville skyline and Cumberland
River from Shelby Street Pedestrian Bridge,
© Malcolm MacGregor.
Title page photo: Honkytonking on Lower Broad is an
essential Nashville experience, © Melanie Meadows.

Front color section: pg. 2 © Lorraine Archer/123RF;
pg. 14 (top) © Henryk Sadura/123RF; pg. 14 (bottom)
© Andriy Kravchenko; pg. 15 (top and bottom left),
16 (left), 17, 18 (right), 19, 20, 21, and 22 © Courtesy
of Nashville Convention & Visitors Corporation;
pg. 15 (bottom right) © Kristin Barlow; pg. 16
(right) © Natalia Bratslavsky; pg. 18 (left) Courtesy
of Cheekwood; pg. 23 © Bob Bernstein; pg. 24
Courtesy of Jeni's Splendid Ice Creams.

Printed in Canada by Friesens

KEEPING CURRENT

If you have a favorite gem you'd like to see included in the next edition, or see anything
that needs updating, clarification, or correction, please drop us a line. Send your com-
ments via email to feedback@moon.com, or use the address above.